RECONCEIVING NATURE

RECONCEIVING

NATURE

Ecofeminism
in Late Victorian Women's Poetry

PATRICIA MURPHY

UNIVERSITY OF MISSOURI PRESS
Columbia

Copyright © 2019 by
The Curators of the University of Missouri
University of Missouri Press, Columbia, Missouri 65211
Printed and bound in the United States of America
All rights reserved. First printing, 2019.

Library of Congress Cataloging-in-Publication Data

Names: Murphy, Patricia, 1951- author.
Title: Reconceiving nature : ecofeminism in late Victorian women's poetry /
   Patricia Murphy.
Description: Columbia : University of Missouri Press, 2019. | Includes
   bibliographical references and index. |
Identifiers: LCCN 2018043080 (print) | LCCN 2018058830 (ebook) | ISBN
   9780826274298 (e-book) | ISBN 9780826221872 (hardcover : alk. paper)
Subjects: LCSH: English poetry--19th century--History and criticism. |
   English poetry--women authors--History and criticism. | Ecofeminism in
   literature.
Classification: LCC PR595.W6 (ebook) | LCC PR595.W6 M87 2019 (print) | DDC
   821/.8099287--dc23
LC record available at https://lccn.loc.gov/2018043080

∞™ This paper meets the requirements of the
American National Standard for Permanence of Paper
for Printed Library Materials, Z39.48, 1984.

Typefaces: Garamond and Trade Gothic

To all who act to protect our environment

CONTENTS

ACKNOWLEDGMENTS

THANKS ESPECIALLY GO TO MY brother, Jim Murphy, and my sister, Sue Roche, for the endless encouragement they have given me in my scholarly pursuits. I am also very grateful to K. Schoenbrod, whose sage counsel has been so important in my academic endeavors. Also much appreciated are the many opportunities that colleague Joe Sutliff Sanders provided me to discuss this project.

I also wish to thank two professors from graduate school at the University of Iowa years ago whose expertise and teaching have been so valuable to me. Florence Boos shared her vast knowledge of Victorian poetry, which gave me a solid foundation for approaching this book. Garrett Stewart helped me attend to the intricate nuances of language, which has guided me in analyzing all literary forms.

Additionally, I thank two scholarly journals for permission to publish modified material from my essays: *Interdisciplinary Studies in Literature and Environment* (*ISLE*), which published my essay on L. S. Bevington, and *Nineteenth-Century Gender Studies*, which featured my articles on Mathilde Blind and Augusta Webster.

RECONCEIVING NATURE

Nascent Ecofeminism

Ecofeminist insights emerged insistently in the late nineteenth century, as six women poets in particular demonstrate abundantly in their perspicacious work. These writers' verse compellingly challenges conventional ideas that demeaned the nonhuman world and rationalized its exploitation and degradation. The poetry reveals a prescient attentiveness to ecofeminist issues that have become so significant in the modern era, with its horrifically expanded environmental threats as well as its ongoing denigration of women. *Reconceiving Nature* focuses primarily on the "eco" aspect of ecofeminism, examining poetic responses to Victorian estimations of the natural world and its marginalization. Although other late Victorian women poets also articulated conceptions of nature, and may have crafted verses touching upon ecofeminism, this study's six poets notably and prolifically explored such matters and presented their ideas in especially astute ways that show their keen perception of Victorian views on nature. To today's readers, these important poets represent both the familiar and the obscure: Augusta Webster, Mathilde Blind, Michael Field, Alice Meynell, Constance Naden, and L. S. Bevington. Grappling with crucial ecofeminist concerns, the writers heightened awareness of and dispelled misconceptions about the nonhuman realm. As M. A. Stodart declares in her 1842 essay "Poetesses and Fleshly Poets," "The power of poetry is not confined to those who take rank and precedence as the poets of the land," for such a stance would manifest "a cold and an inglorious doctrine."[1]

Ecofeminism encompasses many diverse approaches that cover a wide spectrum of occasionally competing perspectives, yet all firmly embrace the same premise: cultural discourse has closely allied and virtually equated nature and women, augmenting their shared oppression in male-dominated civilization. "Women and nature," Ynestra King remarks in "The Ecology of Feminism and the Feminism of Ecology," represent "the original 'others.'" Ecology and feminism encounter the selfsame hostile sources of repression, Catriona Sandilands argues in an environmental journal. As Susan Griffin states in "Ecofeminism and Meaning," "[T]he social construction (exploitation, destruction) of nature is

3

implicit in and inseparable from the social construction of gender."[2] The inferior status accorded both nature and women derives partially from their presumedly commensurate characteristics, notably an immutable susceptibility to domination, an apparent passivity rather than agency, a marked distance from culture, and a deserved denigration in Christian thought. These supposed traits underlie the poetic responses assessed in this book.

In effect, the six featured poets were *reconstructing* nature in their verse, contesting and revising flawed perceptions. Thus, the poets approached cultural estimations of the nonhuman world as constructions rather than verities, which created a space to reimagine and recuperate nature as a vital presence deserving respect, not oppression. As theorist Luce Irigaray comments in a discussion about perspectives on women and nature, "We need to reinterpret the idea of nature."[3] Although Irigaray's extensive writings typically address the female condition, as well as cultural issues, psychoanalysis, linguistics, and other topics of interdisciplinary interest, the call to reexamine nature is just one of the numerous observations relevant to ecofeminism that thread through her multiple texts and that inform *Reconceiving Nature* as well, a point to which this introduction will return.

Ecocritical commentators underscore the constructed nature of nature, as it were. In "Ecocriticism," for example, Kate Rigby identifies culture as the agent determining perceptions of nature, originating when a subject enters the symbolic order, and Chris J. Cuomo's *Feminism and Ecological Communities* states that nature represents "a relative, socially-constructed concept." Addressing feminist ecology, Karen J. Warren and Jim Cheney argue that ecofeminists appraise the subjugation of nature, and the analogous control of women, "as social problems rooted in very concrete, historical, socioeconomic conditions, as well as in oppressive, patriarchal conceptual frameworks that maintain and sanction these conditions." As Scott Hess mentions in his book on early environmentalism, various scholars have argued that "natures," rather than a sole "nature," exist as a consequence of cultural formulations grounded in discrete temporal moments reflecting "different, historically specific constellations of social, discursive, and materialist practices." Ecofeminism, Gretchen T. Legler explains in "Ecofeminist Literary Criticism," targets such constructions and expresses interest in literary appraisals of nature. Considering nature to be a dangerous antagonist indicates a response that Simon C. Estok calls "ecophobic," a term he defines in an essay on ecocriticism as "an irrational and groundless hatred of the natural world." As the connotative elasticity of the term "nature" makes evident, Raymond Williams's identification of the noun as "perhaps the most complex word in the language" is certainly an insightful statement.[4]

Regarding the linguistic component, Stacy Alaimo comments in an essay about the humanities and the environment that language intersects with material nature, which blurs the distinctions between them. As Erika Cudworth reminds in *Developing Ecofeminist Theory*, discourses "concretize themselves in specific practices, processes and institutional formations"; because "[d]iscourses constitute forms of power and domination," they represent not "merely sets of ideas but also institutionally rooted social practices" that carry repercussions. Legler additionally asserts that interactions with nature broadly shape and reflect language, manifesting themselves syntactically, figuratively, and conceptually. Whether overt or concealed, language carries a presumed power over the natural world, Griffin contends.[5]

The implicit equation of nature and women is deeply embedded in Victorian thought, of course, and the perceived equivalency represents the overriding presumption that ecofeminism challenges in seeking to undermine the domination of both. Thus, the nature-woman identity offers the crucial starting point to contextualize the prevalent views that the six poets encountered. The subsequent chapters each explore a particular component of constructed nature addressed in an individual poet's work, with the concluding chapter on L. S. Bevington bringing together the thematic elements of the previous chapters. The following sections briefly examine the topics to provide a preview, aided by extensive commentary from influential theorists who have helped to shape the various arguments, along with other relevant writings. Because it affects nearly every other aspect of ecofeminist thought, the supposed equivalence between nature and women begins the discussion.

The Nature-Woman Linkage

"Nature is . . . never simple, in that it is always marked by gender," asserts Irigaray. Indeed, the connection forged between nature and women represents "an age-old association," Carolyn Merchant observes in *The Death of Nature*, and it bespeaks "an affiliation that has persisted throughout culture, language, and history." As Griffin indicates, nature and women have been closely intertwined, and the boundaries between the two entities have blurred. Rosemarie Tong's *Feminist Thought* similarly states that "because women have been 'naturalized' and nature has been 'feminized,' it is difficult to know where the oppression of one ends and the other begins." A society that disdains nature also abhors women, King notes. The conviction that nature and women are intimately allied indicates that a culture offers them neither power nor inclusion, Val Plumwood argues in *Feminism and the Mastery of Nature*.[6] The equivalence assumption, which Augusta Webster challenges in the first chapter, justifies joint subjugation through a posited inferiority.

Perceptions of the land as feminized space provide an illustrative example of the ostensible nature-woman equivalence. Thomas Carlyle, for instance, accepted the nature-woman connection, remarking, "The Land is *Mother* of us all; nour-ishes, shelters, gladdens, lovingly enriches us all." He also exclaimed, "[I]n how many ways, from our first wakening to our last sleep on her blessed mother-bosom, does she, as with blessed mother-arms, enfold us all!"[7]

Legler points to a literary tradition that deems both the land and women as lacking agency, speech, and the ability to resist. Additionally, both the terrain and the female have been considered as property deserving an objectifying gaze and a required submission. A presumption exists that the two entities are pleasingly at-tractive and undoubtedly useful, comments Donna Coffey in discussing "a sense of place." Coffey relays Dorothy Dinnerstein's assertion that women represent "a 'natural resource'" and "an asset to be owned and harnessed, harvested and mined."[8]

Nature and women have customarily represented the unprivileged part of a binary that at its other pole valorizes culture and men, a dichotomy that unfortu-nately continues to exist. Their imagined bond has created the belief, in Western culture, that nature and women evidence emotionality, physicality, and illogical-ity, whereas men can enviably claim intellectual, conceptual, and ratiocinative capability. Indeed, males "mark their own transcendent subjectivity by separat-ing themselves from the natural world," Alaimo maintains in *Undomesticated Ground*, aptly subtitled *Recasting Nature as Feminist Space*. Nature, Alaimo says, carries the mark of "otherness" that women likewise bear. The nature and women equivalence partially stems from women's reproductive function, considered their primary role, whereas men, and culture, presumably further and enhance the projects of civilization. In "Oppressive Dichotomies," Penelope Brown and L. J. Jordanova explain that nineteenth-century texts, like their eighteenth-century predecessors, reveal a widespread conviction that nature is both female and ma-ternal, as Carlyle likewise supposed. Decades later, Victorian sexologist Havelock Ellis contended, "The female animal everywhere is more closely and for a longer period occupied with that process of reproduction which is Nature's main con-cern," and he stated as well that "Nature has made women more like children in order that they may better understand and care for children."[9]

Key moments in the long and disturbing history evidencing the nature-woman equivalency offer valuable background. Biblical references in Genesis provide an appropriate start in that the Fall precipitated Eve's alignment with nature, as op-posed to Adam's affiliation with civilizational activity. In Genesis 3:1, Eve's link to the elements signifies her bond with nature since she rather than Adam heeds the serpent initially. As Merchant describes the relationship between the human fore-bears, "fallen Adam becomes the inventor of the tools and technologies," while "fallen Eve becomes the nature that must be tamed into submission," a concept that has shaped beliefs for centuries. Eve assumes triadic representations, Merchant relates, comprising the prelapsarian pure woman, the postlapsarian sinister woman, and the compassionate maternal woman. In fatefully tasting from the tree of the knowledge of good and evil, Eve "becomes one with nature and knows nature," Merchant says.[10]

Early secular history continued to forge the nature-woman linkage. Western culture viewed nature as a caring maternal presence until the Scientific Revolution brought dramatic change, Tong advises. Other exceptions to negative views of nature also existed, such as Romanticism's large-scale regard for the nonhuman world. Merchant traces positive formulations of nature during the early centuries that were countered by the destruction and chaos associated with natural phenomena, and this negativity was applied as well to women through the assumed similitude. Nevertheless, the picture of nature as a beneficent female remained prominent, Merchant says. The medieval and Elizabethan eras not only allied nature with these nurturing qualities, she remarks, but also considered it as signaling a divine intention. The Renaissance brought an implicit injunction to protect nature and a belief that nature provided "an escape backward" and "a return to an unblemished Golden Age" foregrounding the maternal figure's benignity. Pastoral literature continued such admiring impressions and disseminated the idea of benevolence, Merchant indicates. Yet lurking throughout the positive depictions was a negative undertone that framed the nonhuman world as an unruly environment needing control; Merchant argues that this view became prevalent as the Scientific Revolution began.[11]

Assorted luminaries over time promulgated the concept that nature is a feminine presence. Nicolaus Copernicus, for example, designated the powerful sun as masculine and said that "Earth conceives from the Sun, and is made pregnant with annual offspring." Alchemist Paracelsus averred that "[w]oman is like the earth and all the elements."

> [W]oman in her own way is also a field of the earth and not at all different from it. She replaces it, so to speak, she is the field and the garden mould in which the child is sown and planted, then growing up to be a man. . . .
> A woman is like a tree bearing fruit. And man is like the fruit that the tree bears. . . . The tree must be well nourished until it has everything by which to give that for the sake of which it exists.

Centuries later, Friedrich Nietzsche accepted the long-standing supposition that women are closer to nature than are men, and he contended that woman shares the "carnivora-like, cunning flexibility" of a wild animal, with "her tiger-claws beneath the glove" and her "innate wildness." Gerard Manley Hopkins thought that nature's "Heraclitean fire" evidences "her" endless changeability and chaos. As the latter example suggests, the female pronoun is abundantly present in Victorian writings, often essentializing nature and presenting it both positively and negatively. For example, Carlyle mused in 1843,

> Nature, like the Sphinx, is of womanly celestial loveliness and tenderness; the face and bosom of a goddess, but ending in claws and the body of a lioness. There is in her a celestial beauty,—which means celestial order, pliancy to wisdom; but there is also a darkness, a ferocity, fatality, which are infernal. She is a goddess, but one not yet disimprisoned; one still half-imprisoned,—the articulate, lovely still encased in the inarticulate, chaotic. . . . Nature . . . is as a heavenly bride and conquest to the wise and brave, to them who can discern her behests and do them; a destroying fiend to them who cannot. . . . Nature is a dumb lioness, deaf to thy pleadings, fiercely devouring. Thou art not now her victorious bridegroom; thou art her mangled victim, scattered on the precipices, as a slave found treacherous, recreant, ought to be and must.[12]

Victorian texts broadly evidence such essentialist elements when depicting nature, which frequently emerges as inferior to human intellectual endeavor, resistant to control, obstructive to civilizational activity, and difficult to escape.

Perhaps unexpectedly, feminized nature appears in scientific work as well, notably in Charles Darwin's writings. His work, explains Gillian Beer in *Darwin's Plots*, "retains the idea of *natura naturans*, or the Great Mother, in its figuring of Nature." In one edition of *On the Origin of Species*, Beer relates, Darwin indicates the challenge of not presenting Nature as if a human presence. Beer reports, additionally, that the feminine pronoun invariably appears despite the fact that natural selection remains ungendered in varied references; she comments that feminized wording is present in Darwin's most famous work. "Man selects only for his own good: Nature only for that of the being which she tends," Darwin states in *Origin*. Referencing the age-old practice of feminizing nature, Beer identifies another Victorian scientist who used the feminine pronoun, John Tyndall, who averred, "In the application of her own principles, Nature often transcends the human imagination." Additionally, sexologist Ellis pronominally opined in *Man and Woman* that "Nature . . . has taken women under her special protection," insisting that "[t]he interests of women may . . . be said to be more closely identified with Nature's interests."[13]

If the nature-woman linkage were to become destabilized, however, the supposed justification to subordinate either entity would necessarily dissolve; no substantive difference then would characterize female versus male relationships to the natural world. Thus, the rationale underlying the domination of nature in a gender register would fall apart, enabling both sexes to respond positively and analogously to nature. The binary schematic traditionally existing between nature-women and culture-men would not exist in this ecofeminist model. The two sexes would experience the same relationships with culture and the natural world, Plumwood suggests. When "humans and nature [are] meeting on a common ground," Alaimo explains, "nature and culture merge, overlap, and collide."[14]

Domination

Domination of nature brings inexorable destruction, as Mathilde Blind's poetry, analyzed in chapter 2, forcefully reveals. Like the supposed equivalency of nature and women, the rationale for the pair's domination extends back to Genesis. The divine command to humanity is to "replenish the earth, and subdue it: and have dominion over the fish of the sea, and over the fowl of the air, and over every living thing that moveth upon the earth" (1:28). As Tong relates, the biblical injunction leads to interpretations that nature is merely a vehicle. Genesis explicitly addresses the domination of women by men through the dictum to nature-associated Eve that her spouse "shall rule over thee" (3:16). In Christian belief, humans also received naming authority for all beings, which additionally sanctioned control over nature, Lynn White Jr. contends in "The Historical Roots of Our Ecologic Crisis." To Christians, White indicates, the divine plan exclusively promoted human authority and interests. Moreover, in believing that it mirrored the divine image, humanity separated itself from the nonhuman world, White says. When Christianity replaced pagan belief—"the greatest psychic revolution in the history of our culture," White contends—humanity justified using nature as desired without considering the latter's own interests and discarded the view that innate spirits protected the natural world. Consequently, "old inhibitions to the exploitation of nature crumbled" under Christianity, which White designates as "the most anthropocentric religion the world has seen."[15]

The Scientific Revolution strongly reinforced the judgment that nature rightly falls under human control and exploitation. Francis Bacon became a pivotal figure in reshaping appraisals of nature. In analyzing his philosophy and pronouncements, Merchant indicates that Bacon valorized efforts to manipulate nature so that it could serve human interests. Merchant notes that Bacon considered feminized nature basically a pecuniary benefit suitable for exploitation and domination, ignoring the benevolent quality that nature formerly held and exploiting its mysteries to promote monetary objectives. Bacon even opines that torture is an appropriate fate for female nature, Merchant says. The feminization of nature offered Bacon a convenient vehicle for his project of environmental abuse, Merchant observes.[16]

Bacon's numerous comments on nature present a jarring picture of his philosophy. For example, Bacon argues that one should not accept that "the inquisition of nature is in any part interdicted or forbidden." He advocates that nature be "under constraint and vexed; that is to say, when by art and the hand of man she is forced out of her natural state, and squeezed and moulded." Referring approvingly to one parable's "chief aim," Bacon contends, "Man, if we look to final causes, may be regarded as the centre of the world; insomuch that if man were taken away from the world, the rest would seem to be astray, without aim or purpose." He further avers that "the whole world works together in the service of man." He maintains that for "a true son of science . . . when he has left the antechambers of nature trodden by the multitude, an entrance may at least be discovered to her inner apartments." He chides,

> Some in their simplicity are apprehensive that a too deep inquiry into nature may penetrate beyond the proper bounds of decorum, transferring and absurdly applying what is said of sacred mysteries in Holy Writ against those who pry into divine secrets, to the mysteries of nature, which are not forbidden by any prohibition.

Bacon approvingly quotes Democritus, who said, "[T]he truth of nature lies hid in certain deep mines and caves." Explaining that two types of natural philosophy exist, Bacon identifies "[t]he one searching into the bowels of nature, the other shaping nature as on an anvil."[17]

Other famous voices over the centuries have also denigrated nature by claiming that the earth is flawed, which has lent support to proponents of domination. Martin Luther, for example, declared that "[t]he world is the Devil and the Devil is the world." John Locke, John Calvin, and other Protestant figures believed that the divine plan included human dominance of the nonhuman realm, Merchant says. René Descartes opines in *Discourse on Method* that humans can become "the lords and possessors of nature" through their knowledge of its forces, which "is a result to be desired." Griffin discusses a nineteenth-century paleontologist and theologian, William Buckland, who considered that nature's purpose was to be useful, citing such supposed evidence as coal's being found where it can be extracted and animals' having four feet so that they can readily carry loads; as Griffin also explains, Buckland believed that women's role was merely to reproduce. With the development of industrial society, King relates, nature represented an instrument that humanity could manipulate for its own ends and exploit as it wished. As Irigaray indicates, Westerners have enacted "a violent domination over the natural universe" rather than demonstrating "a respect for, a contemplation of, a praise for or an alliance with it."[18]

The sense of being entitled to dominate the environment stems from the presumption that humanity is far superior to nature and thus is authorized to treat the environment however desired. Not surprisingly, in our own time, domination has been a major focus of ecofeminist attention, as an array of comments reveals. In fact, ecofeminism stems from the dual control exerted on nature and women, King explains. A belief that humanity is entitled to command nature means that women deserve domination as well because of their supposed connection, Tong says. Identical views and activities support patriarchal control over nature and over women, Patrick Curry indicates in *Ecological Ethics*. He emphasizes that the assumed nature-woman linkage means that efforts to undermine domination need to involve the two entities, not simply a single one. Tong calls for a rejection of bias based on the suppositions of humanity in general, and of males in particular. As Lori Gruen remarks in an essay on female and animal repression, domination enables a society to apply the label of inferiority and to rationalize subjugation of others. Cuomo cites "hierarchical, dualistic thinking" as characteristic of those in authoritative positions, propped up by untenable binary distinctions that likely provide the foundation for domination and subjection. Although a binary may seem unrelated to hierarchical positioning, Cuomo adds that the relationship can change when domination is the objective.[19]

Various dominative models have emerged to discern the complexities of the power relationships affecting nature as well as women. Karen J. Warren, for one, examines a "logic of domination" that relies on "a substantive value system." Humans claim superiority over nature to rationalize domination, a conclusion that relies on two related ideas, Warren contends: humans enjoy "moral superiority," and this characteristic provides the justification for controlling the nonhuman world. To Warren, "value-hierarchical thinking and value dualisms" are part of "the logic of domination." She defines the first term as "'up-down' thinking," which privileges one element of a binary, and the second term as binaries that validate male-associated rationality, or the mind, over female-linked emotionality, or the body. Cudworth assesses the "multiplicities of domination," positing three aspects that indicate different levels of control, as follows. Marginalization, which may seem less severe than the other forms, actually may cause greater damage because it can be so difficult to detect. Exploitation provides a means of achieving one's own goals by manipulating something else. Oppression entails an especially forceful domination. Cudworth employs the word "anthroparchy" to designate the intricate means by which humanity controls nature.[20]

Passive versus Active

Denying activity and agency allows nature to be objectified and rendered, as Donna Haraway puts it in "Situated Knowledges," "the raw material of culture, appropriated, preserved, enslaved, exalted, or otherwise made flexible for disposal by culture." The feminization of nature advances such projects since all the negative traits associated with women are also conferred upon the natural world, with passivity high on the list. Legler encapsulates the Haraway perspective by urging a reassessment of nature so that it can "be conceived of as more than inert matter that is probed and penetrated; that it have metaphorical status as a speaking, feeling, alive subject," not an immutable object. Assumptions that nature is static, fixed, and ahistorical are deeply flawed from an ecofeminist perspective. Spring, for example, reveals multiple agentic aspects, which Irigaray cites in characterizing its many forms of activity, such as blooming. Moreover, the earth will "laugh," "rustle," and "quiver" as it is "inhabited by an invisible growth," she says. As Murray Bookchin contends in discussing a "green future," the mistaken belief that the natural world is invariable "belies its fecundity, its wealth of change, and its richness of development." In brief, "[n]ature is turbulently active."[21]

For centuries, the dismaying perception has existed that feminized nature is passive, a notion that fosters a propensity toward domination by an agential entity. Aristotle remarked, for instance, that women are not only passive but also serve as ready receptacles, Griffin notes. In contrast to the passive female, he opined that "the male, as male, is active, and the principle of movement comes from him." Centuries later, in the Renaissance era, Merchant advises, this attitude continued to be promulgated. Passivity became attached to the natural world and to women, making them ready targets to be exploited, Merchant comments. Such an attitude toward a passive and exploitable nature remained entrenched in the Victorian era as well.[22]

Ostensibly scientific conclusions in the nineteenth century reaffirmed female passivity. Darwin maintains in *The Descent of Man, and Selection in Relation to Sex*, for instance, that men are more "energetic than woman," with "more inventive genius." The widely read *Evolution of Sex*, appearing at the *fin de siècle*, asserts that females are "anabolic," in contrast to the "katabolic," or more active, males. The authors, Patrick Geddes and J. Arthur Thomson, extrapolate these traits to mental as well as physical ability because the sexes are so dissimilar. Among other effects, Geddes and Thomson contend that "masculine activity lends a greater power of maximum effort, of scientific insight, or cerebral experiment with impressions," and "a stronger grasp of generalities." In contrast, zoologist W. K. Brooks believed in 1879, passivity means that "the female mind is a storehouse filled with the instincts, habits, intuitions, and laws of conduct which have been gained by past experience." The male, however, represents "the originating element" who has "the power of extending experience over new fields." As these examples indicate, the activity attributed to males was far more desirable than the passivity accorded to females.[23]

Considering the tight connection drawn between nature and women, it follows, under a distorted logic that assumes passivity in women, that nature would seem passive compared to an active humanity, a conclusion that Michael Field's poetry strongly belies, as discussed in chapter 3. Legler remarks that male-dominated societies consider nature and female corporeality "as passive, interceptive, docile, as mirror and complement." Curiously, the contention that nature is passive conveniently ignores the undeniable force that the nonhuman world can wield, with potent storms, mighty winds, and other intensely active manifestations. Ecofeminist theory has denounced the cultural presumption of passivity and urged a dramatic reassessment of the nonhuman world as agential rather than static. Alaimo, for instance, seeks a new definition of nature that eliminates stagnancy. In *Material Feminisms*, Alaimo and Susan Hekman identify nature's active quality and the ramifications that this agency carries for nature as well as for humanity. Approaching the issue from the human rather than nonhuman standpoint in describing one view, Noël Sturgeon states in *Ecofeminist Natures*, "If women are equated with nature, their struggle for freedom represents a challenge to the idea of a passive, disembodied, and objectified nature."[24]

Haraway discusses agency in a context that could usher forth a redemptive analysis of nature. Feminists, Haraway argues, have opposed the notion that "an 'object' of knowledge is a passive and inert thing" as a means for countering efforts to appropriate, manipulate, and dominate that enable the natural realm to be "reduced to [a] resource for instrumentalist projects of destructive Western societies" or to be "seen as masks for interests, usually dominating interests." Haraway's approach offers insights applicable to ecofeminist thought, for example, in maintaining that "the object" demonstrates agency rather than simply existing as an exploitative possibility or an insignificant background. Haraway credits ecofeminists for their emphatic claim that the earth is itself an agent instead of an object suitable for masculine usurpation and utilization, calling the ecofeminist approach a "rich feminist practice."[25]

Nature versus Culture

The longstanding dichotomy crafted between nature and culture, as briefly mentioned earlier, has invariably privileged the latter term, with nature deemed a wild, disorderly, and material entity in contrast to the cultural arena's status as measured, rational, and cognitive. Alaimo comments on the seemingly unbreakable hold that the nature/culture distinction possesses as well as the dichotomy's vital role undergirding the West's belief system. This prevalent assumption, Alaimo says, has created an energetic culture but a stagnant nature. Sherry B. Ortner writes in an essay on gender, culture, and nature that "men are identified not only with culture, in the sense of all human creativity, as opposed to nature; they are identified in particular with culture in the old fashioned sense of the finer and higher aspects of human thought—art, religion, law, etc." Supposedly, as Plumwood indicates, their unruly corporeality firmly locates women within the natural realm, according to the dichotomy distinguishing culture and nature. Victorians strove to reinforce a definitive boundary between nature and the supposedly oppositional pole of the binary with culture. Yet Alice Meynell's poetry, discussed in chapter 4, takes the very different position that nature is an integral cultural component.[26]

Providing a helpful lens on the nature/culture issue, contemporary scientific presumptions held that women could not participate robustly in cultural projects because of their inferior minds. An especially vitriolic and misogynistic scientist, anthropologist J. McGrigor Allan, blithely asserted that "[t]he inventing, discovering, creating, cogitating mind is pre-eminently masculine," which conforms to his declaration that "the history of humanity is conclusive as to the mental supremacy of the male sex." Anthropologist and criminologist Cesare Lombroso decided that women cannot be geniuses because only men can claim such intellectual strength. Allan surmised that men have been responsible for "[t]he ideas on which depend all the marvellous acts of human intelligence," which accorded with his logic that "in intellectual power, woman will always fall far short of man." Zoologist Brooks attributed to "the male mind . . . the ability to pursue original trains of abstract thought, to reach the great generalizations of science, and to give rise to the new creations of poetry and art." Grant Allen, a biologist and novelist, succinctly proclaimed that "the males are the race," in that "[a]ll that is distinctly human is man." Positivist Frederic Harrison confidently remarked that "no woman has ever approached Aristotle and Archimedes, Shakespeare and Descartes, Raphael and Mozart, or has ever shown even a kindred sum of powers." To psychologist Harry Campbell, not even unequal opportunities could entirely account for the dearth of female accomplishments, since "we cannot doubt that, had a woman Shakespeare or Beethoven potentially existed, the world would have heard of her in spite of unfavouring external circumstances."[27]

Ortner's detailed analysis of the nature/culture dichotomy is especially relevant here, for her account references the binary's prevalence in all societies. Ortner explains that societies fashion varied creations to elevate themselves over the natural world and shape it to their own needs and desires. Culture thus provides the instrument for dominating nature, Ortner says. Not unexpectedly, the preeminence of culture is presumed in its separation from nature through the former's claim to higher status. "[T]hat sense of distinctiveness and superiority," Ortner argues, "rests precisely on the ability to transform—to 'socialize' and 'culturalize'—nature."[28]

Ecofeminists have demonstrated that the nature/culture binary cannot hold, for women undeniably participate in culture. Even though societies relegate women to the nature side, Ortner comments, women obviously are "full-fledged human being[s] endowed with human consciousness just as a man is." Of course women are involved in cultural activities, Ortner stresses, even though a culture may position females on a hierarchical ladder somewhere between the two poles of nature and culture but pointedly lower than the males' level. As King puts it, society considers women to occupy a "bridge-like position between nature and culture."[29]

Assessing language and ecosystems, Griffin maintains that cultural claims to superiority over nature produce distance and division, but she argues that the supposed gap is merely illusionary: language cannot be separated from nature since nature itself provides the linguistic source. Griffin selects as an example the term "culture," which derives from cultivation of the land. Thus, "what we think of as transcendent thought is not only dependent on nature," Griffin concludes, "but reshapes the very substance and manner of significance through an understanding of natural processes it nevertheless describes as separate from intelligence."[30]

Embodied Spirituality

"Ecofeminist spirituality" constitutes a comprehensive term, for many distinct and sometimes antithetical philosophies exist. In general terms, as Warren notes, ecofeminist spiritualities question patriarchal convictions and replace them with "nondominating and life-affirming beliefs, values, behaviors, and relationships among humans and toward nonhuman nature." However, ecofeminism encompasses varied views on the role that spirituality plays, she observes. For example, some ecofeminists embrace the possibility that conventional religious thought can be reimagined in ways that value rather than deride both nature and women, Warren explains.[31]

Ecofeminist theological approaches have taken issue with the traditional Christian acceptance of God as a detached, disembodied, and male divinity whose followers believe that a chasm exists between spirituality and materiality. Christianity has invariably elevated the spiritual component, appraising the materialist aspect as besmirched and degraded. As a result, the human body has accumulated negative associations that establish physicality as a route to sinfulness.

Gillian McCulloch argues in *The Deconstruction of Dualism in Theology* that "patriarchal spirituality" stresses a separation from corporeality as well as from nature "to achieve a superior God-like status." Consequently, Christianity has credited divine authority with enabling control of women and nature, McCulloch says. With its materiality, nature also falls into the unprivileged category, a condition that, as shown in chapter 5, Constance Naden adamantly opposes in her poetry. Prominent theologian Sallie McFague encapsulates multiple arguments in saying that "Christian tradition is and has been not only deeply androcentric . . . , but also deeply anthropocentric." An important path in ecofeminist theology follows a far different line, seeking to reject the assumed fissure between spirituality and materiality through the notion that God is a body and that the whole universe experiences the divine embrace. Regardless of a woman's spiritual inclinations, says Tong, it is crucial that embodiment, not ethereality, be the core for belief and significance. Ecofeminists have carefully examined religious belief systems that encourage the repression of both nature and women, Carol J. Adams writes in *Ecofeminism and the Sacred*.[32]

Suitably, ecofeminist spirituality endeavors to deconstruct dualisms and hierarchies as a vital priority. McCulloch asserts that the ecofeminist stance strives both to repudiate dualistic thought and to embrace "a 'holistic' concept of the God-world relationship." Ecofeminist theologian Rosemary Radford Ruether encourages a reassessment of Western theological support for a "hierarchical chain of being and chain of command" through which humanity subordinates the nonhuman world. The hierarchical approach, Ruether explains, "starts with nonmaterial spirit (God) as the source of the chain of being and continues down to nonspiritual 'matter' as the bottom of the chain of being and the most inferior, valueless, and dominated point in the chain of command." Instead, Ruether urges the dismissal of a "view of nature as 'dead matter' to be dominated" and seeks "an understanding of nature as living beings in dynamic communities of life." The objective, Ruether explains, is to convert nature and humanity into partners.[33]

The idea that God is a body offers recuperative possibilities in ecofeminist spirituality, for instead of exclusion, nature would participate in a comprehensive design. The universe becomes the divine corpus, McFague says in the appropriately titled *The Body of God*, and the universe's multifarious components, "from the most distant galaxies to the tiniest fragment of life," are interrelated. Thus, the concept of the divine body would encompass all things, human and otherwise, McFague affirms, so that "body" includes all material forms. If God is a body, she argues, the "monarchical model," which situates God at the apex of a domain based on rank, can be discarded. Humans become nature's partners rather than the centralized "goal of creation." McFague stresses that humans are part of an extensive ecological populace connected by close interrelationships. This revised schematic strongly contests the Christian disparagement of materiality, McFague asserts. Rejecting the supposition of disembodiment would end the bias against materiality, she believes. As Roger S. Gottlieb succinctly summarizes the issue in *This Sacred Earth*, "Ecofeminist spirituality tends to celebrate the body and the earth."[34]

Ecofeminist Principles

The term "ecofeminism" has been widely attributed to Françoise d'Eaubonne's 1974 "The Time for Ecofeminism," although this origin has been contested. In a 1991 book review, Ariel Salleh argues that the 1970s saw the term "spontaneously appearing" around the world, and related literature emerged. Greta Gaard, who considers ecofeminism to be an aspect of feminism, likewise maintains in *Ecological Politics* that ecofeminism did not arise from merely one source, noting that ecofeminism's beginnings extend back to Rachel Carson's significant efforts. Regardless of the terminological disagreement, ecofeminism began to make its mark in the 1970s, when concerns about the treatment of both nature and women especially took hold; as d'Eaubonne asserts, feminist environmental concerns were still in their earliest stage before 1973, when ecofeminist activity was gaining ground. Merchant credits a greater understanding of the nature-woman linkage for ecofeminism's growth and d'Eaubonne's charge to women that they protect the earth through "an ecological revolution." Nonetheless, as Gaard remarks, feminist ecological ideas had appeared in the nineteenth century, a historical aspect that definitively underlies this study. Indeed, an ecofeminist lens has illuminated not only writings then but also those crafted during the eighteenth century, Coffey says. In the twentieth century, as Andrea Campbell states in *New Directions in Ecofeminist Literary Criticism*, the final decades saw "ecofeminism struggl[ing] to find its place." With numerous factions articulating diverse standpoints across a broad spectrum, ecofeminist particularities have been the subject of much debate. Since multiple approaches exist, Warren considers the word "ecofeminism" an "umbrella term" that covers the range of ideas.[35]

Nevertheless, the underlying premise among the many articulations has continued to be the shared oppression of nature and women, which various descriptions of ecofeminism reveal. "What *all* ecofeminists agree about, then, is the way in which *the logic of domination* has functioned historically within patriarchy," Warren remarks, "to sustain and justify the twin dominations of women and nature." In *Nature Ethics*, Marti Kheel observes that oppression becomes vulnerable and mutable when understood as historically grounded. Cudworth advises that ecofeminism encompasses varied viewpoints that assess a culture's perception of both gender and nature, adding that ecofeminism strives to identify the linkages and the mechanisms that cause "difference and domination [to] interlock." Curry maintains that "the same *logic*, the same *processes*, and, by and large, the same *people*" are responsible for the treatment of both nature and women. For Timothy Clark, writing about environmental literature, ecofeminism's central principle concerns ecological devastation and female subjection as well as their close connection. Kate Sandilands views ecofeminism as a connector in that it "locates itself as a theory and movement which bridges the gap between feminism and ecology, but which transforms both to create a unified praxis to end all forms of domination." Some comments about ecofeminist priorities point especially to the positioning of nature. Referencing the breadth and changeability of the word "nature," Plumwood suggests that the term has experienced colonization manifested in numerous ways, and she seeks analysis of subjugation in its multiple configurations to provide a full picture.[36]

Various criteria have been applied to assess the differences in ecofeminist positions, and a few examples follow here. Plumwood considers the diversity based "on how and even whether women are connected to nature, on whether such a connection is in principle sharable by men," as well as on "how the revaluing of the connection with nature connects with the revaluing of traditional feminine characteristics generally." Sandilands cites a pair of historical analyses in ecofeminism that Plumwood had identified: the first concentrates on damaging dualistic thought based on hierarchical judgments that promote subordination, while the second focuses on Enlightenment-era changes that validated mechanistic approaches to nature. In *Ecofeminism*, Carol J. Adams and Lori Gruen list significant dualisms that valorize culture, human beings, males, and intellectuality over nature, nonhuman entities, females, and the body, respectively. Cuomo situates ecofeminist attitudes across a broad range that at one side essentializes a nature-women connection while at the other side assumes a poststructuralist stance focused on linguistic linkages. Sturgeon delineates several positions, which may be interwoven: the nature-women relationship can be said to involve exploitation, judgment of inferiority, attentiveness to environmental issues, biological correspondence to nature's rhythms, and spirituality grounded in nature.[37]

The 1990s constituted an important moment in ecofeminism, with the charge of essentialism undermining the movement's impact. Indeed, Cuomo contends that essentialism is likely the greatest criticism leveled at ecofeminism. Although agreeing that essentialism has figured in numerous ecofeminist positions, Catriona Mortimer-Sandilands asserts in "Eco/Feminism on the Edge" that essentialism has often been absent in ecofeminist argumentation. Repudiating ecofeminism as a whole ignores the field's variety, and "ecofeminism has become a favorite straw-woman for a one-dimensional, anti-essentialist postmodern feminist attack," Cuomo concludes. A restrictive viewpoint characterizing some influential feminist circles informs the readily made judgments of essentialism, Alaimo maintains. The early 1990s saw ecofeminism virtually rejected, Gaard explains. Shortly thereafter, Charis Thompson remarks in "Back to Nature?," feminism had pushed ecofeminism aside. So strong was the backlash against ecofeminism that academics were advised to avoid making the term "ecofeminist" prominent in their writings, Gaard relates. By 2010, she states, "poststructuralist and other third-wave feminisms portrayed all ecofeminisms as an exclusively essentialist equation of women with nature," and those movements rejected the wealth of ecofeminist thought so broadly that almost no relevant initiatory collections carried essays about ecofeminism or related issues. The term was "irretrievably tainted," says Mortimer-Sandilands. Consequently, Gaard reports, a new vocabulary emerged to recuperate positive ecofeminist contributions, and such terms as "feminist environmentalism," "social ecofeminism," and "ecological feminism" appeared. Not all, however, agreed with the rejection of the original term.[38]

Another word, "ecocriticism," replaced the discarded "ecofeminism" and in the process removed the foundation that feminism had provided, says Estok. Ecocriticism, as Clark indicates, offers a methodological spectrum, not a specific approach. Estok asserts that ecocriticism considers ecofeminism to be a dead approach offering few contributions rather than appraising it as "a work in progress." He argues, however, that feminism needs to inform ecocriticism, and that such a relationship characterizes all effective ecocriticism. Estok further questions the creation of the term "ecocriticism" since it shares ecofeminist goals. Distancing itself from its ecofeminist beginnings may mean that ecocriticism is actually hostile to feminism, he posits. Interestingly, Clark believes that ecocriticism's most advanced form may be ecofeminism.[39]

Despite assaults on and departures from ecofeminism, there have been efforts to recuperate its significant contributions. Gaard says that aspects of ecofeminism could be recovered and a sense of history regained, which would enhance contemporary approaches. Various individuals have retained the term "ecofeminism" to revive the word and its past, Gaard notes. In fact, she argues, "[t]he first task . . . involves recuperating the large history of feminist ecocriticism, and the contributions of ecofeminist literary criticism within ecocritical thinking." Adopting the valuation that Gaard presents, *Reconceiving Nature* employs the term "ecofeminism" rather than its substitutions.[40]

The Victorian Environment

Ecofeminist ideas become particularly relevant in evaluating the effects of the Industrial Revolution during the Victorian era. The modern concept of the current Anthropocene, an unofficial geological era, provides a helpful perspective as well in that the term blurs the division between the natural world and humanity's effects upon it. The starting date given for the Anthropocene varies in disciplinary studies, Tobias Menely and Jesse Oak Taylor report in *Anthropocene Reading*, but they indicate that the term's creators identified the late eighteenth century as the origin with the invention of the steam engine. Taylor coins the term "abnatural" in *The Sky of Our Manufacture* to indicate that "[n]ature in the Anthropocene exists in a state of perpetual withdrawal," noting that the term "speaks to both nature's absence and its uncanny persistence." In an ecological context, the concept involves "the experience of dwelling in a manufactured environment, wherein everything . . . bears the traces of human action." The "abnatural" concept is particularly applicable to ecofeminism in general and to this book in particular, for human activity in the male-directed Victorian culture brought grave harm to the natural world through its material effects as well as the damaging attitudes it fostered.[41]

The ravages of industrialization were broadly evident in the nineteenth century, with pollution of both air and water an especially appalling result. Indeed, Friedrich Engels says of a Manchester region in his famous *The Condition of the Working Class in England*, "Everything in this district that arouses our disgust and just indignation is of relatively recent origin and belongs to the industrial age," endangering "the health of thousands." Engels condemns the English for an indifference to the conditions that industrialization had wrought: "English society *is fully aware* how dangerous is this environment to the health and life of the workers, and yet takes no action to reform the situation."[42]

Coal was a primary culprit, and its imprint on the environment was especially apparent. In *An Environmental History of Great Britain*, I. G. Simmons presents devastating facts about widespread pollution from coal use in multiple locales. "The burning of coal in homes, workplaces and railways, together with the by-products of the chemical industry, were led off into the air in a more or less uncontrolled fashion until enforceable legislation began to take effect after mid-century," Simmons relates. Surprisingly, domestic use accounted for roughly 85 percent of smoke output, Simmons notes, and it did not see regulation until the twentieth century. By the middle of the nineteenth century, Simmons reveals, 10 million tons of coal had been burned, and the figure rose to 167 million tons by 1900. A distinctive, putrid odor emanated from some industrial sites and could spread twenty-five kilometers, says Simmons, and sewage contributed to the horrible aroma. "[T]he nineteenth-century city was not a place of high nasal amenity," Simmons remarks. In the century's final decade, Simmons reports, smoke caused fogs that reached their highest levels in London.[43]

As Alice Meynell commented in 1898, the city's air was "more than half an artificial climate" as a result of "our own handiwork" in creating "the smoke-mingled sky." Mathilde Blind wrote in *The Ascent of Man* of "the black sky, redly glowing," which "[l]oomed over the city one ominous glare, / As dark yawning funnels from foul throats for ever / Belched smoke grimly flaming, which outraged the air." Late Victorian London provides a key example of the Anthropocene; the city constituted "a novel ecosystem," which references the ecological effects brought by human intervention, as Taylor explains. He defines this London ecosystem as "a manufactured environment in which every scrap of ground and breath of air bore traces of human action."[44]

Engels spoke of London air pollution, among the city's other ills, causing the "unwholesome atmosphere of the working-class quarters." Contributing to the terrible air quality were "[t]he filth and the stagnant pools in the working class quarters," which initiated disease-causing gases intensified by "the miasma exuded by foul streams." Engels blamed pollution for the unhealthy demeanor of numerous Londoners, as well as their susceptibility to consumption. These individuals were the "pale, emaciated, narrow-chested and hollow-eyed ghosts who are to be met with in such large numbers every minute in London."[45]

The evils of pollution also spread to rural areas, in part causing lichens to decline, which signaled a problem with air contamination, Heidi C. M. Scott explains in a study of British ecological literature in the nineteenth century. Coal use spewed acids and other noxious chemicals into the air that damaged crops and brought grave harm to trees, Simmons states. As James Winter comments in a book on the Victorian environmental situation, there was a "perception that the city was intruding everywhere, sending out its tentacles to grasp even the most precious of the remaining natural sanctuaries." By the 1870s, steam plows had a decided presence on sizable farmlands, and forty thousand mechanical reapers were in operation in England, Simmons reports.[46]

Trees suffered another assault in being extensively sought by industry, Winter says, and forest devastation received little attention except from prescient observers. He writes of one geographer who contended in 1879 that technological use jeopardized the planet's forestation and would create unforeseeable changes to plant systems. The fueling of steam engines was "leaving behind in the remaining wildernesses a path of destruction," he indicates. Speaking of deforestation in *Capital*, Karl Marx maintained, "The development of culture and of industry in general has ever evinced itself in such energetic destruction of forests that everything done by it conversely for their preservation and restoration appears infinitesimal." Acid rain was identified midcentury in the Manchester area, Scott says. In 1893, Scott relates, a chemist said that evergreens and deciduous trees could not survive in cities with large pollution outputs, citing the harm from air contamination and insidious deposits.[47]

Energy production left its injurious mark on water as well as air, and Simmons cites the following effects. Because of pollution, Yorkshire waters in midcentury looked like ink, a canal could catch fire, and sewage odors caused Parliament to break off a workweek one year. Pollution devastated and ruined wetland habitats. Sewage, various industrial effluents, and coal products entered waterways, and river inhabitants perished. Although sewers existed, London waste emptied into the Thames, Simmons explains of these various pollution events. The *Illustrated London News* decried the decline in the river's water quality in an 1858 editorial titled "The Purification of the Thames."

> The Thames, which, fifty years ago, ran through London in a clear and lim-pid stream, over whose current it was a pleasure to be rowed, in whose waves it was delightful to bathe, and of whose pure waters it was wholesome to drink, has, by sheer neglect on the part both of the people and the Govern-ment, become a foul sewer, a river of pollution, a Stream of Death, festering and reeking with all abominable smells, and threatening three millions of people with pestilence as the penalty of their ignorance and apathy.

The periodical was not alone in its indictment. An 1858 commentary in *House-hold Words* by Edmund Saul Dixon lamented the wide-ranging injury that pol-lution caused, making the Thames "the receptacle of outcast filth" and damaging other waterways as well.

> [W]e have utterly polluted and defiled one of the noblest watercourses in the world. This has occurred in the metropolis. As a natural consequence, in the provinces, we have more or less polluted and defiled other watercourses . . . of great positive beauty and utility. We have banished fish, . . . we have destroyed water-weeds, which would absorb noxious elements, and give out pure oxygen, if we would permit them to exist; we have left no living aquatic type remaining, except the lowest and the most rudimentary.

Not surprisingly, considering the abundant industrial activity in northern me-tropolises, water pollution was especially prevalent there. Among his writings on Manchester, Engels presents a startling portrayal of the Irk waterway, seen stag-nating rather than robustly moving. He depicts the Irk as "a narrow, coal-black, stinking river full of filth and rubbish which it deposits on the more low-lying right bank." Even without rainy weather, Engels relates, there was a "spectacle of a series of the most revolting blackish-green puddles of slime from the depths of which bubbles of miasmatic gases constantly rise and create a stench which is unbearable." The presumed sources of pollution were the nearby tanneries, dye-works, gasworks, and bone mills from which "[a]ll the filth, both liquid and solid, . . . finds its way into the River Irk." Only in 1876 did England pass the Rivers Pollution Prevention Act, and definitive laws did not exist until the mid-twentieth century, Simmons relates.[48]

The many destructive results of widespread pollution garnered opposition, of course, as the previously cited pronouncements make clear. In fact, the Victorian age was witnessing signs of ecological sensitivity in the wake of the Industrial Revolution. As Engels warns in *Dialectics of Nature*, for instance, "The animal merely *uses* external nature . . . man by his changes makes it serve his ends, *masters* it." He adds, "Let us not, however, flatter ourselves overmuch on account of our human conquests over nature. For each such conquest takes its revenge on us."[49]

Literary figures were no exception in entering the environmental conversation, and among the most prominent was John Ruskin. Ruskin succinctly presented his perspective in observing, "The light, the air, the waters, all defiled!" Mark Frost in "Reading Nature" characterizes Ruskin as "[u]niquely gifted in reading the signs of a healthy environment" as well as "unusually sensitive in discerning environmental breakdown." In various writings, Ruskin strongly denounces the destruction from pollution. He asserts in *Fors Clavigera*, for example, that his myopic contemporaries "have shut the sun out with smoke" and converted a landscape painted "in green, and blue, and all imaginable colours" into a bleak brown terrain. Indeed, "the horrible nests, which you call towns, are little more than laboratories for the distillation into heaven of venomous smokes and smells." Instead of "planting in all soils the trees which cleanse and invigorate earth and atmosphere," Victorians had caused harm "by ravage of woods"; instead of English waters teeming with life and beauty, self-serving Philistines had created "a common sewer." Railway construction through one valley "blasted its rocks away, heaped thousands of tons of shale into its lovely stream," with the result that "[t]he valley is gone." Discussing a particular English road in "Fiction, Fair and Foul," Ruskin declares that "no existing terms of language known to me are enough to describe the forms of filth, and modes of ruin, that varied themselves along the course of Croxted Lane." Railway builders had decimated the land by digging and lacerating the terrain. Consequently devoid of grass, the lane was "bordered on each side by heaps of—Hades only knows what!—mixed dust of every unclean thing that can crumble in draught, and mildew of every unclean thing that can rot or rust in damp." With the extensive environmental degradation, Ruskin charges in *Fors Clavigera*, "you have turned the Mother-Earth, Demeter, into the Avenger-Earth, Tisiphone." In *Modern Painters*, Ruskin muses upon the "infinite wonderfulness there is in this vegetation, considered, as indeed it is, the means by which the earth becomes the companion of man—his friend and teacher!" Ruskin decries cities in *Praeterita*, calling them "the very centres of pollution, of avarice, and impiety" and condemning contemporaries for "blasting the cultivable surface of England into a treeless waste of ashes."[50]

Other literary figures also harshly criticized the changes that industrialization and environmental degradation had brought. In "Signs of the Times," for instance, Carlyle designates his era "the Age of Machinery." He contends, "Only the material, the immediately practical, . . . is important to us," with merely "a calculation of the Profitable" valued. Listing numerous alterations to quotidian life, Carlyle objects that "[w]e remove mountains, and make seas our smooth highway; nothing can resist us." Moreover, "[w]e war with rude Nature; and by our resistless engines, come off always victorious, and loaded with spoils." Carlyle claims, "Our true Deity is Mechanism. It has subdued external Nature for us." He argues that "we are but fettered by chains of our own forging" and adds, "This deep, paralysed subjection to physical objects comes not from Nature, but from our own unwise mode of *viewing* Nature." Suggesting environmental respect, Carlyle in *Sartor Resartus* asks of nature, "Art not thou the 'Living Garment of God'?" Noting "the Volume of Nature," he asserts that its "Author and Writer is God" and wonders, "Dost thou, does man, so much as well know the Alphabet thereof?"[51]

Later in the century, Hopkins laments in "Binsey Poplars" the destruction of aspen trees, "[a]ll felled, felled, are all felled," with none "spared, not one." He adds, "O if we but knew what we do / When we delve or hew— / Hack and rack the growing green!" The regrettable result becomes evident when "[a]fter-comers cannot guess the beauty been." In "Inversnaid," Hopkins raises a dismal scenario in wondering, "What would the world be, once bereft / Of wet and of wildness?" He pleads, "Let them be left, / Oh, let them be left, wildness and wet; / Long live the weeds and the wilderness yet." William Morris voices his ecological concerns in the utopian novel *News from Nowhere*, considering the past and looking to a better world. In fact, Morris is characterized as "[t]he linchpin of the 'back to nature' movement" in Peter Coates's Western history of nature. Morris's novel poses the question, "[D]on't you find it difficult to imagine the times when this little pretty country was treated by its folk as if it had been an ugly characterless waste, with no delicate beauty to be guarded?" The speaker wonders, "How could people be so cruel to themselves?" The ideal England presented in the novel had overcome its environmental assaults. Speaking of England's "second birth," one character proclaims, "The spirit of the new days . . . was to be delight in the life of the world; intense and over-weening love of the very skin and surface of the earth." The narrator describes the contrast in the eras by saying, for instance, that on the shores of the Thames, "[t]he soap-works with their smoke-vomiting chimneys were gone; the engineer's works gone; the lead-works gone." In another area, "the sprawling mess with which commercialism had littered the banks of the wide stream" had been removed, so that "certainly everything smelt too deliciously in the early night for there to be any of the old careless sordidness of so-called manufacture." Another futuristic novel, *After London; Or, Wild England*, by naturalist Richard Jefferies, focuses on "the nature that civilization had replaced," observes Taylor. "Jefferies' London," Taylor adds, "is not simply extinct but inimical to life."[52]

Victorian ecological awareness benefited from that of its Romantic predecessors. Indeed, Romanticism coincided with the Anthropocene's "onset of carboniferous industrialization," writes contributor Thomas H. Ford in Menely and Taylor's *Anthropocene Reading*. The era showed its ecological consciousness, as Jonathan Bate states in *Romantic Ecology*, by promoting a positive relationship with nature. William Wordsworth, after all, is universally deemed a nature enthusiast, and verse by William Blake, Samuel Taylor Coleridge, Percy Bysshe Shelley, and others demonstrates an attentiveness to and respect for nature. Romantic progenitors have positively influenced current ecocritical approaches also, David Pepper contends in *Modern Environmentalism*, adding that the two eras reveal definitive connections regarding their environmental outlooks. Clark credits Romanticism for generating modern ecocritical consciousness, referring to that period's rejection of the damaging Enlightenment desire to subdue the nonhuman world. To Bate, "Romantic ecology" presumes the existence of "'one life' within us and abroad, that the earth is a single vast ecosystem which we destabilize at our peril"; for Clark, present-day ecology echoes the Romantic claim that nature is "a holistic living agent or spirit in which all participate and interact." As Bate notes, Romanticism denigrated the high valuation placed on economic gain. Romantic ecology influenced not only modern ecocriticism but ecofeminism as well, Clark contends, for Romanticism opposed an excessive turn to rationalism and elevated the importance of corporeality.[53]

Of course, Wordsworth has become the seminal literary figure in Romantic ecology. As Bate comments, Wordsworth was the "Poet of Nature" in Shelley's phrase and held that status with Victorians as well; Wordsworth influenced numerous followers in advising "how to walk with nature." Victorian adherents to Wordsworth included such prominent writers as Ruskin, who credited the poet with giving him the ability to perceive nature, Bate relates, and John Stuart Mill, who said Wordsworth's briefer verses "addressed themselves powerfully to one of the strongest of my pleasurable susceptibilities, the love of rural objects and natural scenery." Although Bate indicates that Wordsworth did not initiate the ecological "tradition," the poet nevertheless markedly shaped its contours. Yet, as Hess contends, Wordsworth exhibited a "possessive relationship to landscape."[54]

Although Romantic ecological consciousness affected the Victorians, there was a notable difference in the environmental conditions of the two periods. The Romantic era experienced an earlier phase of industrialization in which environmental degradation was considerably less intensive than it would become during the Victorian era. As John Parham reminds in writing about Victorian environmentalism, the later nineteenth century saw a magnification of the earlier industrial repercussions. At the same time, urban growth brought a host of difficulties, not only employment and lodging challenges but also a range of "ecological problems—sanitation, air quality, disease, deforestation." Moreover, the Romantic impulse to focus on the self created an impediment to a greater ecological consciousness. The year 1830 became a critical one, says Linda K. Hughes, for "nature changed" then; the new railways ushered forth "the death of older configurations of nature," aided by the vast expansion of geological history and Darwinian natural selection.[55]

From a modern standpoint, the nineteenth century undoubtedly represents a significant period of ecological awareness. For example, Frost credits midcentury and later developments for influencing modern ecology. Coates remarks in his book on Westerners' approaches to nature that "proto-ecological ideas attached to evolutionary theory were in the mid-nineteenth century air." Indeed, the term "ecology" originated in 1866 and Ernst Haeckel, a German zoologist, penned a description in 1870, Coates mentions.[56]

Victorianists have attended to environmental developments. As Barri J. Gold comments in an essay on nineteenth-century ecology, modern critics have successfully scrutinized the era for environmental connections. In fact, Gold maintains that the Victorian period has had a substantial influence on modern conceptions of the nonhuman realm. Moreover, Laurence W. Mazzeno and Ronald D. Morrison advise in *Victorian Writers and the Environment* that "the field is still being shaped." Parham suggests that "'Victorian ecology' . . . offers a rich mine of sources for the 'tradition of environmental consciousness'" and advocates expansive consideration of the subject. Parham identifies aspects that led to the idea of Victorian ecology: it occurred near the time frame of modern ecological activity; it reflected views about society and the sciences; it influenced Victorian literature; it revealed ideological resonances; and it became a movement during the century's penultimate decade. Speaking of Victorian poetry specifically, Nicholas Frankel states that "one can sense in Victorian ecological verse a discernible effort to dissolve the confines of self in the dynamics of environmental interaction."[57]

Modern ecocriticism about Victorian literature includes disparate views, Parham observes, and the environment influenced much verse, Frankel argues. Nonetheless, a perception exists that ecocritical commentaries are lacking in Victorian studies, Taylor says. He speculates that a possible reason for the supposed paucity is that critics have not included the specific terminology but have none-theless embraced such work for an extended time. Much ecocritical endeavor has developed from the study of Romanticism, with Victorian coverage frequently evolving from that, he says. Citing the work of Ruskin, Hopkins, and Morris, Gold states that "recently, scholars have begun to argue for the environment or ecological concerns in what may seem unlikely places." The poems of the six women in this study perhaps represent some of these "unlikely places."[58]

Common Ties

Aside from their ecofeminist approaches, the six women poets featured in *Reconceiving Nature* are connected in several other ways as well. For example, Augusta Webster, like Alice Meynell, Mathilde Blind, and Constance Naden, passionately supported the rights of women, as subsequent chapters will address. Blind "identified most closely" with Michael Field, the pseudonym adopted by Katharine Bradley and Edith Cooper, and others contesting the status quo, says Blind biographer James Diedrick. Arthur Symons praised Blind's *Ascent of Man* to Field and Blind knew of Field's collection *Long Ago*, Diedrick indicates. In fact, Blind expressed interest in meeting Field, Diedrick notes, and the poets did have the opportunity to do so. Meynell admired Field and also wanted to be introduced to the pair, though the meeting did not occur, Angela Leighton indicates. Constance Naden and Edith Cooper were cousins, Emma Donoghue reports, and Naden wanted Cooper to visit, Leighton says.[59]

Other linkages abound. Blind and Meynell both attended the Literary Ladies club, Hughes remarks. Webster visited salons, and Blind attended a gathering that Webster herself held, Patricia Rigg observes. Webster and Blind were both *Athenaeum* reviewers, and Webster even reviewed work by Blind and Field. Moreover, Blind reviewed Webster's collection, *Yu-Pe-Ya's Lute*, and spoke admiringly of "the songs and stories of a people, revealing as they do those profounder human emotions." Blind also indicated that through this collection "we are daily realizing a more vital imaginative unity with peoples alien from ours." L. S. Bevington, Meynell, Webster, and Blind were members of "coteries of women poets" whom Victorian anthologist Elizabeth A. Sharp valued, Ana I. Parejo Vadillo says in a discussion of the late-century salon.[60]

Moreover, the various poets also generated and encountered similar intellectual currents. For example, Blind, Naden, and Bevington departed from traditional Christian thought and revealed an antitheist outlook, which informed their ecofeminist work. Darwinian thought most definitely influenced the work of Naden, Bevington, and Blind. Herbert Spencer's ideas affected Bevington and Naden, Leighton says, and Naden even started a Spencer society, Philip E. Smith II reports. Both Naden and Blind felt the influence of George Eliot's poetry and philosophy, Charles LaPorte argues, and Blind wrote a book on Eliot.[61] Other similarities involving the six poets' perspectives on various topical issues exist as well.

Another connection among the six poets concerns their status as New Women, evidenced in varying degrees and perhaps surprisingly in certain cases. The linkage is significant in that the fundamental precept of ecofeminism is the shared oppression of women and nature, so the poets' perspectives on women's issues intersect in their verse. Their work appeared when female resistance to social constraints on voicing their opinions, on conducting themselves as they chose, and on demanding opportunities erupted in the controversy that would be focused on the New Woman. This iconoclastic individual argued for improvements in educational opportunities, vocational possibilities, and marital conditions that would broaden the limited scope facing a late-century female. The writers' links to the much-debated figure range from the tenuous to the robust, with the poets expressing New Woman ideas in their writing, acting to achieve change, or following both pursuits. Hughes comments, though, on "the relative invisibility of poets among recognized New Woman writers," which she believes stemmed from the poets' own "desire to be recognized *as* poets" rather than as "propagandists."[62] The paragraphs that follow here, presented in chapter order, adumbrate the New Woman identifications of the six poets under discussion.

Webster earned extensive bona fides as a New Woman through both her writing and her activism. Among the significant issues to Webster, "[a]n outspoken feminist and social critic," as Leighton calls her, were voting rights, educational improvement, and suitable employment for women.[63] Because the next chapter focuses on Webster's problematization of the nature-woman presumption, additional information appears there.

Blind made "pioneering contributions" to New Woman ideas and "sought to challenge the ways in which the gendered subject was 'envisioned' under patriarchy," Diedrick explains. Her interests extended to the decadence movement as well, and the translation she penned of a Russian artist's writings led to an intense controversy regarding the New Woman's connections to decadence, he asserts. Moreover, Diedrick observes, Blind's important *Dramas in Miniature* and *The Ascent of Man* also entered the contemporary conversation about the New Woman. An advocate of women's suffrage, Blind put her name to a *Fortnightly Review* piece supporting voting rights that thousands of other proponents also signed, Diedrick reports.[64]

Critics have both included and excluded Field from New Woman ranks. In the first case, Field's verse appears in Hughes's 2001 *New Woman Poets: An Anthology* because of the writers' focus on female sexuality. As Sally Mitchell points out, "Literary reviewers of the 1890s described any female character with sexual knowledge or desire as a New Woman," and such a judgment logically would extend beyond fictional personae to women authors whose poetry displayed interest in erotic matters. In the second case, Bradley and Cooper do not fit a New Woman designation, Marion Thain argues, even though they "*did* feel the injustices committed against women" before joining to become Michael Field. Mary Sturgeon's book on Field comments that the women also supported suffrage. Thain states, however, that the pair's interests turned to artistic endeavor, which became the priority. Thain quotes Cooper's 1892 statement that she "should never fight for any freedom" that "would perturb my art"; Cooper added, "I have only so much energy—if the god demands it—the cause of womanhood must go hang!"[65]

Of the six poets, Meynell seems the least likely New Woman. Yet, as Talia Schaffer makes clear, Meynell was quite a paradoxical figure. Meynell appeared to be "the incarnation of housewifery"—despite a lack of attentiveness to such matters—but also an individual "passionately concerned with women's changing roles." Meynell "certainly performed femininity," presenting a "spiritual, fragile, lovely, mysterious public persona," Schaffer writes. Nevertheless, Meynell supported women's rights, and Vadillo includes her among New Woman poets. Although Meynell's feminine persona contrasted sharply with the usual estimations of New Women, the female condition was a profound interest of hers, Schaffer explains.[66]

Naden, a scientist as well as a philosopher and poet, could be termed a New Woman through her advocacy of women's rights. As Emily R. Anderson relates in a biographical sketch, a feminist perspective infuses Naden's oeuvre. A vigorous supporter of women's rights, Naden also opposed a woman's unquestioned submission to social pressures, says Anderson. Thain identifies the poet as a New Woman, calling her "a socially- and philosophically-engaged thinker." Although not included in Hughes's New Woman anthology because of time frame and inclusion in other collections, Naden's work apparently would otherwise have fit the volume's parameters.[67]

Like Meynell, Bevington may seem a rather unexpected candidate for New Womanhood. Women's concerns are "rarely" specified in Bevington's work, Jackie Dees Domingue indicates, for the poet sought better conditions for males as well as females. Bevington also devoted herself to anarchist interests, which her various writings make clear. Nevertheless, Bevington's social activism seems to account for her identification as a New Woman. The poet's work appears in Hughes's anthology and includes what Hughes calls "two stinging polemics" related to organized religion and capitalism. Vadillo also includes Bevington in a brief list of New Woman poets.[68]

Additionally, the six authors, to varying degrees, share a measure of obscurity today, as many of their female contemporary poets do as well. Christine Sutphin comments that Webster's invisibility might stem from a lack of "the powerful literary connections that would have kept her reputation alive," along with changing cultural interests in the late Victorian period and early twentieth century. These reasons could be extrapolated to cover the other poets as well. Sutphin attributes Webster's returning popularity in modern times to scholars' work in recuperating women's poetry.[69]

On a spectrum delineating the recognition accorded the six poets in the modern era, Field would occupy the most prominent position, while Bevington would hold the least. Field's distinction may be due, in part, to the burgeoning interest in queer theory in recent times. Meynell, Webster, Naden, and Blind would likely follow Field, in that order. These writers do not fit the traditional contours of canonical status, if such a designation even applies anymore with the widespread challenges to the canon in recent decades. The poets do not abundantly appear in anthologies, which offers one clue as to the academic acceptance of a writer's literary contributions. The void is especially evident in anthologies that include work by both male and female authors, although the situation has improved somewhat in recent years. Critics have given more attention to the six poets, resulting in several journal articles, chapters in analyses of Victorian writers, and an occasional biography.

Perhaps these poets, as well as their female contemporaries, will receive more Victorianist attention as new theoretical approaches emerge and enable new interpretations of their work to unfold. In the past, fresh literary theories have generated productive applications for Victorian texts that have widened hermeneutic possibilities in intriguing ways and magnified our understanding of literary creations. Currently, various theoretical methodologies are garnering interest, and the opportunities for broadening interpretive paths in Victorian scholarship offer exciting directions for new readings. For example, interest in the Anthropocene era has brought innovative approaches to interpreting literature, and *Anthropocene Reading* raises the question of "how the Anthropocene might require us to read differently." The editors comment that the book's contributors deploy multiple methodologies, demonstrating "a range of conceptual tools, theories, and practices." Similarly, contributor Benjamin Morgan references "arguments . . . which seek to secure a place for literary criticism in conversations about the Anthropocene."[70] It is likely that additional theories will continue to enter the critical discourse and spur more and more enlightening interpretations.

With so many poets writing throughout the nineteenth century, why are the authors under discussion here such noteworthy creators of ecofeminist verse?

Perhaps the best response is a historically based one, since the late nineteenth century was a significant period of ecological awareness. In *Early Green Politics*, Peter C. Gould identifies the time as a vital moment in ecological consciousness. "[T]he most fecund and important period of green politics before 1980 lay between 1800 and 1900," Gould stresses. In the century's final decades, however, he maintains, "the philosophy of industrialism, the relationship between the individual and the social and physical environment, and the functions and successes of the city received an extraordinary degree of critical examination." Such scrutiny, Gould argues, occurred when the status of the city was coming under question, rural life and its cultural contributions were ebbing, unemployment was increasing, and social concerns were growing. Gould cites the century's waning years as a moment when "the call for a return to natural society received serious attention again."[71]

Trajectories of the Chapters

The following chapters concentrate on the short verses that the six authors crafted, though ecofeminism also informs their longer poems. The short poems allow for a similar analytic approach toward all the writers as well as enable interesting groupings and correspondences within a chapter; extended poems would require different treatment. Moreover, the shorter works allow a detailed investigation of related poems rather than a cursory analysis that multiple selections of long works would necessitate. Where relevant, the study does note a longer poem evidencing ecofeminist ideas to illuminate the shorter selections.

Also evident in the chapters, as in this introduction, are occasional references to Irigaray's work, which enrich the poetic analyses with their ecofeminist suggestions. Irigaray asserts, for example, that "the starting-point of the Western tradition was mastery of the natural universe and the construction of a world which precisely used nature in order to separate itself from it." Indeed, Irigaray surmises that male subjectivity is actually formed by distancing the self from nature.[72] Irigaray's ecofeminist perspectives provide *Reconceiving Nature*'s theoretical approach and intersect with the key issues that this study investigates: the supposed special relationship between nature and women, the masculinist drive for domination, the agential identity of nature, cultural dependence upon the natural world, and the crucial role that nature plays in spirituality.

Commentators on Irigaray's work see a definite linkage to ecofeminism. Karen I. Burke, for instance, maintains in "Masculine and Feminine Approaches to Nature" that Irigaray's various writings reveal an ecological attentiveness. Among other points, Burke refers to a 1986 speech in which Irigaray faults masculinist perceptions of nature. Christopher Cohoon asserts in "The Ecological Irigaray?"

that "Irigaray's engagement with the natural makes her work a rich resource for environmental philosophers and ecocritics" and that her ideas reveal "at least three veins of ecological attunement." Irigaray recognizes the related oppression of the natural world and women, Cohoon adds, as well as the disrespect accorded nature in masculinist projections. Such disrespect, as Margaret Whitford affirms in *Luce Irigaray*, accords with ecofeminist concerns.[73]

Another point informing this study is that even when a poet discussing nature does not make an apparent reference to women, the connection likely exists because of the assumed equivalence. An analogous situation provides an instructive model: the abhorrence that Victorian women expressed for vivisection. Coral Lansbury speaks of how women identified with the unfortunate animals, as numerous individuals "saw their own condition hideously and accurately embodied in the figure of an animal bound to a table by straps with the vivisector's knife at work on its flesh." Various female physicians, Lansbury reports, embraced the antivivisection cause because of the experiences undergone by impoverished women who received outrageous treatment as hospitals' charity patients.[74] The elision of mistreated women and vivisected animals offers a suggestive parallel with the equation of nature and women in that abuse of either implies maltreatment of the other. With the ostensible nature-woman similarity, the demeaning cultural response to nature could apply as well to Victorian women, whether a text overtly presents the point or not. Thus, the nature poetry analyzed in subsequent chapters, even if not directly addressing women, may suggest interpretation in a broader framework.

As the individual chapters show, the poets penned many fascinating and diverse poems that evoke ecofeminism. Because of the pivotal importance of the nature-woman equation that ecofeminism contests, chapter 1 focuses on Webster's relevant work. In the 1881 work *A Book of Rhyme*, Webster challenges the belief that a profound linkage exists between nature and women. She undermines essentialist perceptions by indicating the differences between the nonhuman residents of the natural world and the women who live within it. Additionally, Webster's work contests her culture's widespread tendency to equate nature and women.

Chapter 2 analyzes the ways in which Blind assailed the human proclivity to dominate nature. Her poetry demonstrates that nature is not an inferior "other" that should be exploited. Moreover, Blind's verse maintains that human activity is taking a dire toll on the environment and its inhabitants. Blind's work especially targets agricultural machinery and conveys in disturbing tones the damage that it causes. Industrialization also receives harsh treatment because of the destructive effects it imposes upon its environs. Like Webster, Blind demonstrates the problematic equation of nature and women, pointing to its deleterious results.

Field's poems confer an erotic cast upon nature to foreground its agency. Echoing ancient poetic predecessors whose verse invests nature with eroticism, Field's work also resonates with the erotic elements of the Linnaean system, which was so influential in England, emerging especially in the lengthy poem *The Loves of the Plants*, by Erasmus Darwin. Multiple Field poems featured in chapter 3 craft nature as a highly active entity rather than the passive realm that individuals across history had often assumed. This nature poetry charts Field's particular aesthetic path, which both accords with and departs from the aestheticism that influential contemporaries championed.

Meynell's work ushers forth an ecopoetics that implicitly disputes the widely assumed dichotomy between nature and culture. Meynell's nature poetry proceeds from the idea that nature not only participates in culture, it also enables it. As chapter 4 discusses, nature serves as a guide, and the poet, in effect, becomes its instrument. The authentic poet is immersed in nature, while the flawed poet views the nonhuman world as a vehicle to pursue a self-aggrandizing objective. Moreover, nature acts like a collective unconscious, which provides a generational bridge furthering poetic creativity.

Naden's version of embodied spirituality undermines conventional Christian belief, as chapter 5 articulates. Rather than envision God as detached from matter, Naden rejected dualistic interpretations of spirit and body. In her theory of Hylo-Idealism, which she describes in multiple essays, mind and matter are indivisible. Matter, which includes nature, thus is recuperated from the negative associations that traditional Christianity applied. Beginning with a detailed discussion of Naden's Hylo-Idealism, the chapter proceeds to an analysis of several related poems.

Chapter 6 looks at Bevington's verse in *Key-Notes* and provides a conclusion to this study in addressing the issues that the preceding five poets raised. The implicit message in Bevington's work is that people must craft a harmonious relationship with nature. *Key-Notes* endorses certain ideas but counters troubling contentions in Ralph Waldo Emerson's influential *Nature*, rejecting the notion that humanity is entitled to dominate nature in self-serving ways that assume superiority over the nonhuman realm.

A Final Comment

Among this study's objectives are three pursuits of special import. First, *Reconceiving Nature* endeavors to direct attention to women poets who have received less critical examination than they deserve, especially compared to more prominent counterparts of their time. Second, this book hopefully will increase interest in the ecological concerns and themes in Victorian literature, with special attentiveness to ecofeminism. Such work would provide valuable insights into efforts to grapple with the destruction and dangers the Industrial Revolution unleashed. Third, this project strives to stimulate interest in women's nature poetry, especially from the latter part of the century, which represents a crucial resource for understanding the period. *Reconceiving Nature* turns, then, to the ecofeminist poetry itself.

CHAPTER ONE

Augusta Webster:
Interrogating the Nature—Woman Link

In a response to Aristotle's perception of a connection between nature and women, Luce Irigaray alludes to the vexing issue of essentialism that has plagued them both: "The substance of the plant, like that of any (female) being, cannot move, or move beyond, the ontological status assigned to it. Once and for all. It is not capable of any less or any more."[1] The ramifications of this traditional assimilation become especially troubling when considering the faulty logic that confers upon both the unprivileged traits of passivity, materiality, and other markers of inferiority to justify domination of the ostensible analogues. Intervening in this societal verity, however, Augusta Webster provides an iconoclastic perspective in her 1881 *A Book of Rhyme* whereby essentialist presumptions become unsettled through complex strategies that break the supposed ontological linkage between nature and women, instead illuminating difference and undermining commonality. Additionally, *A Book of Rhyme* illustrates the harsh situation of a conventional Victorian woman whose prospects of self-fulfillment are dashed by a constrictive society. Webster adopts an unusual approach for pursuing her sweeping agenda in that the poem deploys nature imagery itself, in multifaceted and mutable permutations, to accentuate difference as well as to foreground the repression of Victorian women experiencing stifled potentiality and thwarted development.

Webster's challenges to deleterious gender presumptions extended beyond her poetry to a dedicated advocacy of women's rights. Webster took public stances through her essays and participated in activities to promote educational improvements, suffrage, and other pressing claims for women. As modernist novelist Vita Sackville-West remarked, Webster was "a woman who was deeply concerned with the lot of women throughout her life." Webster's feminism, as characterized by Angela Leighton, was an "essentially practical" approach. A writer for both the *Examiner* and the *Athenaeum*, Webster lent her voice to a host of topical subjects, with many of her articles subsequently gathered in the curiously titled *A Housewife's Opinions*, an eclectic blend that Theodore Watts characterized in an *Athenaeum* obituary of Webster as "a miscellaneous collection . . . in which criticisms upon Greek drama are oddly mixed up with discussions upon domestic matters." As Leighton remarks, *A Housewife's Opinions*, "under the guise of homely wisdom, . . . ironically mocks many of the cherished opinions of the day." In the collection, Webster took issue with the wrongheaded repression of women, especially regarding education and suffrage.[2]

Webster's work to improve female education addressed inequities on both the university and girlhood levels. Her critiques of university education, presented in *A Housewife's Opinions*, targeted examinations and degrees. In the first case, Webster assailed the practice, as at Cambridge, of holding separate examinations for women and preventing them from competing with men in the evaluation process. Webster argued that examinations exclusively for women treated them "as a class apart" and were suitable only for prospective governesses. This approach, Webster maintained in the essay "University Examinations for Women," was without value since the learning that a woman attained was compared only "to that of other weak vessels." Instead, Webster sought a meaningful standard that would apply to both women and men so that examinations would "represent for Mary what they represent[ed] for John." Webster additionally defended young women "who [had] felt the restlessness of intellectual faculties unnaturally cramped, the weariness of unsatisfied hunger of mind." Rather than encouragement, they faced "on all sides hindrance." In the related second case, Webster attacked the system preventing women from attaining degrees at Cambridge except through the women's colleges. Unlike the man with a degree, who "goes forth to the world stamped and warranted," Webster asserted in "University Degrees for Women," a woman was merely "politely assured that she would have had the degree if she might." She therefore gained no status in the public eye, with repercussions for earning an income since she lacked "the degree's plain voucher for her competence among the incompetent host of untrained women struggling for wages." In the essay "Keys," Webster criticized another educational issue, the focus on teaching women various foreign languages, saying this should not be "a chief and ultimate object, ignoring altogether the art of having anything worth saying in them." The capacity "to think soundly in one language" matters more than being able "to talk sillily in a dozen."[3]

Without adequate education and other training in a society where women outnumbered men, single females were seriously disadvantaged in endeavoring to support themselves, Webster stated in "The Dearth of Husbands," a piece in *A Housewife's Opinions*. Webster did note, though, that improvements had been made. She wryly noted a recognition that "the Unprotected Female," like "the Habitual Criminal," needed education. Yet many women still lacked decent education, she asserted, especially "gentlewomen" without an inheritance.[4]

Webster's efforts to improve the educational situation for girls came through her consequential position on the London school board, "where her influence was considerable," her contemporary Mackenzie Bell reported after her death. As Patricia Rigg relates, Webster fought efforts to expand coverage of domestic matters in the girls' curriculum, wanted the girls to receive physical education, and believed that girls should learn mechanical drawing. Webster also sought an expanded female membership on the board to improve education and to oversee female instructors, Rigg details, and Webster argued against a measure to prevent married women from being hired to teach.[5]

In addition to her educational endeavors, Webster fervently championed the suffrage cause, both as a participant and as a writer. She was a dedicated member of a suffrage organization, but her goal to expand the vote remained elusive in her lifetime. As Rigg reports, Webster's actions included supporting a petition to Parliament, advocated by John Stuart Mill, calling for women's voting rights. Indeed, Webster even attempted to persuade Christina Rossetti to support voting rights, although the poet "preferred not to do [so]," her brother William revealed. Webster's essays in *A Housewife's Opinions* backed the vote for independent women ratepayers and envisioned success for the suffrage movement. In "Parliamentary Franchise for Women Ratepayers," Webster argued that "commonplace justice" demands that these individuals should have the same right as men. She contended that "no earthly reason" existed to prevent the "special class of women whom our laws and customs recognise as qualified citizens in all other respects" from attaining the vote. Although these ratepayers were taxed as were their male counterparts, the women had no political recourse, Webster argued. Writing more generally about the suffrage effort, Webster labeled its advocates "an irrepressible army" in an essay with that phrase as its title and predicted that the movement would triumph. Although legislative measures had proven unsuccessful, she declared that "[t]he phalanx stands united." Webster ridiculed others' expectations that success would cause women to "become coarse-featured un-mannerly hybrids, men-hating, and hateful to men," who would "wear coats and trousers, . . . be Bishops and Judges, and . . . break all the commandments."[6]

A Housewife's Opinions also examined other contentious social issues affecting women, such as employment and marriage, and denounced oppressive conditions. For example, in "Protection for the Working Woman," Webster attacked overprotectiveness aimed at preventing women from gaining adequate employment, arguing that "such formidable power" would actually enslave them. Webster cautioned that foreclosing labor opportunities would cause grave harm. Without the benefit of reasonable opportunities, Webster warned, women would need to battle poverty through vice. Moreover, such factors as tradition prevented women from engaging in various types of work, she argued in "The Dearth of Husbands," but those occupations were "perfectly suitable for them" and even better undertaken by women than by men. In "Matrimony as a Means of Livelihood," Webster decried the sentiment that "any marriage [is] better than none." She castigated "women who marry to be married . . . and be taken care of" rather than suffer the indignity of being an "old maid" or facing poverty.[7]

Webster's unstinting assaults on female repression are compellingly evident in *A Book of Rhyme* through her contestation of the nature-woman bond that so intensively limited a woman's potentiality. As Bell stressed, Webster's "mature poetry" displays "her intense and passionate study of Woman's position and destiny," and such attentiveness is certainly evident in *A Book of Rhyme*. Although Webster wrote numerous nature poems that follow a more conventional trajectory, several verses in *A Book of Rhyme* illustrate difference by pointing to the unique aspects of the natural world and allowing the oppression of conventional Victorian women to stand apart from the workings of nature. During a period when the propriety of topics chosen by women writers raised debate, Webster elided criticism by situating her forceful stance within the customarily noncontroversial contours of the nature poem. Isobel Armstrong remarks generally on a "doubleness of women's poetry," a point that could apply to Webster's work. Armstrong explains that "conventions are subjected to investigation, questioned, or used for unexpected purposes"; additionally, "[t]he simpler the surface of the poem, the more likely it is that a second and more difficult poem will exist beneath it." Similarly, Marysa Demoor sees a modernist component threading through Webster's verse, "that of her elaborating the worn, cliché images of Victorian poets and novelists only so as to subvert them" and "especially target[ing] those stilted images that have been used in connection with women."[8]

The first group of poems from *A Book of Rhyme* that will be examined in this chapter reveals diverse and complex strategies to undermine essentialism. In the first poem, "The Swallows," nature breaks away from essentialist cultural truths to become reimagined in liberatory ways, contrasting startlingly with Victorian women, whom those cultural verities constrain. The next two verses, both centered on springtime—"The First Spring Day" and "A Song of a Spring-Time"—negate supposed reproductive similarities to illustrate difference instead. The second section of this chapter addresses poems deploying floral imagery, particularly the rose, as the crucial focus and controlling mechanism to convey the disturbing societal appraisal of Victorian women. The third group of poems addresses the conflation of women and nature, delineating undesirable results. Finally, "The Old Dream" depicts the damaging effects wrought by essentialist perspectives transmitted across generations.[9]

Substantive Dissimilarities

In "The Swallows," Webster advances multiple techniques to challenge the fusion of nature and women by depicting them as dramatically distinct entities, primarily by conferring agency and purpose on nature, in sharp contrast to the passivity associated with a traditional Victorian female ensnared within intellectual and behavioral strictures. The poem depicts nature not in customary terms as a homogenous, readily definable other through an identifiable essence, but as a heterogeneous mixture of discrete and distinguishable elements, exemplified by the fitting choice of the anomalous swallow. In the poem, nature further provides a lesson that biological sex need not determine destiny, for the male and female of the eponymous creatures significantly participate in identical activities, as figuratively opposed to the gender-specific pursuits underlying nineteenth-century culture. At first consideration, the poem may seem to present nature in conventional feminine images, but such portrayals instead demarcate the deathlike condition that essentialized Victorian women's, and not the energetic swallows', experience. Narrated by a speaker with a marginalized presence, "The Swallows" serves as a lament of sorts; the stanzas trace the free movements of the avian travelers embarking on their migratory journey to emphasize the antithetical condition of a moribund Victorian woman.

Opening with a plaintive question posed to the swallows, the poem reveals the speaker's naïveté about her dismal condition and her underlying but unattainable hope that a desired change in Victorian society's version of natural law could occur and thereby enable the speaker's own version of a dying summer to revive.

> Ah! swallows, is it so?
> Did loving lingering summer, whose slow pace
>   Tarried among late blossoms, loth to go,
> Gather the darkening cloud-wraps round her face
> And weep herself away in last week's rain?
> Can no new sunlight waken her again?
>   "Yes," one pale rose-a-blow
> Has answered from the trellised lane;
>   The flickering swallows answer "No."

Feminine pronouns designate the summer, which assumes essentialist traits through extended sobbing and vitiated movement in her reluctance to depart under another entity's volition, effacing herself in the shadowy celestial mantle. Indeed, the ponderous phrasing and necessarily protracted enunciation of the second and third lines mimic the diffident motion. The other feminine entity, the pallid rose, conveys in this brief poetic appearance the attenuated condition of an unfortunate Victorian female through its wan demeanor and irreversible deterioration, for a blown rose has flowered and decayed; moreover, this rose rests in a "trellised lane," suggesting a carceral space, with the lattice of restraining bands situated within a narrow passageway. The answering swallows rapidly negate the rose's expectation that solar ministrations can revive the summer—and by implication, the rose itself. With the sun's traditional literary designation as a masculine power, the vocal exchange provides an allegory of the female condition; no options exist for a metaphorical flowering that would expand the contours of a Victorian woman's life in the debilitating male-controlled environment that essentializes her.

The swallows not only function as the carriers of the demoralizing denial, but as the major characters in the poem they also provide an incisive commentary on and illuminating counterpoint to nineteenth-century gender roles. As Thomas Bewick notes in *A History of British Birds*, the authoritative tome on avian behavior that a youthful Jane Eyre embraced, male and female swallows are nearly indistinguishable in their plumage, which even a casual observer would consider an unexpected trait among feathered creatures. This visual androgyny extends into conduct, for both sexes of this highly social species participate in vigorous activity, "almost continually upon the wing." The poem's swallows are never discerned by biological sex, but all thrive in a disencumbered and active atmosphere, with their "flickering" movement indicating constant animation and robust agency, as the subsequent stanzas demonstrate. In conferring agency upon the swallows, Webster anticipates Donna Haraway's view in "Situated Knowledges" that there needs to be an interest in "granting the status of agent/actor to the 'objects' of the world."[10]

Unlike the poem's feminine summer concealing herself in the murky clouds that evoke a burial shroud, in the next two stanzas the swallows burst through the suffocating confines and begin their southward trek.

> From out the dim grey sky
> The arrowy swarm breaks forth and specks the air,
>   While, one by one, birds wheel and float and fly,
> And now are gone, then suddenly are there;
>
> Till lo, the heavens are empty of them all.
> Oh, fly, fly south, from leaves that fade and fall,
>   From shivering flowers that die;
> Free swallows, fly from winter's thrall,
>   Ye who can give the gloom good-bye.

The stanzas split the nine-line format of the first stanza, as if figuratively breaking apart the supposed similarity between nature and women. Yet in initially occupying the same obscured space as does the cloaked summer, the swallows at this moment apparently emblematize feminine nature as well. The spatial placement carries a presumption of nature as homogenous—whereby any entity aligned with nature, including women, can be unproblematically aggregated within an undifferentiated category, like "the dim grey sky"—but the supposition simultaneously dissipates. With its prepositional beginning, the second stanza's opening line quickly signals departure from the enveloping environs, and a profound sense of movement ensues. As an "arrowy swarm," the swallows replicate the definitive launching entailed in the unusual modifier that invokes the noun form of an arrow, and the phrase's subsequent actual noun "swarm" subsumes the predicate version as well. The language takes on a slippery quality here, in that adjective slides into noun while another noun slips into a predicate, creating a sensation of incessant activity that provides a definitive deviation from the sluggish summer. Moreover, the arrow's shape duplicates the straightforward, linear time "readily labeled masculine," as Julia Kristeva observes, as opposed to the cyclical temporality often linked to the female and nature.[11] The ensuing phrase "breaks forth" establishes the impression of both irrepressible force and confident advancement as the swarm makes its own mark upon the sky when it "specks the air," as if writing its story rather than having a narrative imposed upon it.

Also undermining the sense of feminine nature as a homogenous essence is the individualistic wording of the next line, whereby the birds proceed "one by one"; thus, although part of the larger swarm, each bird constitutes an individual being as well. Alfred Tennyson's "The Princess" provides an illuminating connection here, for one character in that poem chides another that in perceiving women, "you clash them all in one, / That have as many differences as we. / The violet varies from the lily as far / As oak from elm."[12] Vigorous verbs, such as "wheel" and "fly," maintain the effect of ongoing motion in Webster's stanza, as do the swallows' sudden presence and absence. Successfully escaping the negative associations allied with the overcast sky, the swallows entirely vanish from this space ("the heavens are empty of them all"). At this point, the poem ceases its particularized references to the sky, clouds, and heavens, shifting the focus from a virtually inert setting to the motion of flight, importantly occurring, as a later stanza reveals, in the companionable masculine sunlight that will not nurture the feminine rose.

The poem begins to build upon the gendered dichotomy between a masculine height and a feminine ground that quietly emerged in the first stanza, when the summer was positioned on the earth as it "[t]arried among late blossoms" and the pallid rose was dying in the lane. As Karen J. Warren comments about the shared oppression of women and nature, the "'up-down' thinking" characterizing male-dominated culture "places higher value, status, or prestige on what is 'up' rather than on what is 'down'"; under the prevalent conceptual framework, "[w]hatever is identified with nature and the realm of the physical"—that is, women—"is inferior to ('below') whatever is identified with the 'human' and the realm of the mental"—that is, men.[13] The poem's sky appears to have changed its gender identity from the opening stanza, in which the feminine summer is tied to the somber clouds; however, the identical gender distinction inheres in both stanzas through the contrast between the clouds' darkness, suggesting the night, with its traditionally designated feminine moon, and the sunlight. Moreover, the "last week's rain" that the first stanza associates with the clouds entails a descent to the feminine ground. The third stanza reinforces the gendered opposition between height and ground, signaling the pattern through its punning "lo" metonymically and obversely attached to "the heavens." Helping to form the alternating pattern is the alliterative /f/ play, which, for example, refers in the third stanza both to the soaring swallows that "fly, fly" and the dying leaves that "fade and fall."

The poem shifts in the fourth stanza to include the speaker's first direct indication of self-referentiality, extending the import of the previous stanza's closing line whereby the birds, by their implicit variance, "can give the gloom good-bye." The refocused attention points more directly to the plight of essentialized Victorian women, partly by explicating the numbing effects that winter imposes upon the earth. Without the propitious sunlight that the southbound swallows will eventually encounter, the earthbound Victorian female lies entrapped within winter, associated with masculinity as both the counterpart to the feminine summer of the first stanza and an emblem of male authority marching "towards his throne."

> But what for us who stay
> To hear the winds and watch the boughs grow black,
>   And in the soddened mornings, day by day,
> Count what lost sweets bestrew the nightly track
> Of frost-foot winter trampling towards his throne?
> Swallows, who have the sunlight for your own,
>   Fly on your sunward way;
> For you has January buds new blown,
>   For us the snows and gloom and grey.

Although the speaker has inserted herself into the poem, the appearance of "us" extends her situation to women generally while effacing the speaker as an individual, an appropriate maneuver because of the prevalent nineteenth-century presumption of an amorphous female essence. Furthermore, "us" exists as merely a prepositional object rather than as the subject of its own sentence and figurative destiny. Predicates associated with the Victorian female sharply counter the vigorous verbs indicative of the swallows, in that the former almost entirely designate inertia: the women will "stay," "hear," and "watch," with their activity limited to an unassertive counting of the victims that winter's inhospitable cold destroys, themselves becoming passive since the winter "bestrew" them upon the ground. Conversely, the masculine winter is attached to muscular verbs as well as alliterative puissance through the /f/ and /t/ wording in the fifth line, which in enunciation iterates the "trampling" sound the line describes. Two stanzaic references expand the swallows' solar connection, for the birds both possess the sunlight—it is "your own," the speaker informs them—and continue to pursue their "sunward way." The stanza's final two lines draw a contrapuntal contrast between the swallows and a repressed Victorian woman through parallel prepositional beginnings that stress the very different fates meeting the two entities. The masculine sunlight portends opportunity; the lack of winter sunlight brings paralysis.

The height motif proceeds into the final stanzas--which together compose another nine-line stanza. These last two stanzas establish an unbridgeable gap between the unrestrained swallows and the earthbound speaker, along with her female counterparts, as the first line indicates in emphasizing the distance.

> On, on, beyond our reach,
> Swallows, with but your longing for a guide:
>   Let the hills rise, let the waves tear the beach,
> Ye will not balk your course nor turn aside,
>
> But find the palms and twitter in the sun.
> And well for them whose eager wings have won
>   The longed for goal of flight;
> But what of them in twilights dun
>   Who long, but have no wings for flight?

Marginalized subjectivity additionally inheres in the phrase "our reach," for the speaker's reference to herself and others sharing her condition rests in an adjectival form, a far less potent pronoun than one occupying the subject position. The birds, however, will ultimately succeed in their quest, despite obstacles that may complicate their journey, for they have left the material world associated with the

bleak images of femininity (e.g., black boughs, "soddened mornings") to escape
and triumph even if the earthbound hills could rise or the sea could ravage.
Victorian females trapped by essentialist perceptions faced a foreclosed future,
however; even though the speaker poses the question as to the destiny of those
"[w]ho long," the answer implicitly comes as the poem's final line reveals the
impossibility of their flight. The pronoun alteration in the last two stanzas from
"our" to the penultimate line's "them," coupled with the latter's placement as a
prepositional object, adds to the dismal fate in that the syntactic change suggests
detachment and a lost sense of being, as if any prospect of vibrant subjectivity
is chimerical. As in earlier stanzas, the world that entraps the traditional female
brings greyness and an accompanying gloom, which the final stanza manifests in
the doubly emphatic "twilights dun."

In its contextualization within the natural world, the poem pessimistically implies that the prospect of a Victorian woman's escaping the restrictive life that her
culture has designated for her is as unlikely as that natural law will overturn; for
the speaker, Victorian culture exists as irrevocable law. Fittingly, masculine rhyme
blankets the poem, demonstrating the apparently unbreakable restraints that an
androcentric realm imposes upon a woman. Nevertheless, the poem's inconsistent stanza structure disrupts the supposition of equivalence between nature and
women by breaking apart the rigid nine-line components that would otherwise
suggest an immutable future.

Moreover, in individualizing elements of nature, as with the swallows and the
topographical inhabitants they leave behind, the poem provides a shred of hope,
albeit one not realized within the verse itself. In suggesting that perceptions of
nature as a homogenous mass are faulty, the poem by analogy implies that an
unproblematic equation of women with nature, relegating them to a shared otherness within that amorphous concretion, is equally flawed. As Gretchen Legler
observes in "Ecofeminist Literary Criticism," "reimagining what nature is . . .
is part of the elimination of institutionalized oppression" that informs gender
relationships.[14] Without overt gender differentiation as an identifying trait, the
swallows, regardless of biological sex, participate in the same endeavors to realize
their driving objective. A suppressed Victorian female, the poem hints, could
attain her own form of freedom as well.

In some respects, "The First Spring Day" employs techniques characterizing
"The Swallows" but creates a picture of unrelenting grimness and depressing
comparison, as if presenting an elegy to the irredeemably ruined hopes of a constricted Victorian woman. Like Thomas Gray's famed verse set in a churchyard,
wherein the fading day "leaves the world to darkness and to me," the Victorian
woman speaker implicit in the Webster poem is doomed to her own version of

opacity because her aspirations cannot be reborn and realized. The fact that a pronoun does not personalize the voice adds to the marginalization that the effacing effect of essentialism causes; the distanced third-person perspective provides additional evidence of inhibited subjectivity. The nature-women equivalence defined by ostensible essence is undermined not by demonstrating individualism, as in "The Swallows," but by disrupting the traditional perception of similarity stemming from reproductive cycles. As Sherry Ortner writes in her essay referencing gendered nature, a woman's bodily operations, which are "more involved more of the time with 'species life,' seem to place her closer to nature, in contrast to man's physiology." To some, "woman's body seems to doom her to mere reproduction of life."[15] In the poem, however, the reproductive connection is metaphorically detached; the rebirth that nature experiences does not hold true for the speaker since the prospects for improving women's conditions are utterly foreclosed.

Solar imagery permeates the poem to accentuate the substantive difference between women and the natural world they supposedly mirror, serving as the initial contextualizing and subsequent controlling image.

> The sunshine died long ago,
>   Stifled out long ago,
> And the waste of the world was grey,
>   And night was the best to know,
> For night was to doze and forget the day,
>   To be warm and forgetting and still,
>   And need not the sun and know not the chill:
> But oh, for the day that was darkened so!

Through the traditional designations that confer gender identity upon it, the sun not only functions as a masculine presence in the poem but more pertinently can be extended to serve as an emblem of the masculine world that promises stimulating opportunity and fulfilled potential. The sun's death in the first two lines both announces and reiterates the speaker's sad plight. In an essay on language and poetry, Armstrong speaks of repetition as "always contemplating redefining, a prior form of itself,"[16] which Webster's poem insinuates in its second utterance through a kind of tolling that pronounces lifelessness. In fact, the two-line repetition beginning the stanza creates a poetic pattern, signaling an immutable permanency that the reiterated words are enacting. In the first stanza, repetition of "long ago" augurs a kind of eternal present that ushers in an unbearable world marked by the enduring "waste" that remains of a woman whose dreams have been destroyed. The predicate "stifled" is an apt choice that encapsulates as well the repression of women's possibility and a smothering of subjectivity. The metaphorical annihilation of sunshine suggests the diachronic fate of women from centuries past or from the poem's specific historical moment, the latter of which provides a particularly haunting picture through its immediacy.

As in "The Swallows," greyness pervades the environment, but in incorporating the night, "The First Spring Day" taps a readily identifiable feminine image through the association with the moon. Night, in "The First Spring Day," represents a desired state of living death in which numbness, unconsciousness, and forgetfulness become vehicles for survival. The nocturnal image evokes Charlotte Smith's sonnet of a century earlier, "To Night," wherein "the exhausted heart / Is calm, tho' wretched; hopeless, yet resign'd" within the "quiet gloom."[17] Through the tethering to Smith's verse, "The First Spring Day" provides as well a commentary on women's immutable condition over the centuries while accentuating the poem's sense of an eternal present. During Webster's own era, the unchanging oblivion of her poem positions an essentialized woman as a kind of desolate Lotos-eater undergoing a live burial, "warm and forgetting and still," that enables her to dull the mind and endure rather than suffer from thoughts of what cannot be. In expressing no need for the sun and no sensation of cold, the speaker realizes that she can bear the misery of broken dreams only by pushing away any remembrance of them. Yet in the final line, regret cannot be entirely negated.

In the second stanza, the distinction between height and ground reinforces the speaker's distance from her dreams and incipient opportunities, which the repetition in the first two lines insistently portrays.

> Why gaze on a barren heaven,
>   Void and unchanging heaven,
> On a barren earth in the grime,
>   And not a poor blossom given,
> No thing that was thinking of sunshine time,
>   For a promise, a praise of the past?
>   And so one forgot the sunshine at last;
> And sleep could avail, but what to have striven?

The subsequent reference to the "barren earth" provides an ironic moment in that the line points to the supposed commonality of reproductive patterns among women and nature, but the presence of the "barren heaven" retrospectively dissolves the connection through association to the very different infertility that unrealized expectations bring forth. Recognizing the futility of revived desires, the lamenting speaker remains immersed in a dulling torpidity to ease the pain.

With no prospect of recuperating vanished aspirations—no evidence of even "a poor blossom" that could revive the ephemeral "sunshine time"—the speaker again counsels herself not to dwell on impossibility. Indeed, the /p/ alliteration of the sixth line punctuates the self-given advice with its forceful enunciation. The stanza's final phrase questions the value of even having sought a more stimulating life, as if intertextually nullifying the positive perspective of Robert Browning's Andrea del Sarto when he famously muses, "Ah, but a man's reach should exceed his grasp, / Or what's a heaven for?"[18] Webster's speaker seemingly is responding that such an optimistic viewpoint applies only to "a *man's* reach," since a woman encounters merely a correspondingly sterile firmament.

A thematic shift occurs with the third stanza through a juxtaposition, in that the poem's preoccupation with the speaker's plight recedes into the background to focus instead on nature more literally. This move, as with Webster's other verse according agency to nature and problematizing its supposed homogeneity and essence, alters a cultural construction whereby nature is relegated to the background so that human activity is highlighted in the foreground. As Val Plumwood explains the conventional schematization in a book on the natural world and feminism, nature serves "as the 'environment' or invisible background conditions against which the 'foreground' achievements of reason or culture (provided typically by the white, western, male expert or entrepreneur) take place"; that is, nature comes "to be defined as a *terra nullius*" lacking "its own purposes or meanings."[19]

The recurrent image of the sun loses its figurative focus in the third stanza, for the poem brackets off the solar connection to a masculine world of possibility. Instead, the sun assumes its customary role as the force physiologically essential to renew life in spring.

> The sunshine wakes once anew,
> 　Wakes and is born anew,
> And the Age of the earth grows young,
> 　And heaven has its youth for hue,
> And hope is the tune of the spring-bird's tongue,
> 　And the leaves in their prisons all hark,
> 　And blossoms will know there is end of the dark:
> One hour of the sun, and the spring-time grew!

The predicate associated with sunshine in this stanza's opening line provides a telling deviation from the verb of the poem's initial line, in which the sun expired rather than merely slept. The distinction points to the unbridgeable distance

between an essentialized Victorian woman and actual nature in indicating that a
rebirth does not apply to her destroyed ambitions that have no prospect of revitalization in a constrictive culture. The echo of "wakes" in the next line reiterates
the divergence between women and nature, which a temporal contrast furthers:
the sunshine is "born anew" instead of having "died long ago," as in the poem's
first line, and subsequently fosters spring growth in merely an hour's passage.
The poem similarly reworks other earlier images to emphasize the very disparate
conditions of women and nature. No blossom exists in the second stanza, which
attests to the speaker's lack of life, yet in the penultimate stanza the literal blossoms are preparing for the "end of the dark"; for the speaker, however, darkness
represents a perpetual condition. For a sole moment in the poem, a distinctive
voice emerges, as an avian song conveys "hope" that the persona can never again
know; unlike this example of tuneful nature, a constricted Victorian female effectually lacked a voice within a culture that instead valued her silence. Replete
with references to nature's awakening, growth, and expectation, the stanza bears
no resemblance to the situation of the speaker adumbrated in the previous lines.

The effect continues in the final stanza through persistent images of light and
renewal, with the contrast to the darkness of the first pair of stanzas dispelled,
along with the barrenness that characterized the speaker's heaven.

> The sunshine new on the earth,
>   Heaven to brighten the earth,
> And the deathful dimness gone by,
>   The barren and winter dearth!
> And to-day is the best till the next is nigh,
>   And to-night is to-morrow begun,
>   To-morrow, when blossoms remember the sun!
> Dead hopes, are ye born with the blossoms birth?

As in the previous stanza, temporal progression prevails, as today, tonight, and
tomorrow attest to advancement and optimism along with a sense of agency. In
the process, the temporal movement suggests the realm of masculine linear time
in which the speaker cannot participate. The contrasting image of "deathful dim-
ness" portends the final stanza's dismal reminder of the lifelessness that the first
two stanzas charted to identify the speaker's condition. By reasserting the decided
distinctions between nature and womanhood, the poem allows no answer but a
negative one to the final question posed. "Dead hopes," most certainly, will not
be reborn in accordance with nature's cycles.

The poem's prosodic elements convey the arrhythmic condition in that no pattern in either stresses or syllabic count occurs. The eight-line stanzas represent the only consistent aspect, as if mimicking the presumed commonality of women and nature before demonstrating through disjunction that the comparison cannot be maintained. Although the stanzas on first consideration seamlessly conform to an *aababcca* scheme, the rhyming is occasionally strained through inconsistent shifts between single and double syllabic pairings, as in "ago" and "know." No two stanzas follow the same sequence of syllable counts or stresses but instead disclose a lack of unity. In effect, the consistent pattern of stanza length and rhyme scheme replicates the rhythms of nature; conversely, the disharmonic syllabic and stress aspects intimate that Victorian females should not be unproblematically subsumed within nature and deemed an immutable essence. Instead, like those highly individualistic prosodic components, women need to be recognized as discrete entities entitled to their own subjectivities rather than consigned to enervating roles. Pertinent here is Irigaray's remark that "individuation in the feminine must start again," especially "consider[ing] all the aspects of feminine identity in its complexity and discover[ing] a way to cultivate them."[20]

Another poem addressing the ostensible period of rebirth, "A Song of a Spring-Time," takes a broader perspective than does "The First Spring Day" not only by creating a separation between an essentialized Victorian female and the reproductive rhythms of nature but also by distancing women from the movements and patterns of nature altogether. "A Song of a Spring-Time" criticizes the season's avian harbingers for premature reaction to the titular moment and subsequently implies that the speaker cannot attain her own spring as she addresses the poem's avian chorus. The title's usage of indefinite rather than definite articles signals an atypical response to spring, one that elides the revitalization supposedly heralded by the season in indicating that merely the time, not the promise of renewal itself, has arrived. The title's opening noun inserts an ironic element through the customary connection of women with the sounds of the natural world as well as with mimicry, which singing entails, rather than with the capacity for the originality of language. Composed of a pair of eight-line stanzas, the poem replicates through its brevity the ephemeral prospects of the speaker's version of spring and the distinctive difference between nature and women in responding to the season. For the birds, the spring is a false one because it comes too early; for the speaker, spring will never arrive. Underscoring the lack of commonality between women and nature, the speaker does not engage in a symbiotic conversation but instead chastises nature for its preferable situation.[21]

Images of destruction and death suffuse the first stanza to demonstrate the misidentification of spring and additionally to depict the speaker's own unenviable situation.

> Too rash, sweet birds, spring is not spring;
>   Sharp winds are fell in east and north;
>   Late blossoms die for peeping forth;
>   Rains numb, frost blights;
> Days are unsunned, storms tear the nights;
>   The tree-buds wilt before they swell.
>   Frosts in the buds, and frost-winds fell:
>   And you, you sing.

A note of wistfulness appears in the first line's address to the "sweet birds," as if gently chiding them for their error and incomprehension of a rather apocalyptic moment while wishing that the creatures were correct in their assessment. In portraying the birds as being premature, the poem is metaphorically presenting the situation of the speaker herself, a Victorian woman who effactually is ahead of her time in her own situation of a false spring and thus unable to attain the life for which she longs; the dark images permeating the stanza implicitly replicate the position of the unconventional woman embedded in a society hostile to her desires. Like the arboreal buds that cannot develop, the speaker's hopes "wilt before they swell," annihilated by the harsh environment that the speaker must inhabit. Sadly appropriate for her situation, the days are devoid of sun, suggesting as in the poems discussed earlier that the speaker cannot participate in a masculine world wherein she could develop her own capabilities beyond the narrow confines prescribed for nineteenth-century women. The final line of the stanza seems almost contemptuous, reproaching the birds for their lack of understanding.

In the second stanza, the false spring is retrospectively presented as the speaker's fledgling, but crushed, hopes.

> But let no song be sweet in spring;
>   Spring is but hope for after-time,
>   And what is hope but spring-tide rime?
>   But blights, but rain?
> Spring wanes unsunned, and sunless wane
>   The hopes false spring-tide bore to die.
>   Spring's answer is the March wind's sigh:
>   And you, you sing.

From the speaker's perspective, nature's true spring is false also, as is the prospect of a change in her position. A kind of syllogism develops in the stanza's first quatrain, which reveals that the concept of hope is no more promising than the rime that will eventually dissolve, the blights that through deterioration will bring death, and the rain that will carry all aspirations away. Perhaps "rime" is even acting as a pun on "rhyme" to accentuate impermanence when verse is spoken but not preserved. The stanza becomes unremittingly bleak in the second quatrain, wherein spring seems to move backward in time as it declines without the sun's presence, like an advanced woman who receives only discouragement for seeking a more satisfying life outside the reactionary parameters she confronts. The speaker's repeated remark to the birds at the stanza's ending assumes an even harsher tone than the first iteration, now that the poem has drawn her situation more fully.

Structurally, the poem follows a consistent syllabic and rhythmic pattern, as if creating an unrelenting framework that allows no deviation from the order it has imposed. With the *abbccdda* scheme, each stanza ends where it begins, replicating the lack of growth and forward movement that characterizes the speaker's plight. The diction consists almost entirely of only one or two syllables, creating an emphatic and authoritative sound as if brooking no alteration to the structure; the sole three-syllable word, "after-time," offers merely limited variance since only the tie of the hyphen creates the extra syllable. The aberration at first glance implies that an "after-time" portends a different actuality for future women, yet an optimistic reading readily falls apart through analogies in the two subsequent lines that reveal the prospect to be as unsustainable as the rime.

Focusing on Floral Imagery

In other poems featured in *A Book of Rhyme*, the differences between nature and women also indicate that a woman's hopes to alter her situation in a restrictive culture cannot be sustained. The implication arises with flowers, particularly the rose, as the central imagery. A longtime literary emblem of women, the rose provides a particularly appropriate vehicle for enacting this function. Like the personae in the verses addressed above, women whose ambitions are definitively dashed face lives without adequate fulfillment, with no glimmer of substantive cultural change. Instead, restraints on potentiality appear overwhelming and unassailable.

In "Once," for example, promising aspirations devolve into unattainable desires, as two floral images, the lily and the rose, portray. The pair present a timeline of sorts that encompasses both the speaker's youthful innocence and her later experience. In the first of three eight-line stanzas, the lily signifies a treasured dream that briefly flourished before ultimately being eviscerated. The opening lines chart the creation of the speaker's vision: "I set a lily long ago; / I watched it whiten in the sun; / I loved it well, I had but one." The lily's ripening in the masculine image of sunlight suggests that the speaker's anticipated outcome would be situated within a conventionally male register. Yet the whitening suggests not only the lily's progressive development but also a movement toward death through the searing effect that a perilous exposure causes. The speaker's dream cannot reach fruition, the blanched hue implies, for her ambition exists within the hostile confines of a male-controlled culture that resents and rejects female participation. In the subsequent lines, the destruction of the dream parallels the seasons; although they will ultimately return in the final stanza, the speaker's aspiration is gone forever, as the next lines foreshadow: "Then summer-time was done, / The wind came and the rain, / My lily bent, lay low." The result brings suffering and despair as the speaker emphatically laments, "Only the night-time sees my pain— / Alas, my lily long ago!" The reference to night evokes the presence of the moon and its perceived connection to women through the orb's regular cycles, which in the poetic context restricts the speaker to an essentialized position.

The sequence of events unveiled in the first stanza basically repeats with the fate of the rose in the next stanza. The initial trio of lines traces the early floral life and the pleasure it generated. "I had a rose-tree born in May," the speaker recalls. "I watched it burgeon and grow red, / I breathed the perfume that it shed." Summer again flees, this time even more ominously, with the hint that winter is coming. "Then summer-time had sped," the speaker recounts in an almost identical statement to the fourth line of the first stanza ("Then summer-time was done"), which projects a sense of inevitability through repetition. The floral life then "died away," leaving an even more forlorn speaker than in the first stanza, when summer had merely finished its seasonal journey. The regret imparted in the second stanza's concluding line projects greater force than in the previous stanza, as if a reiteration of death evidences an intensifying and unstoppable assault on a dream: "Only the silence hears me weep— / Alas, lost rose-tree! lost, lost May!" Again, a stanza ends with an oblique reference to women, in this case through the speaker's weeping, and alludes to the speaker's own rigid placement within a culture that stifles a female voice.

As the poem moves into the closing stanza, the resolutions for nature and the speaker are antipodal, with one reinvigorated and the other enervated.

> The garden's lily blows once more;
> The buried rose will wake and climb;
> There is no thought of rain and rime
> After, next summer-time.

But the heart's blooms are weak;
    Once dead for ever o'er.
Not night, not silence knows me seek
    My joy that waned and blooms no more.

The loss of the metaphoric dream traced in the stanza brings an annihilation of the speaker as well, for she becomes invisible, in contrast with the previous two stanzas. In those stanzas, each line of the opening triad begins with "I," projecting an impression of subjectivity and agency. The predicates that follow the "I" are active—the speaker sets, watches, loves, possesses ("had"), and breathes. Subjectivity gradually dissolves in the two stanzas, which is logical in that the intensity of the dream's loss expands as the poem ensues. Thus, in the first stanza, the possessive pronoun ("my") initiates the sixth line, but in the last two lines the pronoun moves from that prominent site to a less powerful one located more distantly in each line. In the second stanza, the first positioning of the possessive pronoun again introduces the sixth line. However, the personal pronoun devolves in the stanza's penultimate line into a direct object, "me," which demonstrates a loss of authority from being the possessor to being merely an object. No personal pronoun appears in the final line of the second stanza as subjectivity erodes. The worsening destinies of the flowers also chart the decline of subjectivity, for the lily had stooped but the rose-tree instead "died away." Moreover, the nearly identical fourth lines of the two stanzas impart an acceleration of the decline, for the summer of the first stanza is simply "done" but in the second stanza the summer has "sped."

The final stanza charts further deterioration in that the first three lines completely lack a pronoun, in decided contrast to the "I" that appeared in the comparable lines of the previous stanzas. Personal pronouns emerge only in the last two lines, with the object form in the penultimate line even less prominent than the "me" of the previous stanza since not even the silence, which had earlier heard the speaker's weeping, recognizes her presence or intent ("not silence knows me seek"). The possessive form in the final line provides a decided shift from the stanza's opening three lines, which focus on nature's agency and promise, as opposed to the speaker's loss of both, portended by the titular "once."

Also noteworthy is the placement of the flowers and the speaker within the feminine space of a garden. Her confinement within a feminine locale underscores the reason for the death of her dreams. The feminine boundaries signified by the garden preclude the speaker from entering the masculine register that her dreams would require for realization. The fact that the garden is not mentioned until the last stanza, wherein the speaker confirms the impossibility of successfully reviving her dreams, imparts an impression of inescapable confinement.

The poem's formal structure reinforces content through an unvarying rhyme scheme and syllabic count. The two features mimic male control of the speaker and limited opportunity. Indeed, the incessant masculine rhyme dominates the poem, as if exerting authority, with no feminine rhyme present. Triadic groupings in each stanza bracket six-syllable lines between eight-syllable counterparts so that the longer lines restrain the lesser line between them.

Equally bleak as "Once," the thematic trajectory of "My Loss," as the title anticipates, similarly follows a progression from optimism to misery. In "My Loss," however, despair stems from the realization that an essentialized woman's desired pathway in Victorian society concludes with her finding fulfillment through a proper romance. Yet once the attachment has shattered in "My Loss," nothing remains for the speaker, who belatedly recognizes her "folly" in placing all hope in a loving union and ignoring her potential in other pursuits. The variance between nature and the speaker is enacted through the prevailing image of the rose and the gap between the two entities. In "My Loss," only the roses in nature flourish and seemingly exist forever through seasonal rebirth, whereas the speaker's own roses die horrifically. The first of four stanzas, though, fashions an idealized picture:

> In the world was one green nook I knew,
>   Full of roses, roses red and white,
> Reddest roses summer ever grew,
> Whitest roses ever pearled with dew;
>   And their sweetness was beyond delight,
>   Was all love's delight.

The "green nook" is a green world, an edenic setting where nature assumes almost impossible perfection in evidencing the most intense colors and the most appealing fragrance. The repetition of "roses" in the second through fourth lines mimics a mantra in revealing the force that the flowers exert on the speaker, reminiscent of the sensuous catalog beginning Christina Rossetti's "Goblin Market" and its array of appealing fruits. As the third line of "My Loss" indicates, nature seems virtually immortal, returning yearly in all its splendor. The reference to ardor in the last line ("love's delight") definitively identifies the reason for the speaker's immersion in the green world; no other possibility for attaining this heightened state of elation obtains. In Victorian society, the stanza reinforces, only the gratification that derives from a respectable union matters as an essentialized woman heads toward marriage and the stability it purportedly furnishes to the society at large.

The second stanza continues the speaker's rapturous account of the nook and its pronounced impact. "Wheresoever in the world I went, / Roses were," the speaker proclaims in recalling that they existed "in my heart." Again, the aura of a green world abides, this time in "[l]ove's far summer nook," where "Roses never with the summer spent, / Roses always ripening in that nook." The speaker appears intoxicated by emotion, immersed in its sway to such an extent that she appears disoriented and unable to project her thoughts in other directions; nothing else takes on significance as she is overcome by the roses' "bewildering scent" and the consuming quest for marital success.

The poem turns in the third stanza, however, as the romance ends and the speaker's life degenerates. Funereal images depict her fate whereby the green world becomes a graveyard and a corpse-like coldness inescapably pervades her existence.

> In the world a soddened plot I know
>   Blackening in this chill and misty air,
> Set with shivering bushes in a row,
> One by one the last leaves letting go:
>   Wheresoe'er I turn I shall be there,
>   Always sighing there.

Departing from the picture of nature crafted in the first two stanzas, in this one rebirth will not occur; importantly, this setting is indicative of the speaker herself, not the natural world in general. She has increasingly lost her illusions about love, "letting go" of them like the leaves falling to their demise. A relentless, incessant quality characterizes the speaker's suffering, with the predicates' progressive form reflecting the ongoing process of death through the "blackening" and "shivering" of the site. Even the bushes' positioning "in a row" produces an unnerving effect in this linear pattern, resembling a narrative outcome for the speaker that leads invariably and systematically toward her unenviable state. She cannot escape her doleful plight, forever implanted in her memory so that it incessantly molds her life.

As the final stanza unfolds, the speaker fully comprehends the enormity of her miserable situation, wrought by the cultural illusion that marriageability makes a woman's life meaningful. "Ah, my loss, my pain!" she exclaims about the surcease of romance. "Dead, my roses that can blow no more!" As in the previous stanza, the distinction between a natural world existing unto itself and the speaker's personal emblem of nature ("my roses") is irreconcilable through the apparent permanence of the former, with its yearly resurrection, and the transience of the latter. Although not specifically mentioned, the inference that marriage represents the crucial objective is apparent, since a wedding is the necessary outcome for a Victorian woman to reach her presumably highest accomplishment in life.

Relevant here is Webster's reference in *A Housewife's Opinions* to "the position of our multitude of fresh unpremeditating girls with no particular office in life except to be marriageable."[22] Ultimately, the poem's speaker is unmoored, and her titular "loss" assumes another dimension besides the romantic dissolution as she appears unable to advance. Since all her previous behavior centered on the romance, she can only look back and realize that a new path is undiscernible.

> Wherefore looked I on our nook again?
> Wherefore went I after autumn's rain,
>   Where the summer roses bloomed before,
>   Bloomed so sweet before?

Lacking any ambitions beyond romantic success, the speaker faces a bleak existence devoid of hope or direction. Considered from this perspective, the speaker's absorption with the roses could signal the danger inherent in the culture's binding of women and nature together; the speaker lives within the narrow parameters judged acceptable for the presumed passivity, inferiority, and malleability of an essentialized Victorian woman. Furthermore, the poem's distressing conclusion suggests that the situation remains inescapable unless the culture reconceptualizes female subjectivity as vibrant and irrepressible. Adding to the pessimistic ambience is an aura of inescapability that the rhyme pattern provides, for each stanza's concluding pair of lines ends with an insistent repetition of the final word, as if brooking no deviation from a standard.

Nature as Woman

Two verses from *A Book of Rhyme* incorporate nature imagery in somewhat different fashion. In this poetic pair, nature imagery solely represents women—rather than also comparatively delineating the natural world at large as a means of asserting difference—to depict the grim outcomes resulting from the nature-woman conjunction. By not developing a contrast to nature in its wild forms but instead solely signifying a female speaker, the two verses can concentrate on the damage caused by cultural presumptions that a woman's supposed essence is a mimetic rendering of the unenviable traits accorded to nature.

Like the two previous poems discussed, "Not to Be" employs a rose as a prevalent image, this time in conjunction with a lark. Both images signify frustrated women wanting to break through social restraints on their prospects and fulfillment. If a woman does not recognize the need to be figuratively separated from nature and instead exists under the illusion that such a bond is acceptable, she is denying an inevitable outcome, the poem shows. The discouraging title prepares for the poem's judgment that such a misapprehension precludes meaningful subjectivity. Instead, the nature-woman equivalency consigns a female to a metaphoric death.

The first of three six-line stanzas explores a personified rose and its assumption that entrance into a better situation—participation in the pursuits of a masculine society—is destined.

> The rose said "Let but this long rain be past,
>   And I shall feel my sweetness in the sun
> And pour its fullness into life at last."
>   But when the rain was done,
>   But when dawn sparkled through unclouded air,
>   She was not there.

The lengthy rain represents the difficulties involved in such a passage, and the gender-inflected image of sunlight sought by the rose establishes the connection to the male-dominated realm. Through the influence of the sunlight, the rose will reach its potential ("sweetness") through the outcome ("fullness") that the flower wishes to experience. The final segment of the stanza, however, carries the distressing note that such a prospect will not occur. Indeed, not even the weakest glimmerings of light, issued by the dawn, alter the rose's prospects. Instead, the rose becomes invisible, which suggests that a desirable sense of subjectivity cannot be achieved for this emblem of a woman, designated by the feminine pronoun ("she"), in a societal context wherein a female is equated with nature.

The pattern repeats in the second stanza, with its portrayal of the lark as the female marker. In this case, winter produces the same impact as did the rain upon the rose and presents an obstacle to female acceptance into a masculine space, which sunlight again indicates.

> The lark said "Let but winter be away,
>   And blossoms come, and light, and I will soar,
> And lose the earth, and be the voice of day."
>   But when the snows were o'er,
>   But when spring broke in blueness overhead,
>   The lark was dead.

Another gendered image, the earth, represents women through their customary identification with unenviable materiality. The positioning of the earth and the sunlight holds significance through contrast here, for the sunlight linked to masculinity will enable the lark to "soar" and leave the denigrated ground behind. The fact that the lark will become "the voice of day" is doubly important. In a culture where a woman's voice traditionally is muted, where women are discouraged from expressing consequential ideas in favor of maintaining a supposedly womanly silence, the lark instead anticipates becoming a voice. Moreover, the voice would proceed from within the masculine realm, indicated by the reference to "day"; a diurnal setting, with its accompanying sunlight, is implicitly distinguished from the antipodal night, which is associated with the moon and by extrapolation with women. As with the rose in the first stanza, however, the lark's expectations are decimated and even more alarmingly. The rose's fate of invisibility ("She was not there") more harshly resolves into death in the second stanza.

The final stanza establishes a comparison between the representations of vanquished women described earlier in the poem and a host of other roses, which are existing under the illusion that they have reached their ultimate level of fulfillment through their flowering and song.

> And myriad roses made the garden glow,
>   And skylarks carolled all the summer long--
> What lack of birds to sing and flowers to blow?
>   Yet, ah, lost scent, lost song!
> Poor empty rose, poor lark that never trilled!
>   Dead unfulfilled!

These roses initiate no attempts to alter their situation and do not even recognize the need to do so. Instead, they are confined within the feminized space of a garden. The concluding lines, however, read like a eulogy for the rose and lark that failed in their emblematic quests for true selfhood.

The poem "Belated" also explores a lack of personal satisfaction and an accompanying regret. In this poem, the speaker realizes that a desire to alter a stagnant life has come too late for substantive change to occur. The first of four quatrains addresses a "[b]lithe summer blossom, born too late" and poses the question "Wilt make my desert garden fair?" This particular locale not only conveys the speaker's judgment on her arid existence but also places her within the confines of the feminized garden. A sense of urgency emerges as the blossom faces death: "Winter's hand is on the gate, / His breath is in the curdling air."

The second stanza indicates that the speaker's flower recently appeared promising and capable of extending indefinitely. "Still yesterweek, but yesterweek, / Thou hadst, unfolding in warm light" offered such hope, amplified by the blossom having "[s]pread ripening" and produced "seed to make the next year bright." As in "My Loss" and "Not to Be," cold weather and rain mark the end of the growing season and presage the blossom's demise, which the closing stanza describes:

> Oh flower too frail, too late of birth,
>   There is no sun for such as thou:
> Droop down upon the barren earth;
>   What boots it to have blossomed now?

Again the temporal factor appears, with the fragile flower arriving "too late." Despondency fills the stanza, suggesting that the speaker has realized too late in life the need to chart a different path leading to fulfillment. Perhaps she missed an opportunity, or the relentless passage of events—a marriage or motherhood, for example—foreclosed change. As in the poems above, the speaker's loss likely issues forth because, as a female, she cannot participate in the masculine world of possibility or achieve a robust subjectivity ("There is no sun for such as thou"). The speaker instead is consigned to the "barren earth," which indicates through the noun the material designation applied to women and through the adjective an utter dearth of opportunity. In fact, the speaker will "[d]roop down," as her lack of prospects represents an inevitable descent. The closing line projects a searing regret that unconventional ambitions ever surfaced, with "boots" not only making that point as a predicate but also by its noun form implying crushed hopes through a forceful pressure.

Unhealthy Perpetuation

Unlike the verses investigated thus far, "The Old Dream" focuses on the unhealthy transmission of traditional perceptions through a conventional mother. The reproductive process creating the Victorian daughter does not carry the sense of renewal seen in the natural world but instead perpetuates outworn and damaging ideas in a dispiriting heritage. An unenlightened Victorian mother thus functions as a destructive rather than a nurturing figure to her hapless daughter. The underlying concept of "Mother Nature" assumes two meanings here, neither of which carries positive associations because of the linkage to the natural world and the Victorian mother's role in continuing harmful beliefs. Although the poem could seem a lament for lost love, "The Old Dream" more compellingly assails a mother's indoctrination of a daughter into a culturally appropriate life that sunders a dream offering an alternative path.[23]

"The Old Dream" brings to mind Webster's sonnet sequence *Mother and Daughter*, penned over several years beginning the same year as *A Book of Rhyme* appeared. Yet the approaches are quite different. *Mother and Daughter* presents a complex tracing of an intense maternal bond, involving an emotional range as the speaking mother ponders the daughter's path from childhood to adulthood. This exploration reveals not only the depths of mother-love, but also the lessons imparted, the discipline accorded, and the concerns surrounding the daughter's maturation. As Emily Harrington describes the sequence, "The mother's nurturing presence is meant to prepare the daughter to be separate from her" and "emphasizes the mother's anxieties about the passage of time and inevitable changes and developments in the relationship between mother and daughter." Melissa Valiska Gregory speaks of the mother's determined scrutiny and discipline of her child, in some cases so marked that "the monitoring and correcting of her child's behavior" resembles "voyeuristic absorption, an unhealthy form of parental surveillance that leads to an almost fanatical watchfulness."[24] It is the disciplinary component of the mother-child relationship from which "The Old Dream" builds, depicting a daughter's resentment at being molded within the traditional parameters of female behavior as well as a painful understanding of the process.

As the speaker in "The Old Dream," the daughter initially condemns the mother and refuses to recognize that her parent unquestioningly followed what she perceived as her maternal duty and therefore should not be judged harshly.

> Nay, tell me not. I will not know.
>   Because of her my life is bare,
> A waste where blow-seeds spring and grow
> Then die because the soil is spent,
>   And leave no token they were there;
> A soddened mere where marsh-lights gleam,
> But no star sees the ray it lent
>   Because of her despoiled and bare.
> What then? she did a wrong unmeant.
>   Leave me my dream.

The knowledge that the daughter will not accept in the first line discloses an angry refusal to forgive the mother for conforming to traditional responsibilities and in the subsequent line places all blame on maternal misdirection. Nature imagery illustrates the concomitant harm in this first stanza, inverting the customary perception of both nature and mother as cultivating entities and reproductive forces that bring fresh life. Instead, the imagery depicts a sterile environment in which the daughter's fate is one of waste and barrenness. The spent soil on which the seeds cannot thrive intimates a worn-out tradition unable to sustain a present generation, whereby even small steps toward progress will end in oblivion, "leav[ing] no token they were there." The redundant image of the "soddened mere" not only evokes a place of unhealthy and insubstantial torpidity but also connects an analogous intellectual sluggishness with the noun that in a French context identifies the mother. In noting the presence of marsh-lights, the speaker stresses both the insubstantial foundation upon which traditional gender practices rest as well as their illusoriness and deception; such lights form a mirage of sorts, unassociated with any star, and thus hold forth a false promise. The mother's adherence to tradition causes her daughter to become "despoiled and bare," in another inversion of reproductive allusions. In the stanza's penultimate line, the daughter pauses to reconsider her ire, recognizing at least momentarily that the mother represents a victim also in following tradition that caused her to initiate "a wrong unmeant." Nevertheless, as in two subsequent stanza endings, the daughter pleads for the memory of her dream that portended a fulfilling existence, knowing that such remembrance offers the only possibility of attaining it.

As the second stanza opens, the speaker can no longer bear even momentary forgiveness and blames the mother for the gentle demeanor that belied the harmful advocation and transmission of conformity.

> Tell me no more. I will not know.
>   My life, if she had harsher eyes,
> Did her sweet voice not deepen so,
> Had maybe missed this bitterness;
>   Maybe I should have been more wise
> If she were sterner, or could seem,
>
> If she could have been pitiless.
>   Too sweet low voice! too trustful eyes!
> What then? she could not judge their stress.
>   Leave me my dream.

With her soft eyes, quiet voice, and tranquil behavior, the mother smoothly accords with the ideal of Victorian womanhood. In demonstrating valued maternal traits and conduct, the mother conveys no warning that her daughter should reject the motherly instruction. The third stanza again presents a fleeting moment of forgiveness; the same phrase of "What then?" in the penultimate line also arose in the first stanza, as the daughter realizes that her mother lacked awareness of the effect her behavior and indoctrination would cause.

The final stanza charts an unmistakable alteration in attitude toward the mother, in that the speaker mourns her lost dream of fulfillment and realizes that a loss of affection would compound the sense of deprivation.

> I will not know. Rob not my heart:
>   It is too poor to lose yet more.
> Leave the old dream where she was part:
> Are all smiles ill, all sweetness lies?
>   One blossom once my life-time bore
> It wakened at her April beam,
> Then froze; yet dead 'tis still some prize
>   It shows mine blossoms were of yore.
> Let be: I need some memories:
>   Leave me my dream.

Margaret Homans's comment about nineteenth-century women applies here: "It is the mother's cultural powerlessness that the daughter is rejecting, not the mother herself"; also pertinent is Leighton's remark about the "tempt[ation] to detect . . . matrilineal yearning in the many poems about mothers, mourned or celebrated, by Victorian women."[25]

The ironic adoption of nature imagery equates the speaker's dream with a transient blossom, now forever gone. The knowledge that the daughter refuses to accept includes a recognition that the mother has cruelly betrayed the speaker's dream. One surmises that the mother initially encouraged the daughter's aspiration—"It wakened at her April beam"—only to understand that the dream was inappropriate for a Victorian female and so stifled its realization. The speaker assumes a rather rueful tone in comprehending that a lesson has been learned, for the dream can never be restored. In effect, the speaker experiences an odd gratitude in the "prize" of being forced to recognize the severe realities of her culture and the impossibility of her aspirations. All that the daughter can retain are the vanished moment of hope, captured in the eternal present of memory, and the belief that her mother unwittingly erred.

The poem's recurrent rhyme scheme echoes the speaker's agitation, for the *abacbdcbcd* structure seems ragged and disharmonious. The rhythmic repetition through the stanzas creates a sense of dullness, as if the loss of the dream has brought an unpleasant sameness marked by hopelessness. In fact, each line, barring the line "Leave me my dream," follows an eight-syllable format to convey immutability. The line "Leave me my dream" carries only four syllables, as if to demonstrate that the memory of the dream holds only marginal comfort, lacking the fullness of an aspiration that has actually been realized.

As the compelling poems addressed in this chapter reveal, the nature-woman bond is fraught with damaging assumptions, invalid conclusions, and biased judgments. Webster approached the problematic linkage from two standpoints to question the delimiting connection. In the poems explored in the first section of the chapter, nature and women reveal substantive differences rather than sweeping similarities. Deconstructing flawed assumptions enables a far more valid reckoning that avoids conferring presumptive traits on one entity merely because that characteristic is wrongly ascribed to the other entity. By severing the connection, Webster opened up a space whereby both nature and women could be refigured in considerably more accurate and productive ways. In the poems investigated in the second section of this chapter, Webster foregrounded with flower imagery the dangers to subjectivity that an essentialized Victorian woman undergoes and the depressing limitations governing her conduct as a result. At the same time, the poems reinforce the point of the previous verses that women and nature are not equivalent. The next poems discussed deploy nature imagery to underscore the constraints imposed upon women, who are unable to escape an identification with nature and are prevented from participating in the projects and purposes of the masculine realm. The final verse reveals the harm caused by essentialist thought continuing across generations. Yet, to return to the Irigaray quotation beginning the chapter, "the ontological status" conferred on women, as on nature, need not be immutable.

CHAPTER TWO

Mathilde Blind
Contesting Domination

To MATHILDE BLIND, FOR WHOM nature "had always been an inspiration" and the source of "exquisite delight," as a memoirist recalled, unimpeded dominance over the environment created a dangerous and indefensible position. Recognizing the social construction of nature, Blind assailed the disturbing version that Victorians were fabricating to meet self-serving ends, and she eloquently challenged such cultural approbation of authority as a decidedly destructive prerogative. Blind spoke of "the view of Nature, which is essentially the product of [an] age and nation," and she decried the Victorian sense of entitlement that rationalized domination based on a presumed human superiority. Also the product of an era, of course, are perceptions of women, which Blind found in her own time to be utterly stultifying. Blind said of "the present social conditions" that "the wish to live, of letting whatever energies you possess have their full play in action, is continually thwarted by the impediments and restrictions of sex." The poet referred to "feminine nature, of which as yet we know so little," and averred that "most of our knowledge comes to us second-hand, through the medium of men with their cut-and-dried theories as to what women are or ought to be."[1] In her work, Blind deftly spoke about the oppression of both nature and women in subtle yet convincing fashion, building from the cultural binding of the two concepts that the term "feminine nature" inadvertently foregrounds.

Blind's disdain for dominance echoes the writings of nineteenth-century environmentalist George Perkins Marsh, who alluded to its perils in speaking of "the hostile influence of man." Marsh, credited with "launch[ing] the modern conservation movement" through his 1864 *Man and Nature*, insisted that "man is everywhere a disturbing agent." He added,

Wherever he plants his foot, the harmonies of nature are turned to discords. The proportions and accommodations which insured the stability of existing arrangements are overthrown.

. . . The fact that, of all organic beings, man alone is to be regarded as essentially a destructive power, and that he wields energies to resist which, nature—that nature whom all material life and all inorganic substance obey—is wholly impotent, tends to prove that, though living in physical nature, he is not of her.

Marsh further noted that civilizational achievements bring increasing destruction to nature. The natural world will take its revenge, however, for the ruinous interventions that upset its equilibrium will unleash powerful forces, he averred.[2]

Luce Irigaray's diverse writings more than a century later provide an illuminating lens through which to view Blind's environmental stance. As Irigaray contends, "man" seeks to wrest power from nature so that he can hold it himself. "Men always go further, exploit further, seize more, without really knowing where they are going," she says. Irigaray argues that men consider their relationship with nature as adversarial and aim to battle it. Conquest becomes the driving force and the sole objective, she explains. Instead, she stresses, nature "must be safeguarded as the place of existence for living beings" as well as "preserved in its present and future possibilities."[3]

In contrast to this aggressive approach of men, Blind expressed a deep appreciation of nature. As a friend's account reports, Blind was "a free-spirited traveler in communion with the natural world." Blind speaks stirringly of pristine nature in describing a tour of the Alps, for instance.

For once I felt truly free. My body, pliant to my soul, moved rhythmically to the sound of the rushing stream. The sky, of a deep sapphire, was alive with clouds, high white clouds changing chameleon-like as the sun and wind touched their ethereal substance. Sometimes they stood on tiptoe on the top of a mountain peak like columbines balancing themselves on the shoulders of a giant. Innumerable waterfalls came rushing from invisible glaciers—sometimes in a broad torrent that dashed foaming down to the stream; sometimes in a soft froth like the milk with which the Alps, those Mothers of Europe, were feeding the land.

A very few things in this life have exceeded my expectations. The Alps . . . beckon[ed] something deep down usually ignored or apparently non-existent, in some depth of being below an habitual consciousness—something latent within leaping up, irresistibly yearning to that glorified region as if they two belonged to each other from everlasting to everlasting. What a sensation, momentary and yet to be kept through life as one of its treasures!

Moreover, biographer James Diedrick credits nature with being a substantive influence on Blind's feminist perspective. The confluence of the two attitudes appears, for example, in Blind's response to a question about whether women are doomed to dependency. Blind answered with a reference to nature that demonstrated equality between the sexes: "There seems very little difference in the habits of male and female eagles, seagulls and swallows."[4]

Domination of women, like that of nature, brings great harm, Blind believed. Theodore Watts-Dunton stated in Blind's obituary that "the chains with which women are loaded by convention irritated her, and no wonder." As memoirist Richard Garnett recalled, Blind reviled the legal presumption of female inferiority and the perpetuation of that view. From early adulthood onward, Garnett said, Blind was preoccupied with the female condition in both her spoken and written commentary. On one occasion, as "A Lady Representative" reported in a *Pall Mall Gazette* piece titled "Women Who Write," Blind presented at a Literary Ladies' Dinner "a noble and eloquent speech on the dreams, needs, hopes, and aspirations of woman now that there is a general up-lifting of her nature to new aims and ideals."[5]

Blind took an emphatic stance against women's supposed inferiority in her signature work, *The Ascent of Man*. The poem "is one deserving of high praise," an *Athenaeum* reviewer said, adding that Blind "hurries her reader along, breathless and perspiring perhaps, but never anxious to stop." The long narrative poem contests the ostensibly scientific views proclaiming male intellectual superiority. As this study's introduction related, writings by Darwin and other Victorian scientists insisted that biological processes ordained female deficiencies and that women's mental flaws doomed them to the periphery of substantive human activity. Men, the arguments claimed, propelled civilizational advancement, while women's role was primarily a reproductive one. *Ascent* dramatically undermines such assertions in presenting extensive details about the many failings of Western civilization under male direction, tracing events occurring across centuries that brought chaos, confusion, and misery. Women, the poem sets out, will be the world's saviors by initiating a rebirth based on love and compassion rather than continuing to promote the competition and aggression that has undergirded male-dominated societies. As the female speaker exclaims in anticipating a revitalized world, "Yea, let earth be split and cloven asunder / With man's still accumulating curse" so that humanity could start anew; past life represented "but a momentary blunder / In the cycle of the Universe."[6]

As critics have discussed, *The Ascent of Man* rewrites evolutional history in responding to Darwin's *Descent of Man* and its contention of male superiority. After *Ascent* delineates civilizational flaws, the poem returns the world to its origins and applies the terminology of childbirth to characterize the reemergence of life within a female register; thus, the earth "[h]eaved convulsive with the throes of birth." The Voice of the earth begs the female speaker to "redeem me" as "my heir and hope of my to-morrow." The presence of the "Voice" brings to mind the Word in Christian belief but provides a gendered reversal so that it is the female who receives the awe-inspiring gift. Says the Voice,

> I have cast my burden on thy shoulder;
>   Unimagined potencies have given
> That from formless Chaos thou shalt mould her
>   And translate gross earth to luminous heaven.

In a further rejection of female inferiority, the poem suggests that the speaker's poetry will bring the vital transformation. Tellingly, *Ascent* in general terms had earlier praised the figure of the poet, who brings "wings to thought," and through "whose shaping brain / Life is created o'er again."[7]

Blind's "Nûît" also challenges presumptions of female inferiority, in this case through a female creative force designated as "[t]he all upholding, / The all enfolding, / The all beholding." The titular night, conventionally associated with the moon and thereby with women through their biological cycles, ushers forth the world's religions in their various permutations. The poem reinforces the divine quality of the night and locates religious origins in the oceans, which corresponds to the way that *Ascent* traces the beginnings of life. Evoking the moon's tidal effects, "Nûît" implicitly credits female force for the oceanic "wild commotion" as "[w]aves upon waves, / Mingling in thunder, / Rise and go under." The female creator holds power over the life and death of religions, the poem intimates, for "Night has her graves" as well as her generative ability. As Bonnie J. Robinson maintains, female night not only replaces the conventional male divinity, but male-directed creeds ultimately answer to her.[8]

Blind's prose additionally attests to her advocacy of women, as several times she wrote about individuals who ardently upheld similar views. Her essay on Mary Wollstonecraft begins as follows:

> Whether our sympathies are favourable, opposed, or simply indifferent to the present movement for securing to women certain professional privileges and political rights, from the historic point of view it should at least not be forgotten that it was Mary Wollstonecraft who, in this country, boldly ventured to raise a voice on behalf of her sex.

Introducing her translation of a journal penned by Russian painter and feminist Marie Bashkirtseff, Blind states that "the same revolts, the same struggles, the same helpless rage, have gone on in many another woman's life for want of scope for her latent powers and faculties." Blind wrote a book on Madame Roland, an early feminist and French Revolution leader, who, soon to be executed by guillotine, lamented the crimes committed in the name of liberty. In a review of William Rossetti's anthology of Shelley's poetry, Blind comments approvingly on Shelley's depiction of a female character in *The Revolt of Islam* and its unconventional treatment of women. Noting that poetic descriptions typically presented women in their traditional roles as wife, mother, daughter, or mistress—"as a supplement to man's nature"—Blind praises Shelley for his departure from such portraits.

> To Shelley belongs the honour of being the first poet who has embodied, in a shape of the loftiest loveliness, the most momentous of all our modern ideas—that of the emancipation of women from this subjection to men. He is thus the poetic forerunner of John Stuart Mill.
>   . . . [Shelley] holds that woman, just as man, is or should be a being whose sympathies are too vast—whose thoughts too multiform to converge to the one focus of personal love, and that in the self-same way it is at once her right and her duty to take an active share in the general concerns of humanity, and to influence them, not only indirectly through others, but directly by her own thoughts and actions.

Blind adds, however, that she supported Shelley's "deep insight" about women's needing to initiate their own salvation. Shelley believed that "the task of the regeneration of woman can only be brought about by woman herself; that it is she who must rouse man's interest, and kindle his enthusiasm in her cause," Blind stresses.[9]

Like Augusta Webster, Blind sought improved education and employment conditions for women, as well as voting rights. In fact, Blind approved of Webster's activities to improve women's status, says Diedrick. Blind believed that the dearth of female educational opportunities led to the demeaning perceptions of women's intellect so prevalent in Victorian society. As memoirist Garnett recollected,

> She seized . . . with real discernment, upon the root of women's inferiority, the inferiority of women's education. . . . It was not from want of talent, or of desire to excel; within the range of her own acquaintances she had seen

numbers of lives intellectually wrecked by parents' obstinate adherence to conventional schemes of education and of life. She felt and wrote admirably upon the subject.

Higher education, Blind contended, would enable women to flourish.

> Now, she who is ambitious to make a dent on the world's surface, writes, speaks, and acts independently, by herself. In old days *man* was the material which the clever woman moulded as a potter does his clay, this way and that, and through whom she attained influence and posthumous fame.

Blind was so committed to women's education that she arranged for Newnham women's college at Cambridge to receive the bulk of her property after her death, Garnett noted.[10]

With her interest in contesting norms, Blind became an ardent proponent of women's suffrage. Her memoirist saw Blind's advocacy of voting rights as a way to counteract the view that women are the inferior sex. Blind was one of hundreds who signed a suffrage petition, which the *Fortnightly Review* discussed in an 1889 response to suffrage opponents. As the article indicates, "Those who support women's suffrage do so, not in any spirit of vulgar antagonism or rivalry with men." The right to vote would not jeopardize the distinctions between the sexes, nor would suffrage produce unwomanly individuals, the article said. Instead, as other events had demonstrated, gaining the franchise would provide "a good influence on character," would undercut views that women cannot "act or think about the concerns of their country," and would fit with other measures that had bettered conditions.[11]

Blind also sought improvements in the employment situation for women to ensure decent wages and career possibilities. She supported women's entry into nearly all professions, Garnett stated, except nautical or martial endeavors. When Garnett questioned Blind about the effect that added workers would have on already full professions, she opined that male emigration would correct the problem. She approved as well of demonstrations that a Marxist group held over a couple of years to aid women in the workforce who were receiving "starvation wages" that were largely causing "wretched degradation." Blind believed that the group's efforts would certainly improve the situation and generate substantive results, Diedrick observes.[12]

Domination and Its Untoward Effects

It is the problematic domination of nature, however, that Blind's short poetry especially interrogates. Blind condemns in her verse such harmful control on several fronts, deploying ecofeminist arguments in such ways as the following. Nature suffers egregious harm, her poetry shows, through the prevalent perception of human superiority and the enthusiastic acceptance of a rigid logic validating masculine domination. Nature is therefore consigned to a passive, vulnerable, and marginalized role deemed an appropriate positioning. As the final portion of this chapter will indicate, Blind soundly condemned the disturbing assumptions applied as well to women because of an ostensible female essence; her poetry assails the faulty beliefs that justified subjugation, stultification, and diminishment. Blind's verses are cautionary tales that offer few prospects for optimism unless cultural attitudes were to drastically change.

Among the earliest of her poems, the 1867 "Entangled" examines, rejects, and overturns the masculine assumption of rightful human dominance over nature while urging a genuine respect for and recognition of the natural world's own integrity. "Entangled" opens with the speaker assuming a definitive stance as the superior element in a human/nature dichotomy and with the privileging of a robust "I" as the initial word and grammatical subject of the stanza-long sentence.

> I stood as one enchanted,
> All in the forest deep:
> As one that wond'ring wanders,
> Dream-bound within his sleep.

The speaker's syntactical positioning—coupled with an authoritative upright physical stance—assumes an unquestioned command over nature. This conviction also takes on a gendered valence in that the speaker invokes a masculine pronoun in a self-reflexive metaphorical comparison to provide another endorsement of the culture's ubiquitous belief in nature's marginalized status. Yet these textual presumptions become destabilized even as they are inscribed. The stanza's final lines presage that a very different response to nature will unfold through a diminishment of the speaker's power and a corollary augmentation of the natural world's potency. The reference to enchantment presupposes an entity able to overwhelm human presence in a manner that escapes rational understanding or effectual resistance. The final two lines of the stanza continue to reveal nature's puissance in that this nonhuman world has already begun transforming the speaker beyond a rigid logic of masculinized thought to an uncertain and impressionable liminality of sleep. In this state, rationality ebbs and otherwise unimagined ideas can quietly emerge.[13]

As the second stanza unfolds, human authority has resumed, for indications of human agency—footsteps and voices—occupy the subject position.

> A thousand rustling footsteps
> Pattered upon the ground;
> A thousand whisp'ring voices
> Made the wide silence, sound.

The footsteps mimic the sounds of a marching army, with soldiers conversing in low tones among themselves. These militaristic images suggest that humanity has regained its dominance, and the supposition carries into the following stanza as the voices sustain their communication. The impression of reinstated authority is breaking down in both stanzas, however, with the second stanza gaining its meaning retrospectively through a teleological reading of the third one.

> Some murmured deep and deeper,
> Like waves in solemn seas;
> Some breathèd sweet and sweeter,
> Like elves on moon-lit leas.

The third stanza evinces an ongoing breakdown of linguistic capacity, a hallmark of ostensible human superiority over the natural world, in that whispers deteriorate into murmurs before speech dissolves into nonlinguistic respiration. The stanzas reveal that, instead of human authority, nature is the agent here. The pattering footsteps elicit the movements of woodland creatures, the whispering voices mimic the sounds of breezes, and the resultant sound emanating from the silence reveals the workings of nature. Furthermore, the poem has moved considerably from the upright posture of the speaker in the opening phrase ("I stood") to the debased level of the leas. The customary designation of nature as female emanates from the stanza as well through the moonlight touching the land. This depiction, coupled with the simile referring to fanciful elves, contributes to a slippage of dominance from the socially accepted masculine discourse on nature to a startlingly different perception. Nature has assumed the subject position in each syntactical unit of the second and third stanzas. The transformation is not to be feared, the soft alliteration of the abundant /s/ and /l/ sounds assures, and the triple similes in the first three stanzas create a symbiotic harmony between humanity and nature rather than a threatening scenario.

As the poem progresses to the next stanza and the beginning of the fifth, the intermingling of human traits with natural elements intensifies, while foliage assumes the subject position.

> Tall ferns, washed down in sunlight,
> Beckoned with fingers green;

Tall flowers nodded strangely,
With white and glimm'ring sheen;

They sighed, they sang so softly,
They stretched their arms to me.

Intriguingly, the "tall" ferns and flowers now exhibit the standing posture of the speaker in the first stanza, yet an ominous note appears with the sunlight's effect. As a traditional masculine image, sunlight counters the influence of the moonlight in stanza three, for the descending movement implied by the "wash[ing] down" of the ferns suggests an overwhelming force. Feminized nature appears resilient to the masculine domination, however, in that personifying predicates and nouns reveal that the ferns summon the speaker with their vegetative digits, like a gestural command; the flowers make a judgment with their nods; and the plants continue to exert agency, again imitating human behavior, as they extend their limbs. Varied predicates contribute to nature's agency by suggesting a precursory human speech—the whispering and murmuring noted earlier, joined by sighing and singing. The sounds signify a form of language, one that must be heeded since nature's utterances not only are foregrounded but also provide the sole form of speech acts traced in the poem. In conferring this linguistic capability, the poem complicates the usual human/nature binary wherein only the former component of the oppositional relationship can speak. Though the two forms of "speech" are certainly distinct, the poem nevertheless calls attention to nature's own unique voice and in so doing signals its consequence. Again the poem builds upon the traditional designation of nature as feminine by invoking predicates that often describe female speech in literary contexts: deprived of words or deemed incapable of independent thought, the female is frequently distanced from language and the authority it confers. Such a female resembles John Keats's unmerciful *belle dame*, with her "sweet moan," "fairy's song," "language strange," and "sigh[ing]," but she never emits substantive language. The *belle dame* ultimately triumphs, however, by vanquishing and virtually destroying the knight.[14] In "Entangled," a similar capacity for underlying control exists, along with the caution to recognize nature's latent power.

The final pair of lines in stanza five--"My heart, it throbbed so wildly, / In weird tumultuous glees"--indirectly conveys such force in its treatment of the speaker, who has devolved from the standing entity and syntactical subject "I" of the poem's first line to simply a body part, the heart. The alteration drains the speaker of unified subjectivity, for the heart signals further depersonalization; the noun deteriorates into the pronoun "it" immediately thereafter, and subsequently the speaker diminishes to a prepositional object. Although the initial line of

stanza six reinstates the speaker's "I" as the grammatical subject, the next part of
the phrase replicates the deprivation of agency in that the speaker "stagger[s]"
before returning to the object position and becoming "drag[ged] down." Again
nature has exerted control, for entrapping mosses cause the speaker's lurching
movements, which in turn impel the persona into more vegetation.

> I staggered in the mosses,
> It seemed to drag me down
> Into the gleaming bushes;
> To fall, to sink, to drown.

Also imparting the influence of nature is a deterioration, albeit slight, in the
speaker's own linguistic ability, for a singular pronoun improperly references the
plural mosses. By the final line of the stanza, the speaker is fully immersed in nature and occupies its lowest level. The speaker's placement connotes marginality,
in that a literal and figurative high ground conventionally indicates the site of
authority. The speaker's descent to an unexpected nadir signifies defeat.

   As the poem moves to the penultimate stanza, a shift in tone augurs the speaker's reconfigured attitude toward the natural world in opening with a fervid
"When lo!" The stanza is tracing the movements of a "lovely bird," which occupies the subject position and superior location as it flies above the speaker, who is
again reduced to a prepositional object.

> When lo! thro' scared foliage,
> A lovely bird did fly;
> And looked at me so knowing,
> With bright and curious eye.

Interestingly, the bird is holding the gaze with its own implications of power and
thereby mimics a human activity that further destabilizes the humanity/nature
antithesis. Moreover, the homonymic resonance of the bird's orb suggests nature's
own "I" and the reverse in authority that the poem has mapped. Appropriately,
the bird serves as the subject of the first line in the final stanza and issues forth
with nature's voice in two iterations:

> It broke out into warbles,
> And singing sped away;
> But I, like one awakened,
> Fled down the mossy way.

The use of the pronoun to reference the bird provides another example of the speaker's imperfect linguistic ability, in that the antecedent is actually the eye. The departure from paradigmatic language structures intimates a breakdown of rigid thought, thereby opening a space for new conceptions.

Although the speaker returns to the subject position in the final stanza's third line, the "I" is an altered form compared to its importance at the poem's commencement. The line resonates with the speaker's slumber-like state in the first stanza as the persona awakens through a newfound realization of nature not as other but as necessarily integral to and in symbiotic accordance with human experience. The poem's closing line bolsters the point and draws upon earlier revelations to leave the reader with such a critical thought. The predicate "fled" illuminates nature's agency in inducing the speaker's rapid movement as well as the persona's own newly discovered compulsion; the speaker heads "down," becoming even more a part of the marginalized low ground; and the path taken proceeds through "the mossy way," which indicates the power of this exemplum of nature that had caused the speaker to stagger and enter what now has become the chosen space. Subsumed within nature, voluntarily rather than unexpectedly, a wiser speaker has come to value instead of diminish it. The speaker no longer dominates the natural world but exists in communion with it, recognizing the false cultural dualism between humanity and nature.

Formal elements reinforce the poem's thematic trajectory as the structure elucidates nature's authority, in part by incorporating the traditional feminization of nature. The lines of the ballad stanzas alternate in syllable count and rhyme sequence, privileging a feminine presence. Each stanza consists of seven syllables in the a- and c- lines and six syllables in the b- and d- lines; the a- and c- lines feature feminine endings, as if imprisoning the b- and d- lines, with their masculine endings. Adding to the control of the feminized a- and c- lines is the indentation of the masculinized b- and d- lines, as if the latter lines carry less significance in being subjugated beneath the feminine lines in a kind of literal as well as figurative marginalization. The rhyme pattern also builds upon a gendered dichotomy; the lines with feminine endings do not rhyme, conveying an openness that contrasts with the rigidity of the rhyming masculine endings, with their reminder of inflexible masculinist perceptions about nature's purported inferiority. The choice of the ballad stanza itself, with the form's connection to song, resonates with and foregrounds nature's own singing voices as well as its exquisite harmony.

The esteem for nature that is embedded in "Entangled" takes a quite different path in the 1889 poem "On a Forsaken Lark's Nest." While "Entangled" carries a primary argument that nature should not be perceived as an inferior other, "On a Forsaken Lark's Nest" warns of the dangers that human presence poses to the natural world. The poem is responding to agricultural developments and human disregard that bring environmental ruin. Beginning with a rather funereal tone, the poem employs harsh vocabulary to trace the movement of a harvesting machine.

> Lo, where left 'mid the sheaves, cut down by the iron-
>   fanged reaper,
> Eating its way as it clangs fast through the wavering
>   wheat,
> Lies the nest of a lark, whose little brown eggs could
>   not keep her
> As she, affrighted and scared, fled from the harvester's
>   feet.

Jarring consonants and devouring images underscore the perils that the machine poses to nature. Guttural and other forceful consonants in "cut," "fanged," "fast," "clangs," and "feet" create an agitating cacophony, while the ravenous machine's appetite propels it relentlessly through the crop in which the lark's nest insecurely rests. In contrast, the consonants associated with nature are gently liquid, with an abundance of /l/ and /w/ sounds. The reference to the lark's nest does not come until the third line of the introductory stanza; the delayed placement amplifies the domineering effect of the reaper as it consumes everything in its path. The use of the weak verb "lies" in conjunction with the nest emphasizes its fragility, as does the adjectival "little" to describe the endangered eggs, while the linguistically violent /f/ of "feet" and "fled" provides the alarming contrast of human devastation. Additionally, the foregrounding of the noun "feet" in reference to the harvester connotes pounding force as the human, like the machine, unyieldingly advances upon the bird and her nest. Indeed, the noun "reaper" in the stanza's first line conflates the human and the machine, making the two destructive entities indistinguishable and suggesting a frightening conjunction of decimating conquerors. Physical positioning further accentuates the lark's vulnerability. The upright human soars above the creature, and she occupies the marginal space of the ground. As in "Entangled," a gendered binary prevails; nature is feminized, with the lark as thwarted mother, in contrast to the masculine figure of the harvester. The binary suggests, as in "Entangled," a prevalent masculine discourse that situates humanity above nature in an assumed hierarchical arrangement that justifies suppression.

The second stanza proceeds to focus on loss, which will dominate the rest of the poem. Human activity brings the coldness of death as opposed to the warmth of fostering nature.

Ah, what a heartful of song that now will never awaken,
Closely packed in the shell, awaited love's fostering,
That should have quickened to life what, now a-cold and
    forsaken,
Never, enamoured of light, will meet the dawn on the
    wing.

Positive images counterpoise nature with its destroyer: "heartful," "love's foster-ing," "quickened to life," "enamoured of light," and "the dawn on the wing" pro-vide a sharp contrast to the human agency connected with "never awaken[ing]," "a-cold and forsaken," and the "never" of birth. The stanza further indicates that the ruination of the bird's nest violates a natural law, in that the eggs "should have quickened to life." Humanity is out of step with the rhythms of the physical world and thus also poses a monstrous menace to its own well-being, as the poem ultimately will make clear.

    If such a violation of natural law does not provide a convincing enough reason for humanity to cease its destructive behavior, the next stanza builds upon cul-tural religiosity—despite Blind's own atheistic outlook—to advise Victorians that divine law is also being transgressed.

Ah, what paeans of joy, what raptures no mortal can
    measure,
Sweet as honey that's sealed in the cells of the honey-
    comb,
Would have ascended on high in jets of mellifluous
    pleasure,
Would have dropped from the clouds to nest in its gold-
    curtained home.

The "ah" initiating the second stanza reemerges here, but the tone shifts in that the rest of the line infuses the word with a feeling of awe reminiscent of a devout supplicant. Subsequent vocabulary choices within the line invoke other religious associations among their definitions: "paeans" denote hymns of praise; "raptures" involve a mystically transcendent experience that provides a connection to divine understanding; and the "mortal" unable to measure such rapturous moments contrasts with the immortal celestial entity. The phrase "mellifluous pleasure" is itself melodious in pronunciation, which underscores the harmonic and majes-tic picture presented. The final line, with its focus on descent from the celestial realm, hints at Christ's presence in evoking his own descent to earth. Divini-ty and nature combine when the being that "dropped from the clouds" then "nest[s]" in the tabernacle-like "gold-curtained home" of the bee's honeycomb.

It is in the poem's final stanza that the harm that humans cause to themselves by devastating nature becomes especially evident.

> Poor, pathetic brown eggs! Oh, pulses that will never
>   quicken!
> Music mute in the shell that hath been turned to a
>   tomb!
> Many a sweet human singer, chilled and adversity-
>   stricken,
> Withers benumbed in a world his joy might have helped
>   to illume.

The /p/ alliteration of the first line echoes the syncopation of a healthy beating heart with the pairing of "[p]oor, pathetic." The throbbing slows, however, through the three words preceding the next /p/ iteration, "pulses," before stopping abruptly as the consonant disappears in the line's continuation. Evident as well is a severance between creature and human. The term "pulses" generally evokes the measurement of human life, and in this line's usage the pulses develop a connection to the nonhuman life that also carries a pulse; in death, a bird cannot quicken the pulses of a human who otherwise would hear its song. The coupled words that open the second line, with their harmonic similarity in initial consonant and vowel, turn an initial impression of a paused song into an eternal silencing within a grave-like enclosure. The startling effect comes about aurally through the harsh /t/ sounds in "turned to a tomb." The third line's reference to "a sweet human singer" reflexively invokes the "sweet" hymns that the dead birds will never sing and in so doing reminds of the broken connection between humanity and nature. The point is immediately reinforced by the chill that the human, like the lost birds, endures. The final line juxtaposes all three primary entities in the poem, which underscores human discordance with the natural and divine worlds through the word "his." The pronoun lacks an antecedent and could refer to the human singer, a dead avian counterpart, or Christ's presence. Clearly, the poem argues, to destroy nature brings disaster to humankind as well. The male pronoun also reveals that the ruination is not simply a gendered matter of a male oppressor violating a female nature but is an annihilative act that a male imposes upon other males, too, and upon humanity in its totality.

A prosodic examination helps to articulate the poem's thematic concerns. The *abab* scheme sounds like a stomping military march, creating the same dismaying effect as the unstoppable footsteps in "Entangled." Moreover, the *abab* format, by virtue of its commonality, insinuates that the wreckage depicted in "On a Forsaken Lark's Nest" is not limited to the unfortunate lark's eternally silent brood but occurs on a broad scale, in diverse ways, within the natural world. The *a*- and *c*-tail rhymes follow a somewhat discordant pattern that reflects the disharmonious relationship humanity has forged with nature, especially since the rhymes appear in feminine endings that bring to mind gendered nature. The syllabic count adds to the poem's overall sense of dissonance, for there is consistency only in the lines with feminine endings (which have fifteen syllables). Even though the *a*- and *c*- lines, with their feminine endings, share identical syllabic counts, the stress pattern in the lines varies between them; the *a*- lines follow a consistent stress pattern, but the *c*- lines do not, suggesting that humanity's appalling effects upon nature threaten its very core.

A similar warning of human destruction surfaces in "The Sower," but this verse imparts a measure of hope in revealing that nature is a resilient entity that may be able to counteract the devastation if attitudes justifying its subjugation change. "The Sower" evidences several components that characterize "On a Forsaken Lark's Nest," most notably the domination over the land that agricultural incursions have brought. Composed of nine *abab* quatrains, with the familiar rhyming pattern again evoking the commonality of the destruction wrought by the agricultural invasion, "The Sower" brings forth numerous references to mastery in its opening stanzas. The poem moves from elevation to lowland as it traces through a sweeping panorama the crushing submission of nature that human interference entails, as if no part of the natural realm escapes its reach.

> The winds had hushed at last as by command;
> The quiet sky above,
> With its grey clouds spread o'er the fallow land,
> Sat brooding like a dove.

The voice of nature, emblematized by the hushed winds and quiet sky, has been stifled and silenced, for the overbearing force of human behavior has created a passive entity. The grey clouds accentuate the oppression since they are so extensive that they entirely cover the landscape below and allow no escape. The land occupies a passive position through the prepositional phrase preceding it, and the adjectival "fallow" conveys through one of its denotations inactivity and dormancy, as does the weak verb form "sat." Contributing to the repressive atmosphere is the gloominess that the "brooding" bird evokes; the modifier ironically reminds readers of the life-giving incubation this gentle creature typically provides but in this instance appears moribund.

The silencing effect of the "command" resulting in a "quiet sky" reemerges in the second stanza to depict a deathlike stillness. The sole connection to sound in the second stanza expands the effect by signifying death when a lifeless leaf drops:

> There was no motion in the air, no sound
>   Within the tree-tops stirred,
> Save when some last leaf, fluttering to the ground,
>   Dropped like a wounded bird.

The final line continues the death imagery, for an injured bird that falls to the soil is almost certainly destined to perish from predators if not from the wound itself. Nature demonstrates no agency here except in a poor imitation thereof as the leaf aimlessly descends to its earthen grave. The poem continues to play with the states of sound in the third stanza, in this case noting the unpleasant shrieks of crows. The contrast between height and depth that characterized the first two stanzas also appears in the third stanza as the crows sweep down from their high perches to the land; the descending movement continues to convey subjugation, with the fourth line's opening "down" providing emphasis.

> Or when the swart rooks in a gathering crowd
>   With clamorous noises wheeled,
> Hovering awhile, then swooped with wranglings loud
>   Down on the stubbly field.

The avian imagery is additionally telling, in that the predatory rooks are vastly different from the peaceful dove or the wounded bird of the previous stanzas; indeed, the deafening rooks appear to represent human harvesters, with their discordant machinery that invades the land and upsets its harmony ("clamorous noises," "wranglings loud").

The first three stanzas create a momentum and then the fourth stanza's opening "For now" provides a shift to the agricultural work itself, to which the poem has been leading. Nature is literally being harnessed as restrained horses prepare the land for planting.

> For now the big-thewed horses, toiling slow
>   In straining couples yoked,
> Patiently dragged the ploughshare to and fro
>   Till their wet haunches smoked.

Diction emphasizes the suffering caused by subjugation as the horses laboriously pull the plow ("toiling low," "straining," "dragged," and "smoked," with the latter term's archaic denotation emphasizing punishment). The ploughshare provides a violent image, for it is the part of a plow that cuts through the soil. Moreover, the word "till," substituting for "until" in the final line, stresses that the misery comes from the "tilling" of the land. The opening of the fifth stanza repeats that connection, along with the fierce tone.

> Till the stiff acre, broken into clods,
>   Bruised by the harrow's tooth,
> Lay lightly shaken, with its humid sods
>   Ranged into furrows smooth.

Nature can resist only passively, as a "stiff" piece of land contesting the plow's power, but that limited opposition is doomed when the land is "broken" both literally and figuratively. In the second line, nature's pain provides the tone, in that it has been "bruised" by the marauding "tooth" of the "harrow," with the latter's archaic meaning of pulverizing, tormenting, and plundering adding to the horrendous picture. The stanza conveys a raping of the land, as the harsh predicates bring pain and subjugation, with the terrain "shaken," its "humid sods" forced into a submissive state ("into furrows smooth").

The sower makes his appearance in the sixth stanza as an omnipotent and omnipresent figure moving incessantly through the land.

> There looming lone, from rise to set of sun,
>   Without or pause or speed,
> Solemnly striding by the furrows dun,
>   The sower sows the seed.

The /l/ and /s/ alliteration that in other contexts imparts graceful motion in this case creates a dirge-like, sinister cadence that resonates with the unthinking momentum of a mighty agricultural machine. That impression of invulnerability and unremittingness gains weight with the repetition of the stanza's final line in the first line of the seventh stanza:

> The sower sows the seed, which mouldering,
>   Deep coffined in the earth,
> Is buried now, but with the future spring
>   Will quicken into birth.

Death and decay become the overriding motifs in the stanza, with the "mouldering," "deep coffined," and "buried" seeds inserting a disconcerting note into the sowing process and an accompanying impression that male agency brings destruction. Moreover, the rape imagery of the fifth stanza continues here with the plunderer depositing his seed in the violated earth. Nevertheless, a rare hint of optimism surfaces in the reference to life developing at a later time, a concept that the closing stanza will revisit. At this moment, however, the sower's domination of nature prevails and extends into the penultimate stanza:

> Oh, poles of birth and death! Controlling Powers
>   Of human toil and need!
> On this fair earth all men are surely sowers,
>   Surely all life is seed!

With the phallic initial noun providing accentuation, the "poles of birth and death" are governed by the "Controlling Powers." These forces suggest the masculine power structure that shaped Victorian perceptions about the relationship between humanity and nature, as well as other human behavior ("human toil and need"). The fact that "all men" fit the category of sowers highlights their master status, as the sole sower's actions have demonstrated in the poem thus far. Women are absent from this equation, in that their role in the process of creating life is excised; it is the men's seeds that generate life. In a corollary way, the poem implies that women are marginalized in determining human activity relative to nature as well. If, as the final line remarks, "all life is seed," then the presumption exists that masculine control is monolithic and permanent.

In the concluding stanza, however, the prospect for eventual change comes forth. The quatrain reminds of the Foucauldian tenet of circulating power and the fissures in authority that allow the marginalized to gain a foothold and eventually end their subjugation.

> All life is seed, dropped in Time's yawning furrow,
>   Which with slow sprout and shoot,
> In the revolving world's unfathomed morrow,
>   Will blossom and bear fruit.

Although the stanza starts by repeating the notion that "[a]ll life is seed," stressing the apparent seamlessness of masculine authority, the stanza immediately opens up the possibility of transformation. An evolutionary element emerges in the stanza's reference to the vast spans of Time ("yawning furrow") that can enable a "slow" development of new life. With evolution comes change, and the new plant may diverge considerably from its predecessors; the "unfathomed morrow" is being shaped by the passage of time inherent in a "revolving world" experiencing its own alterations. The idea gains credence through the adjectival hint of revolution, which counters the impression of consistency that otherwise might characterize the endless revolutions of the earth itself as well as the orbits around the traditionally masculine sun. The seed planted by a tyrannous force not simply may but "will blossom and bear fruit" to generate a different world. The first line predicts female influence on the process with the "yawning furrow," a representation of the land that the sower has subjugated, depositing his seed into its cavernous womb-like space. Even though the prevalent Victorian discourse on evolution posited an ongoing male superiority—Darwin's *Descent of Man* made that idea clear to contemporary readers—a handful of dissenting views expected that women would instigate advances to the human species. The /s/ alliteration that earlier conveyed an unyielding male power shifts in the final stanza to a smooth cadence in detailing the gradual growth of an evolved form of plant, and the vigorous /b/ sounds of the final line resemble a rallying call to victory. Considering that male authority pervades the bulk of "The Sower," the almost unvarying presence of masculine endings provides an expected emphasis. Nonetheless, the last two stanzas break the pattern as each incorporates a pair of feminine endings, appearing at the point where the poem augurs the hope of change. Also making the connection is the fact that the feminine endings appear in the *a*- and *c*- lines, which are substantially longer and thus more dominant, with their eleven syllables, than the *b*- and *d*- lines with masculine endings that carry only six syllables.

Another agricultural poem, "Reapers," shows how human intervention and domination can sever a connection with the natural realm. Although the act of harvesting entails a relatively minimal interruption of nature, in the poem it serves as a subtle admonition that even small incursions can create marked effects. As Irigaray argues, "Life must be respected at the level of the natural world where it is a matter of cultivating it without appropriating or destroying it."[15] In "Reapers," the "toiling" workers occupy the dominant position through their activity on the land and the immediate repercussions on their surroundings. The natural elements become immobile and utterly silent, their cessation of activity on a massive scale contrasting sharply with the movement of the reapers wresting the crop from the soil as they advance through the field. So still is nature that even shadows are immobile, and breath itself seemingly ceases. The extent of the silence indicates that not only are birds "hushed" but so are the trees in which they perch. Cows appear as immovable as statues when not warding off flies, and not even insects seem to inhabit the grasses, as indicated in the second and third quatrains.

> Busy life is still, sunk in brooding leisure:
>   Birds have hushed their singing in the hushed tree-tops;
> Not a single cloud mars the flawless azure;
>   Not a shadow moves o'er the moveless crops;
>
> In the grassy shallows, that no breath is creasing,
>   Chestnut-coloured cows in the rushes dank
> Stand like cows of bronze, save when they flick the teasing
>   Flies with switch of tail from each quivering flank.

Nature and humanity are separated as if they occupy entirely different worlds. The last quatrain underscores the contrast between them through immobility and its opposite. In the first instance, "Nature takes a rest—even her bees are sleeping, / And the silent wood seems a church that's shut." Nature is the valorized entity through its comparison with a place of worship, and, tellingly, it is secured against human entry. In the quatrain's final pair of lines, an opening conjunction differentiates between the two worlds, again accentuating the relentless movement of the workers and the stillness of the environment they dominate: "[b]ut these human creatures cease not from their reaping / While the corn stands high, waiting to be cut." The poem's last line inserts a jarring note as the erect corn resembles a doomed prisoner awaiting execution. Exploitation of nature, the poem in its entirety warns, severs humanity from the rhythms of the natural world and divides it from the surrounding life.

In detailing the discordant effects stemming from human intervention in and domination of nature, "Reapers," like "The Sower," is providing an admonition, one that carries greater urgency when contextualized within the late-century development of ever more damaging agricultural machinery. Thomas Hardy's *Tess of the d'Urbervilles* emphatically makes the point by darkly portraying machines relentlessly pushing through the land. The narrator characterizes a threshing machine as "the red tyrant" that field workers "had come to serve" and declares that the machine "kept up a despotic demand upon the endurance of their muscles and nerves." When the crop supply diminished, "[t]he hum of the thresher . . . increased to a raving" as if an insatiable monster. The soot-covered machine operator resembled "a creature from Tophet" who "served fire and smoke"; he "was in the agricultural world, but not of it." Indeed, his surroundings "might be corn, straw, or chaos; it was all the same to him." The itinerant operator traveled throughout Wessex "hardly perceiving the scenes around him, and caring for them not at all."[16]

Similarly indicting mechanistic invasion, Victorian naturalist Richard Jefferies describes in *The Hills and the Vale* the advent of the steam-powered plow in alarming terms that emphasize its brutal destruction. The machines embody "crude force . . . as may have existed in the mastodon or other unwieldy monster of the prehistoric ages"; the "hissing" steam shrouds nearby berries "with a strange, unwonted cloud"; and "thick dark brown smoke" emanating from "the fiery mouth of the beast" suffocates and disperses wildlife. The machine's unpleasant exhaust "overcomes the fresh, sweet odour of the earth" while "[s]tray lumps of coal crush" fragile vegetation. One machine "comes jerking forward, tearing its way through stubble and clay, dragging its iron teeth with sheer strength deep through the solid earth." Such implements, Jefferies laments, speak "as loudly as iron and steel can shout, 'Progress! Onwards!'" Although Jefferies's account was published posthumously and after Blind's poem was written, the agricultural horrors that Jefferies declaims would have been churning through the countryside during her life. As Irigaray comments about plowing, it is a "kind of violence upon the earth," with the result that "[m]an upsets the rhythm of natural growth."[17]

A poem written in 1913 by Michael Field, included in *The Wattlefold*, reinforces Blind's condemnation of agricultural exploitation. In "Wheat-Miners," Field assails "libertines with senseless / Passion" who ravage the land—"[e]arth corn-bearing, rich, defenceless"—for unworthy profit. The agricultural invaders see the "golden wheat" as merely a source of riches, "[n]othing gold but money; naught / Treasurable, worth a thought / Save what they can work and mine." The poem continues its harsh judgment:

> Sensual, malicious greed
> Of wild infidels, who heed
> Nothing holy in the womb
> Of the prairie-land they doom
> By the lust with which they reap
> From its soil a yearly harvest deep;
> Through each year the ruined earth grows thin
> With the wasting of such wastrels' sin.

As the references to "passion" and "lust" accentuate, the despoilment is a form of rape, which mirrors Blind's imagery in "The Sower"; the Field poem speaks of "[e]arth impregnated by men," who are "violators." These interlopers will assault "the wheat-farms till these shine / With their lustrous corn no more / Than a gold-reef's worked-out store."[18]

Further Repercussions

Several other Blind poems demonstrate the harmful results of a domination of nature on various fronts, as a brief examination reveals. "Hope" provides a good starting point in that it unveils the mind-set of an individual who seeks to dominate nature for his own ends and who assumes that he deserves to possess any part he desires. The first segment of the sonnet sounds like a paraphrase of the biblical pronouncement in Genesis bestowing upon humanity the right of domination (1:26). The sense of entitlement is unequivocally accepted in the opening lines of the octave.

> All treasures of the earth and opulent seas,
> Metals and odorous woods and cunning gold,
> Fowls of the air and furry beasts untold,
> Vineyards and harvest fields and fruitful trees
> *Nature gave unto Man*; . . .
> (emphasis added)

A suggestion of surrender appears in the italicized line of this passage, and the impression of humanity's deserved position of dominator intensifies as the octave continues. The tone becomes one not only of an undisputed right to possess all the earth can offer but also of a disturbing presumption of authority to penetrate, through any destructive means desired, the mysteries of nature to benefit "Man." The diction of the octave's final lines becomes unsettlingly menacing:

> and last her keys
> Vouched passage to her secret ways of old
> Whence knowledge should be *wrung*, nay *power to mould*
> Out of the rough, his occult destinies.
> (emphasis added)

Nature becomes a tool to be manipulated, whereby nature's secrets are appropriated and reconfigured to the individual's own ends, themselves becoming secrets through their "occult" characteristic. The adjective inserts an ominous tone, with its connotative invocation of unsavory arts. This final section of the octave resonates with the disconcerting appraisal of nature that developed with the Scientific Revolution, as recounted in this study's introduction.

In its sestet, "Hope" traces a progression away from nature in favor of self-determination as the subject, bored with nature's offerings, "craved a wider scope." Underlying the alteration is the conventional schism between unprivileged, material nature and valorized, ratiocinative humanity. The poem describes the transformation through a mythological analogy that emphasizes the cognitive factor, for the subject's "own creation" emerged "fair as Pallas from the brain of Jove." Nature's influence thus has been discarded in favor of this "creation," depicted as "[t]he only thing man never wearies of." Interestingly, the "creation" is identified as "visionary Hope," which provides an ironic cast to the poem, for in rejecting nature, the subject has lost, not gained, a sense of vision.

The toll that blithe domination takes on nature is examined from a different standpoint in "The Hunter's Moon," which reveals through the destruction of animal life the deleterious outcome for the human actor, who is left in a lifeless place. In the first of three stanzas, the eponymous orb has reached its peak and images of the sky are characterized in hunting terms: "herded clouds" proceed to "[s]camper tumultuously" as they are "[c]hased by the hounding wind," which, like a hunting dog, "yelps behind." The blending of hunt and sky imagery mirrors the vast effect of human activity on the world. In the second stanza, the "clamorous" hunt has concluded, the cacophonous adjective emphasizing the disconcerting repercussions the activity has imposed on nature. Empty space surrounds a solitary huntsman as a result of the hunt's presumed carnage, for "[h]e wakes a hollow tone" that is "[f]ar echoing to his horn / In clefts forlorn." In the final stanza, the moon has nearly reached its nadir, and an unnerving stillness is all that remains for the hunter and his unfortunate prey. "Where is the panting roe? / Where hath the wild deer fled?" the speaker asks in realizing their absence and the emptiness that abides: "Hunter and hunted now / Lie in oblivion deep: / Dead or asleep."

Two other Blind poems target the harm produced by a separation from nature that a different form of domination causes--industrialization on a large scale, specifically factory mechanization. The first poem, "Manchester by Night," presents a place where the only connection to nature comes from the sky's "[b]lack brows majestical with glimmering stars," a "dewy silence [that] soothes," and a glowing moon. Limiting reminders of nature to the firmament, the poem accentuates human separation from nature through the sky's immense distance from the earth's edifices and inhabitants. The sonnet structure provides an ironic twist in light of the form's associations with Petrarchan love and its romantic literary descendants, as opposed to its usage in the Blind poem to convey bleakness, despair, and suffering.

The octave's diction stresses strife and misery, as the opening line augurs in characterizing Manchester as being "rife with intestine wars." The denotations of the adjective "intestine" are doubly significant, for it refers to a locale's internal affairs and to the bodily part essential for human life. Manchester resembles a voracious predator as a "huge" place that spews forth, as if from "monstrous sacrificial shrines," ominous "[p]illars of smoke." The city resembles a prison, as the moonlight appears "athwart the narrow cloudy bars" that the smoky columns form. The sestet presents a hellish battle for survival in which the town's residents turn upon one another in brutal combat. Choked by the factory's noxious effluent, the adversaries struggle against suffocation as they climb over each other to remain alive. Yet the outcome for conqueror and conquered is virtually indistinguishable as continued existence is merely a form of death in life. Graphic vocabulary conveys the horror of the struggle.

> Now toiling multitudes that hustling crush
> Each other in the fateful strife for breath,
> And, hounded on by diverse hungers, rush
> Across the prostrate ones that groan beneath,
> Are swathed within the universal hush,
> As life exchanges semblances with death.

No nature images appear in the sestet, which imparts the toll that an isolation from the natural world entails. The consequences of dominating nature by favoring industrialization, and all its accompanying ills, are social chaos, misery, and pain. No salutary thoughts appear in the poem, as human life irrevocably spirals downward.

"The Red Sunsets, 1883" presents a slightly more positive picture in that a trio of factory workers enjoys an awe-inspiring moment as they gaze at a magnificent solar event. Unlike "Manchester by Night," this sonnet includes brief references to beauty, all of which proceed from the sky. Although depicting a bleak cityscape of "huddling streets" in "the black fringes of the wintry night," the poem notes the sunset's glimmers of light that provide a transformative effect. An intertextual allusion to the biblical Revelation compares the poem's illuminated city to the "new Jerusalem, coming down from God out of heaven" while the apostle John looked on (Rev. 21:2). The poem speculates, "Such bursts of glory may have rapt the sight" of Christ's disciple, whom "[t]he visionary angel came to show / That heavenly city built of chrysolite." Through the religious connection, the poem positions nature, as emblematized by the sunset, at the highest possible level for a devout Victorian reader and thus amplifies the importance of preserving a bond with the natural world.

The sestet builds on the religious link in opening with the phrase "And lo," as if beginning the poem's own biblical statement. The factory workers react to the sunset's light as they would to a divine vision: they, "begrimed with soot, / Aflame with the red splendour, marvelling stand, / And gaze with lifted faces awed and mute." The poem then indicts an industrial system that severs humanity from nature, as the workers have been "[s]tarved of earth's beauty by Man's grudging hand." Access to the splendors of nature belongs to all, for the "toilers, robbed of labour's golden fruit," also deserve to "feast in Nature's fairyland."

Instead of dominating nature, as detailed in the several poems discussed thus far, Blind calls for humanity to nurture a harmonious relationship, as "The Moat" suggests. The verse resonates with Wordsworth's "Lines Composed a Few Miles above Tintern Abbey," with the earlier poem's depictions of nature and humanity compatibly intertwined. "Tintern Abbey" reveals the linkages in remarking upon "these pastoral farms, / Green to the very door" and the "wreaths of smoke / Sent up, in silence, from among the trees!"[19] Similarly, the first line of "The Moat" references a "lichened home of hoary peace," as if nature has literally bonded with the human construction in a figuratively eternal coexistence. The home, "[i]nvulnerable in its glassy moat," gains this strength through the close union with nature. A nearby herd of cattle, connected with humanity as a source of sustenance, merges smoothly with "[t]he tender slopes" upon which the animals graze. Other meldings of nature and human creations appear in the poem: thus, a natural scene resembles a painting that "an old Master made"; like a man-made object, a peacock is "jewelled" and evidences "rich enamel"; and a "mossy wall" mimics a symbiotic pairing. The positioning of nature in this poetic scenario resembles the positive human perspective on nature in the time before the Scientific Revolution, with multiple associations to benevolence, tranquility, and generosity.

The scene portrayed in "The Moat" likely existed through centuries, the poem implies with a quiet lesson that an ongoing harmony with nature provides humanity with stability and calm. The opening quatrain accentuates the span of time as "[a] breath of ghostly summers" that "seems to float / And murmur mid the immemorial trees." The poem creates an eternal present in this green world that is set apart with its moat, as suggested by the next stanza's comment that, "self-oblivious, Time forgets to note / The flight of velvet-footed centuries." The modifier "velvet-footed" characterizes the passage of time as a gentle progression providing continuity rather than disorienting change. The conjunction of sunlight, a giver of life, reposing languidly alongside the "slow shade" of a yew contributes to the picture of a soothing eternal present. A marker of death, amplified by the double meaning of "shade," the yew is often planted in churchyards. Thus, life and death coexist as if the movement of time is virtually meaningless rather than signaling disturbing mutability. Even a flower appears to exist eternally, in that a "youthful rose / Blooms like a rose which never means to fade." All the poem's markers of a beneficent bond between humanity and nature that create a sense of a peaceful eternal present attest to the value of living in harmony with the surrounding world.

The Nature-Woman Connection

The calm ambience of "The Moat" provides no indication that humanity is dominating the natural realm, in decided contrast to several of the preceding poems addressed. Although the previous verses center on a domination of nature, the wielding of such deleterious authority in Blind's poems also extends in another direction, that of exerting control over women. As this book's introduction emphasized, nature and women were deemed analogous under the ostensible logic of Victorian culture in that both were viewed as inferior entities that shared numerous undesirable traits indicative of weakness and destining their rule by men. Like Augusta Webster, Blind would add a crucial dimension to the churning debate over the Woman Question by addressing the damaging linkage of nature and women evidenced by stifled subjectivity and assumed immutability. In a pair of short poems, Blind speaks about the oppression of both entities, building from the cultural binding of the two concepts. Blind interrogates the gendered designation of nature and the repercussions for women when they are inextricably linked to the natural realm. The subjugated entities are bound to each other such that the oppression of one can serve as a metaphor of and justification for the suppression of the other.

Aptly titled "A Parable," the first poem calls attention to the dangerous effects that women's identification with nature creates, pessimistically suggesting a veritable death of subjectivity through the cultural association that apparently cannot be severed. The four-stanza poem immediately situates its female character, a young girl, literally and linguistically within nature:

> Between the sandhills and the sea
>   A narrow strip of silver sand
>   Whereon a little maid doth stand,
> Who picks up shells continually
> Between the sandhills and the sea.

With the repetition of the first and final lines in the stanza comes a sense of imprisonment, as if the identical lines are constraining bars within which the girl is subsumed by nature, which the opening preposition "between" reinforces. Though the girl has an element of agency in that she is standing, the supposition is merely an illusion. The bar-like stanzaic lines, along with the narrowness of the sand upon which she is located, added to the instability of sand itself as a shifting foundation, limit her so substantially that no escape from the supposed female connection to nature appears feasible; indeed, she is perpetually gathering a representation of that linkage through her incessant collection of the shells. Accentuating her trapped status are the stanza's *b*- and *c*- lines describing her position, for those indented lines are themselves entrapped by the longer lines that surround them.

The inescapability from the nature-female linkage becomes even more established in the second stanza through an element of the sublime and the masculine connotations it carries.

> Far as her wondering eyes can reach
>   A Vastness, heaving grey in grey
>   To the frayed edges where the day
> Furls his red standard on the breach,
> Between the skyline and the beach.

Not only does the sublime component of vastness appear, but the word's capitalization emphasizes its might, a notion underlined by the fact that its depressing grey contours seem to extend infinitely, as the first line indicates. Although the third line reveals that the grey sameness is actually limited by signs of daylight, which inserts itself within the "breach," the girl's entrapment does not cease in that the sun supposedly heralding relief is yet another masculine image. This masculine force, with its militaristic standard signifying conquest, and the flag's redness, proclaiming invulnerability through the blaring visibility of the color, stress the girl's entrapment by her association with nature. The stanza's final line reinforces the linkage by replacing the ground-level sandhills of the first stanza with the infinite boundary of the sky.

The asphyxiating effect that inheres in being trapped between the sky and the beach becomes even more pronounced in the third stanza, as the ocean forms another suffocating barrier that prevents escape from the nature-female bond.

> The waters of the flowing tide
>   Cast up the seapink shells and weed;
>   She toys with shells, and doth not heed
> The ocean, which on every side
> Is closing round her vast and wide.

The girl's obliviousness to her physical danger replicates a conventional Victorian female's inability to recognize the threat that the nature-female bond presents in limiting her own potentiality. That the maid ineffectually "toys with shells" and "doth not heed" the creeping ocean points to a lack of recognition that imperils her very existence. Her toying serves as the only verb in the stanza connoting any form of agency, but it signals impotence. As in the previous stanza, the sublime transmits the magnitude of the threat through the vastness of the menace posed and the ocean's presence "on every side," leaving no avenue for escape.

The final stanza is especially unnerving, in that the girl's innocent toying with the shells contrasts with a sinister ocean that maliciously "creeps" to end her life.

> It creeps her way as if in play,
>   Pink shells at her pink feet to cast;
>   But now the wild waves hold her fast
> And bear her off and melt away
> A Vastness heaving grey in grey.

In implying that the ocean has a malignant intent, the poem insinuates that the masculine linkage of nature and female is itself disingenuous, a cunning maneuver that helps to hold women in a position of weakness and inferiority, since both supposedly are endlessly destined for subjugation. The pinkness of the shells and the girl's feet reminds readers of that equation, and the girl's grim fate is couched as natural; indeed, the pink coloration is an attenuation of the red hue characterizing the masculinist flag. By the final stanza the maid has lost any sense of agency, for only the ocean—that is, the latest representation of her close link to nature—prevails. In fact, the poem's predicates have charted a switch in agency, beginning with the maid's standing posture in the first stanza but altering in the second stanza to reflect her lack of power. Although the second stanza indicates that the maid's eyes "can reach," the fact that the impenetrable haze wholly constrains her vision negates the sense of agency. Thereafter, the predicates relate to forces that act upon her. In the final stanza, the repetition of vastness and greyness introduced in the second stanza stresses the might of the nature-female linkage and the difficulty in comprehending the danger that it poses to a nineteenth-century woman. Indeed, the sequence of verbs in the final stanza creates a crescendo of sorts exhibiting the maid's vulnerability; the ocean first "creeps," then becomes increasingly active in constraining and ultimately carrying the girl to her death. Line endings contribute to the effect of control, in that they are masculine and present an overriding masculine authority.

The second short poem, "The New Proserpine," assails the nature-female equation as well, in this case turning to the detrimental workings of myth in portraying the oppression of women. A female's long-standing links to nature and myth foreground the substantively unchanging situation for women over time through the designation of female essence that the two concepts reinforce. As in "A Parable," the message is grim, for no release from the associations to nature and myth appears possible. Instead, a Victorian version of Proserpine simply repeats the delimiting picture. Indeed, following the final line is the notation "Villa Pamfili Doria," a seventeenth-century edifice in Rome with impressive gardens where Blind penned the poem; the locale, with its lengthy history, confers an ironic element on the story of this Proserpine, for the poem dwells on her veritable removal from history as a model of a supposedly immutable female essence.

"The New Proserpine" draws upon the concept of enclosure, as did "A Parable," but demonstrates the constraint with an enclosed garden, one that is "walled," in a carceral reminder. Although at first glance the vegetation within the boundary appears to have a modicum of agency, that presumption quickly dissipates.

> Where, countless as the stars of night,
>   The daisies made a milky way
> Across fresh lawns, and flecked with light,
>   Old Ilex groves walled round with bay.

The verb associated with the daisies, "made," seemingly there to imply an action, instead serves as a synonym for the passive "appear," for it simply acknowledges their presence rather than conveying any initiative. The type of trees found in the garden contributes to the idea of immutability, for both Ilex and bay are forms of evergreen, which in never altering its appearance presents an unchanging essence. The second stanza introduces the titular character with several disturbing references.

> I saw thee stoop, oh lady sweet,
>   And with those pale, frail hands of thine
> Gather the spring flowers at our feet,
>   Fair as some late-born Proserpine.

Syntactically, the woman becomes the object of a gaze, which situates her in an inferior position that her "stoop" amplifies. The "pale, frail hands" convey both a deathly pallor and an innate vulnerability. The third line becomes even more troubling as her flower-gathering occurs "at our feet" in a reiteration of her lowly situation. By identifying her in the fourth line as a "late-born Proserpine," the poem initiates the link to myth and suggests through the modifier "some" that she is merely one of a multitude—in other words, that women in general carry the unfortunate link to myth and the essence it entails. The opening word, "fair," insinuates an essential connection applicable to all females since the archaic meaning of "fair" is "woman." The mythical Proserpine provides an apt representation of Victorian females in that she was tightly bound to nature in her role as a maiden of springtime and carries an unmistakable redolence of death, not only through her lengthy residence in the underworld but also through her own perpetual demise, occurring every year. The Victorian woman, the poem shows, is simply considered another iteration of female essence, a warning signaled in the poem's title.

The third stanza repeats the connections to nature, myth, and death, along with the inferior position that the character occupied in the previous stanza. She both bends to collect flowers and resides in the underworld, never rising above ground level.

> Yea, gathering flowers, thou might'st have been
>   That goddess of the ethereal brow,
> Revisiting this radiant scene
>   From realm of dolorous shades below.

Accorded an "ethereal" brow, the contemporary woman lacks material substance, which ties her not only to the famed goddess but also to another unearthly figure, the Victorian angel of the house. The /r/ alliteration of the closing two lines combines the ideas of immutability, through the static milieu that Proserpine endlessly revisits, and of death, through the underworld and its anguished ghosts. Ironically, the scene to which Proserpine continually returns is termed a "radiant" one.

In the closing stanza, the contemporary Proserpine is allied to constrictive conceptions of subjectivity that cultural and literary associations of the Victorian era widely assert.

> Thou might'st have been that Queen of Sighs,
>   Love-bound by Hades' dreadful spell;
> For veiled within thy heaven-blue eyes,
>   There lay the Memory of Hell.

First, the title "Queen of Sighs" presents a damaging analogy in that it points to women's separation from language and the implication that women are doomed to silence or mimicry. Second, the reference to being "love-bound" through hellish influence calls to mind a Victorian woman's own hellish constraint in

fulfilling her expected role as provider of unbounded affection and the attendant self-sacrifice required. Third, the veiling evokes self-effacement, as do the
"heaven-blue eyes," with their allusion to the Virgin Mary and her unfailing obe-
dience. Appropriately, then, the new Prosperine is left with a "Memory of Hell"
in considering the perception of female essence she has inherited—a destructive
legacy for the female reader as well.

With "The New Proserpine" and "A Parable," it becomes readily apparent that
Blind contributed a compelling feminist and ecological perspective to the cultural pairing of nature and women in an approach that resonates with Webster's
poetry. Blind's work in the ecofeminist arena provides a crucial window into
Victorian debates on the assessment and treatment of nature as well as the gender
upheaval of the *fin de siècle*. Her contributions in this regard are not limited to
the verses studied in this analysis, for the urgent messages thread through other
short poems in her oeuvre.

As the poems investigated in this chapter have demonstrated, Mathilde Blind
issued weighty admonitions to her contemporaries. If the illusion that humanity
can indiscriminately dominate nature without repercussions is not recognized as
such, the oppression of nature will ultimately bring disaster to humanity itself
for failing to accept the necessity of a companionate, not hierarchal, relationship. Additionally, the view that nature and women are inextricably connected
provided an avenue for the continued subjugation of Victorian females. The implications carry crucial significance not only for understanding the vexing issues
characterizing the Victorian *fin de siècle* but also for recognizing a vital warning
to the current era.

CHAPTER THREE

Michael Field
Eroticizing Agency

A SIGNIFICANT FACET OF THE NATURE-WOMEN equation that Augusta Webster and Mathilde Blind challenged so effectively is the passivity it entails. Focusing primarily on the nature portion of the presumed equivalence, Michael Field forcefully countered the deleterious supposition by foregrounding the agential component that is decidedly intrinsic to and inseparable from the nonhuman world. The oeuvre of Michael Field—the pen name used by the poetic and loving couple Katharine Bradley and Edith Cooper—strikingly demonstrates the agency of nature by insistently linking it to eroticism. Heterosexuality and homosexuality, as well as autoeroticism, enter and complicate Field's poetic corpus. By broadening erotic opportunities, the poetry creates a sense of empowerment so intense that cultural restraints on multiple levels can fall apart.

As Gretchen Legler observes in "Ecofeminist Literary Criticism," nature should be considered "a desiring subject," and the approach to nature in the Field poetry adheres to that designation. The verses also conform to Catrin Gersdorf's call in "Ecocritical Uses of the Erotic" for the "reintegration of the body into metaphors of nature"; Gersdorf emphasizes that an erotic component could alter suppositions about the natural world. Michael Field's poetry anticipates that recommendation as it endows nature with erotic qualities suggesting expansive energy and impressive power to emphasize agency; an active entity can elude suppression and domination. Eroticism extends beyond conventional barriers in an explosion of sensual possibilities. As Gersdorf comments, "A broad variety of erotic possibilities . . . imaginatively disturb[s] the boundaries." In many cases, a particular Field poem can suggest either male-female or female-female desire, and the indecipherability opens interpretive space in important ways through these agential configurations.[1]

The concept of eroticism carries numerous connotations besides sexuality, Greta Gaard contends in an essay on ecofeminism; thus, the erotic can refer to "sensuality, spontaneity, passion, delight, and pleasurable stimulation," and definitions change in different times and cultures. Gaard's catalog of erotic possibilities evokes the qualities that Field embraces in contributing to *fin de siècle* aestheticism, which this chapter will address. Eroticism can be assessed through its relationship not only to nature but to women as well, along with the long-standing efforts to dominate both entities in Western culture. Representing a "lifeforce" and a "source of power," eroticism has been denied to women, Audre Lorde notes in *Sister Outsider*. Instead, women "have been taught to suspect this resource, vilified, abused, and devalued within western society," Lorde states. Catriona Sandilands's discussion of "desiring nature" illuminates the significance of eroticism as an agent that shreds perceptions of nature as being a passive object rather than a vibrant subject. In connecting eroticism and power, Sandilands identifies a decisive, historical association "between the regulation of sexuality and the containment of nature." Sandilands cites "western culture's profound erotophobia" and refers to the ostensible split between a valorized rationality and a degraded physicality. The intense erotophobia, Gaard says of theorists' findings, leads to its rigid control by social pressures. The multiple theorizations of eroticism make abundantly evident that recognizing nature as an active erotic entity means attributing formidable force to it.[2]

Early Beginnings of Eroticized Landscape

The eroticization of landscape has ancient antecedents in Greek and Roman literature, as found in the work of such writers as Homer, Virgil, and Ovid. The first two poets, for example, imbued the image of a cave with sexual suggestiveness. In *The Odyssey*, Homer selects a cave as the site of the hero's sexual encounters with the beautiful Calypso: "they retired, this pair, to the inner cave / to revel and rest softly, side by side." Calypso's cave is surrounded by sensual foliage and populated by avian visitors.

> A deep wood grew outside, with summer leaves
> of alder and black poplar, pungent cypress.
> Ornate birds here rested their stretched wings—
> horned owls, falcons, cormorants—long-tongued
> beachcombing birds, and followers of the sea.
> Around the smoothwalled cave a crooking vine
> held purple clusters under ply of green;
> and four springs, bubbling up near one another
> shallow and clear, took channels here and there
> through beds of violets and tender parsley.
> Even a god who found this place
> would gaze, and feel his heart beat with delight.

Later, Odysseus recalls that Calypso, by whom he had "been detained long," kept him "in her smooth caves, to be her heart's delight." Similarly, Virgil's *Aeneid* applies a sexual taint to a cave where Aeneas and his men are led.

> The rock's vast side is hollowed into a cavern,
> With a hundred mouths, a hundred open portals,
> Whence voices rush, the answers of the Sybil.
> They had reached the threshold, and the virgin cried:
> "It is time to seek the fates; the god is here,
> The god is here, behold him." And as she spoke
> Before the entrance, her countenance and color
> Changed, and her hair tossed loose, and her heart was heaving,
> Her bosom swollen with frenzy; she seemed taller,
> Her voice not human at all.[3]

It is Ovid, however, who weaves eroticized descriptions of landscapes with the most notable frequency; they are often the sites of lustful and violent behavior in his *Metamorphoses*. In discussing Ovid's treatment of landscape, Charles Paul Segal speaks of "peaceful sylvan scenes as the setting for violence, often sexual violence," wherein innocence cannot endure. "The natural scenery reinforces this effect," Segal observes, "by creating in the poem a pervasive sensuous atmosphere, a mood of luxurious lassitude." Tracing Ovidian technique to pastoral predecessors, he remarks, "The woods and groves of pastoral may themselves express a certain degree of erotic wish-fulfilment and libidinal freedom." Because of the sensuality characterizing Ovid's terrain, merely one word can create an intended impression, Segal notes.[4]

Sensuality exists not only in a *Metamorphoses* landscape drawn in broad strokes but also in Ovid's use of natural images to describe the capture of unfortunate innocents. In the story of Daphne, for instance, Daphne sought help in avoiding Apollo's unwanted pursuit; consequently, "her limbs grew numb and heavy, her soft breasts / Were closed with delicate bark." As Apollo observed Daphne, "[h]e placed his hand / Where he had hoped and felt the heart still beating / Under the bark; and he embraced the branches / As if they still were limbs, and kissed the wood." When Pluto captured Proserpina in a wooded setting, the goddess was gathering the "lovely flowers growing" while playing among "[v]iolets, or white lilies." Then, "in one moment, / Or almost one, she was seen, and loved, and taken / In Pluto's rush of love." Pluto ripped her garment, and "loosened flowers fell" as she, "[i]n simple innocence," mourned their loss because of "[h]er ravager." In "The Story of Dryope," the speaker recalls the fate of Lotis, who

"[f]led from Priapus' lust" and "her body / Was changed into this flower." The
tale of Salmacis reverses the biological sex of the aggressor, as a water-nymph
pursues a gazing boy. Ensconced within a natural setting, the nymph would "rest
on the soft greenery, or gather / Bright-colored flowers." While so doing one day
"she saw the youngster / And wanted what she saw." As Salmacis "[c]ontrolled
her eagerness, a very little," she endeavored "to be as pretty / As ever she knew
how" to lure the youth. She embraced him and refused to release him, despite his
resistance. The entrapment parallels the actions that occur in nature, for varied
reasons: a snake coiling around an eagle to make its escape, ivy encircling a strong
tree, an octopus succeeding in capturing its prey. When the nymph ultimately
conquered the youth, "the two bodies seemed to merge together, / One face, one
form. As when a twig is grafted / On parent stock, both knit, mature together."[5]

Michael Field enacts a similar strategy in deploying natural images to convey
sensuality. The eroticization of landscape is abundantly evident in two Venus
poems included in the 1892 *Sight and Song*, a collection based on observations
of museum paintings. With numerous connections to desire, passion, seduction,
and fertility in mythology and literature, Venus offers a particularly fitting choice
for coupling landscape and sexuality. "The Sleeping Venus," based on an eroticized painting with the same title by Giorgione, makes the association unmistakable, through both her telling presence on the land and the scanning of her naked
body as if it were terrain. A comment by Edith Cooper about the Field poets'
viewing of the painting, though following Victorian convention in designating
nature as feminine, nevertheless points to the linkage between the erotic Venus
and the landscape in noting "that ideal sympathy between woman and the land."[6]

In the lengthy poem's opening lines, Venus is positioned as if framed by nature, "resting on the verdant swell / Of a soft country flanked with mountain
domes." Citing her departure from the "archèd shell" of her birth, the poem
establishes a sexual component immediately in contrasting the "barren wave"
Venus left behind and the fecund space within "earth's fruitful tilths" where she
will reside. Natural settings are accentuated, as "sward-lands or the corn-field
sweeps" surround Venus and leave her visible for all to see "on open ground,"
again framed by "the great hill-sides around." It is in the second stanza that the
erotic bond with the landscape is compellingly forged, for Venus as sexualized
avatar takes on the contours of the earth where she rests.

> And her body has the curves,
> The same extensive smoothness seen
> In yonder breadths of pasture, in the swerves
> Of the grassy mountain-green
> That for her propping pillow serves.

Sexual insinuations bracket the passage, with the first line accentuating the shapeliness of a female body and the final line alluding to a bed for conducting erotic activity through the reference to Venus's pillow. In fact, the Giorgione painting situates the pillow, in that case formed from fabric rather than the ground, as a prominent element depicting the supine Venus in her bed-like setting; the Field substitution of nature for Giorgione's crafted material promotes the poem's positioning of the land in eroticized terms. The sexualization of the body continues between the passage's starting and concluding lines, with the "extensive smoothness" bringing forth the tactile sensation that becomes part of the consummatory act. The combination of curves and texture recalls Edmund Burke's theorization of the beautiful and its own underlying interest in the female form. The extensive landscape surrounding Venus underscores the span of her body, and the "swerves," or turns, replicate her curvaceous form. The scopic perspective moves toward Venus, proceeding from a focus on "yonder" fields to an immediate mention of the swerves beneath this mythological deity embodying libidinousness. No impermeable boundary separates the sexualized figure and the landscape, and the stanza proceeds to confirm and heighten their conjunction.

> There is a sympathy between
> Her and Earth of largest reach,
> For the sex that forms them each
> Is a bond, a holiness,
> That unconsciously must bless
> And unite them, as they lie
> Shameless underneath the sky
> A long, opal cloud
> Doth in noontide haze enshroud.[7]

In its capitalization, Earth becomes a personified entity apparently analogous to Venus as sentient figures drawn together to share "sympathy." A sensuous tethering suggesting Venus's body's span is confirmed in specific language, with both entities allied with "the sex" that created them and the firm "bond" that "unite[s] them." The phrasing returns to more opaque configurations through their reposing together without shame as if each has unapologetically engaged in sexual congress. These lines not only validate eroticism but elevate it to a plane of "holiness" and "bless" it, references that coincide with Venus's status as a deity. A "long" cloud suggests that an expansive body is being enclosed. Additionally, the hazy atmosphere calls to mind Victorian bed curtains that set apart a pair within them, immersed in intimate communion, from disturbance.

The erotic agency of the terrain beneath Venus contrasts with the traditional view of land as a feminized other and, as Legler observes, as an "agentless female object." In characterizing one tradition in nature writing, Legler identifies the predilection to perceive the land as "a 'thing-for-us,' not as a 'thing-in-itself,'" whereby it is "rendered an object for the construction and maintenance of the 'self' of the writer," to provide "a mute mirror" rather than an agent. Legler offers an alternative position, one that "emphasizes erotic conversation between humans and the land; a reinvention that constitutes the land as an agent, a 'speaker' with erotic autonomy." This approach offers a corollary benefit for a woman writer, who can express female desire through the medium of landscape. Referencing the work of French feminists, among others, Legler points out that male-oriented language has shaped female desire and precluded women from defining it themselves. Within that linguistic framework, there is no space wherein nature has its own identity and the capacity to desire, Legler observes. By reworking such language, however, a female writer can "converse erotically with the land, to let it 'speak' its own desires," says Legler. In applying Legler's comments to "The Sleeping Venus" as well as other nature poetry penned by Field, the erotic configurations of landscape provide an effective vehicle for reevaluating the natural world, discarding delimiting impressions of passivity and silence in favor of activity and a version of speech.[8]

In the ocular examination of its main figure, "The Sleeping Venus" moves from an overview of the deity's entire body to a scrutiny of individual components. The speaker pans Venus's figure from head to foot in a pattern reminiscent of other literary depictions in the Victorian era that focus on a woman as a collection of somatic components, eroticizing them throughout the fetishistic depiction. Of particular interest here, though, is the sustained accentuation of the sexual Venus joining with the terrain and thereby eroticizing it through contiguity. The poetic segment begins with another reference to extension and the tacit reference to the span of the body, this time with the goddess raising her arm above her head. The poem proceeds to scan the figure from elbow to knees in delineating the connection to nature through simile.

> Down to the crossing knees a line descends
> Unimpeachable and soft
> As the adjacent slope that ends
> In chequered plain of hedge and croft.

During the downward movement, the poem pauses to focus on Venetian breasts with elaborate attention. The language of nature permeates the depiction, beginning with a simile before turning from an implicit distinction to an elision of the boundary between the terrain and the libidinous body upon it. This phrasing initially positions the breasts as distanced from the land, indicating its separation from Venus, since the landscape must travel to reach her. Thus, the passage begins, "Circular as lovely knolls, / Up to which a landscape rolls / With desirous sway." That ascending movement signals the erosion of the barrier between the two through the erotic agency that the land reveals in its "desirous sway." The phrase provides both an overt nexus between the land and eroticism through the adjective and the less apparent link wrought by the customary undulations of breasts in motion. As the poem unfolds, Venus's bosom becomes part of an uneven land.

> each breast
> Rises from the level chest,
> One in contour, one in round—
> Either exquisite, low mound
> Firm in shape and given
> To the August warmth of heaven.

The subsequent section of the poem advances the connection between the erotic body and the landscape, with such references as Venus's "herbage-cushioned foot," a leg resting "[a]gainst the turf," a curled knee hidden by a protuberant incline, ambient shade touching her breasts and neck, and her "body's lower heaves" indicative of a river's movement. The comparisons create a crescendo that leads to not only a sexual act but an autoerotic one that adds yet another overdetermined layer of sensuality to the goddess's body as the poem's descending scan reaches its goal.

> Her hand the thigh's tense surface leaves,
> Falling inward. Not even sleep
> Dare invalidate the deep,
> Universal pleasure sex
> Must unto itself annex—
> Even the stillest sleep.

In the gap of the poem following this last line, sexual satisfaction occurs, for in the next lines, Venus is "at peace" and "enjoy[ing] the good / Of delicious womanhood."[9]

The poem proceeds to assess again the deity's body parts, even to her eyebrow, as if no portion of her form escapes notice in this intensive scopic examination. Previous poetic maneuvers return as the line between eroticized body and landscape remains illegible. Thus, eyelids look like flower buds, which additionally carry implications of virginity and its subsequent loss. Carnations do not simply rest by Venus's face but "mount" it in a sexual mimicry. Her "red lips" conceal secrets, presumably related to passion through the lips' hue and their role in physically expressing the ardent emotion with a kiss. The white cloth upon which Venus sleeps "is stained with shade," intimating sexual experience so abundant that the shadow makes its mark "fold by fold" in a veiled reference to vaginal formation.

In its conclusion, "The Sleeping Venus" reinforces the figure's bond with the landscape, which has been formed so firmly as to endure through the centuries. Not only had Venus rested upon "the solemn glebes" since "ages far ago," she would so remain "till the long, / Last evening of Earth's summer glow." Her fecundity extends to the land upon which she lies, for she exists "[i]n communion with the sweet / Life that ripens at her feet," with the verb underscoring the earth's own fertility. The poem's last lines reinforce the erotic conjunction a final time: "She is of the things that are; / And she will not pass / While the sun strikes on the grass."

Like "The Sleeping Venus," the Field poem based on and titled for Botticelli's "Venus and Mars" repeatedly identifies the erotic relationship to the land, in this case through the deities' illicit affair. The painting presents the pair after they have copulated, "[w]hen love had its sway" and Mars "fell from her caress" in exhausted sleep, splayed across the bed-like ground. Although not as erotically overdetermined as "The Sleeping Venus," this poem incorporates several of the strategies discussed earlier, while adding others. Surrounded by satyrs, themselves associated with lustfulness—one will later display a "jaunty leer"—Venus "lies upon the grass" as the poem opens, and the satyrs seemingly approve of her action in chanting about "what she brings to pass." Her connection to the landscape becomes more apparent when she exists in harmony with the terrain:

> And nature is as free
> Before her strange, young face
> As if it knew that she
> Were in her sovereign place,
> With shading trees above.

Images associated with passion follow thereafter. Venus rests on a "crimson-rose" pillow, which "heaves" beneath her. She leans against laurels, and their connotation as signs of victory suggests the successful coupling with her lover, Mars. She reveals citron protruding through her "cunning plaits," the presence of the fruit reinforcing her link to fecundity. She is steeped in nature, wearing a "dress of crimpled lawn" from which "[f]ine blades of herbage rise," and a simile compares her rising body to a growing stem. The poem's erotic tone intensifies as Mars "lies in perfect death" and appears like "[a] creature that is dead" in a reminder of *le petit mort* indicative of copulatory satisfaction. His desire nevertheless revives, as "his nostrils scent / New joy and tighten palpitating nerves," but he is so enervated that "his naked limbs, their fury spent, / Are fallen in wearied curves." As the poem closes, Venus is presented as the agent in the sexual encounter, musing "[w]ithout regret, [on] the work her kiss has done" as she adds to "[h]er victims one by one."[10]

In both "The Sleeping Venus" and "Venus and Mars," the focus reveals a wide lens, for the landscapes examined have fairly broad parameters instead of lingering primarily on one specific element of the natural world. The approach followed in the two poems provides a connective to eroticized landscapes in earlier literature, as with the verses of Homer or Ovid, for instance. Michael Field turned periodically in their next poetic volume, *Underneath the Bough*, to a more particularized technique that highlights individual flowers rather than more sweeping settings. Through their own activity and various interpretations of their meanings, both contemporary and long-standing, the flowers carry intense erotic charges that depict them as active and vibrant. Before this chapter assesses these Field poems, however, the following section will provide a background for examining floral sexuality.

Eroticizing Plants

A logical approach and valuable context for analyzing the eroticized flowers in Michael Field's poetry involves the scientific interest in sexualizing plant life that developed more than a century earlier. In the 1730s, Swedish taxonomist Carl Linnaeus devised a classification system based on the intricacies of botanical reproduction. He was not the only botanist to do so, Ann B. Shteir says in *Cultivating Women, Cultivating Science*. The Linnaean system became especially influential and remained so into the nineteenth century. In fact, Linnaeus considered himself the "second Adam," Harriet Ritvo writes in an essay on Victorian science. The scientist sorted the plant kingdom according to the numbers of stamens and pistils, which he designated as the male and female parts of a flower, respectively, according to their appearance and roles. The phallic stamen consists of a stalk, or filament, and its anther, which contains the fertilizing pollen. The pistil includes an ovary-like base to contain the eventual seeds, as well as a number of leaflike carpels. Naturalist René-Louis Desfontaines asserted in 1787 that "the action of the pistil itself . . . incites each stamen to orgasm." Indeed, the term "coitus of vegetables" appeared in the discussions of the day, as Londa Schiebinger notes in *Nature's Body*. The male components, Schiebinger explains, paralleled the vas deferens, testes, and semen, while the female components replicated the vulva, vagina, fallopian tube, and ovary. Linnaeus deemed the male element the dominant member and so organized the system primarily according to the number of male parts in the plants. He cited "the importance of masculine sexual organs" for "it is there that the semen, the powder that constitutes the subtlest part of the plant, accumulates, and it is from there that it later flows forth." The Linnaean system, Schiebinger remarks, "imported into botany traditional notions about sexual hierarchy," although there existed "no empirical justification" for the prioritization. Commenting on "the revolutionary role" that botany "play[ed] in the sexual debates of the 1790s," Alan Bewell says in an essay on botany in the decade that "Linnaeus had indicated how botany could be used to talk about sex, gender relationships, and the social order."[11]

In the sexualized Linnaean system, plants fall into twenty-four classes, which in turn split into approximately one hundred twenty orders, themselves into some two thousand families, each of which contains approximately twenty thousand species. Distinguishing the classes are the number and properties of the plants' male members, while the orders reflect the same aspects of the female members. The first eleven classes designate flowers containing both sexes and are labeled according to the number of a flower's stamens. Thus, the first class contains one male member, or stamen, in a flower, the second class contains two male members, and the sequence continues up to eleven; this system leads to such curious class names as Polyandria ("many males"), Gynandria ("feminine males"), Polygamia ("polygamy"), and Cryptogamia ("clandestine marriage"). Among other arrangements are the male-oriented labels of "brotherhoods" (one, two, and many), "confederate males," and "eunuchs." Plants were thought of as engaging in sexual relations, "romantic, erotic, sometimes illicit, sometimes the sanctified love between husband and wife," Schiebinger notes.[12]

Yet, as Thomas Laqueur explains in *Making Sex*, "the immediate, promiscuous projection of gender onto sex in Linnaeus' sexual system made even contemporaries blush." One dismayed individual, although a supporter of the scientific foundation of the system, observed that "the great concourse of husbands to one wife, which often happens" in Linnaeus's description, "is so unsuitable to the laws and manners of our people." Botanist Johann Georg Siegesbeck assailed the "shameful whoredom for the propagation of the reign of plants." Another disconcerted reader, the botanical author William Withering, refused to feature the racy language of Linnaeus in his own tome, as Janet Browne explains in an essay on a Linnaean poem. Withering used euphemisms for stamens ("chives") and pistils ("pointals") indicating "threads" and "columns" in their Greek and Latin forms, Browne relates. A fellow botanical writer, Priscilla Wakefield, crafted her 1796 introductory text with Withering's sanitized vocabulary, and such a modified approach was widely adopted, Caroline Jackson-Houlston writes in an essay on Victorian botany. The sexual aspects of the classificatory approach caused 1773 *Encyclopaedia Britannica* contributor William Smellie to complain that "obscenity is the very basis of the Linnaean system." Such reactions underscore Laqueur's statement that "[p]lant sex was so extremely gendered at its core that in his own day Linnaeus' taxonomy seemed quite indecent." One eighteenth-century critic, Charles Alston, decried "the fulsome and obscene names imposed by sexualists on the different parts of the fructification of vegetables" and called the Linnaean treatment of the pansy "too smutty for British ears." Goethe would complain in 1820 about the system's effect, with "[e]ternal nuptials going on and on, with the monogamy basic to our morals, laws, and religion disintegrating into loose concupiscence—these must remain forever intolerable to the pure-minded."[13]

To opponents, the sexual connections in the Linnaean system were especially troubling since they were modeled on human relationships. Nevertheless, marriage was a prevalent motif, with references to nuptials, spouses, and offspring, for instance. Noted Hugh Rose, the translator of a Linnaean text, about the depictions of floral components, "The calyx then is the marriage bed, the corolla the curtains," along with other comparisons. Following the marital theme, Linnaeus spoke of plants' being "intermixed . . . by their marriages with each other," referred to a subsequent step involving "reciprocal marriages," and reported that "barren" plants resulted from some of these "marriages."[14]

Linnaeus depicted such bizarre relationships in flowery language, as it were.

The flowers' leaves themselves . . . contribute nothing to generation, but only do service as bridal beds, which the great Creator has so gloriously arranged, adorned with such noble bed curtains, and perfumed with so many soft scents that the bridegroom with his bride might there celebrate their nuptials with so much the greater solemnity. When now the bed is so prepared, it is time for the bridegroom to embrace his beloved bride and offer her his gifts; I mean, then one sees how the testicula open and powder the pulverem genitalem, which falls upon the tubam, and fertilizes the ovarium.

Linnaeus also adopted terminology to describe plant behavior in terms of kinship. He asserted, for instance, that "all species of one genus have arisen from one mother through different fathers" and that in some cases a species "should be referred to the mother's genus as her daughters." The Linnaean designations include various domestic arrangements, one being that of "one house," which indicates that the male and female elements appear in "the same house, but have different beds," or leaves; another is the Polygamia class, in which there are "many marriages with promiscuous intercourse."[15]

Despite its controversial aspects, the Linnaean approach proved immensely popular and became the dominant botanical practice. In the mid-eighteenth century, the system spread to England, where it was similarly embraced, leading to the 1788 establishment of the Linnaean Society there. In fact, as Schiebinger reports, "Linnaeus took England by storm." Nevertheless, "bloody and protracted battles erupted almost immediately," Schiebinger relates, over the system's "scientific and moral implications." Linnaeus's eroticized taxonomy was especially intriguing to Erasmus Darwin, grandfather of Charles. The elder Darwin penned an odd poem that built on sexual scenarios, part of an oeuvre that made him an influential figure. Among others, Romantic poets found Darwin and his writings quite intriguing. Desmond King-Hele notes examples: William Wordsworth asserted that he fell under an "injurious" influence from the "dazzling manner of Darwin," and Samuel Taylor Coleridge judged Darwin "the most original-minded" and "extraordinary man." King-Hele also mentions that William Blake's work, such as *The Book of Thel*, reveals aspects of Darwinian thought; Percy Bysshe Shelley's letters show Darwin's influence on the poet; and John Keats's ideas carry parallels to those of Darwin.[16]

Darwin designed his lengthy 1789 work, *The Loves of the Plants*, as an epic poem complete with heroic couplets and an invocation to a botanical muse. Steeped in eroticism, the poem, which was originally published anonymously, consists of four cantos, hundreds of lines, copious explanatory footnotes, and occasional interludes. As Amy M. King remarks in discussing literary usage of plant vocabulary, "Darwin's poem simply amplifies the libertine qualities already present in Linnaeus's system, a system that outlines the many other sexual alternatives to monogamy in the plant kingdom." Lisa L. Moore asserts in "Queer Gardens" that Darwin's popularization of Linnaean concepts in Britain "drew on a long tradition that viewed flowers as strongly suggestive of human eroticism." Moore adds, "Clearly the idea that plants mimicked human sexuality, and even human homosexuality, was part of the British cultural adaptation of Linnaeus's system." The poem became a widely read and reviewed offering in Darwin's time, although it was not received without criticism. Richard Polwhele's 1798 poem *Unsex'd Females* decried the highly sexualized poem as contributing to scandalous conduct, cautioning that "botanizing girls . . . [who] do not take heed . . . will soon exchange the blush of modesty for the bronze of impudence." He proclaimed the following about the plants:

With bliss botanic as their bosoms heave,
[They] [s]till pluck forbidden fruit, with mother Eve,
For puberty in sighing florets pant,
Or point the prostitution of a plant;
Dissect its organ of unhallow'd lust,
And fondly gaze the titillating dust.

Others also censured Darwin's erotically effusive poem. Thomas Mathias, author of a late-century poem titled *The Pursuits of Literature*, assailed the "glittering verses" and "harlotry of the ornaments" in the poem and asserted, "Modern ears are absolutely *debauched* by such poetry as Dr. Darwin's."[17]

The Loves of the Plants begins with an explanation of the Linnaean system and proceeds to a proem addressed to the "gentle reader," where Darwin explains his desire to "restore" flowers and trees "to their original animality" after the mythological alterations of humans and gods into these botanical forms; he laments their "having remained prisoners so long in their respective vegetable mansions." Poet and Darwin's friend Anna Seward characterized the Linnaean approach as "unexplored poetic ground" and said the system "suggests metamorphoses of the Ovidian kind, though reversed." Like Linnaeus, Darwin confers human qualities upon plant life. In the first canto of the overwrought poem, for example, Darwin refers to a "belle," a flower's "slender waist," a "chaste mimosa," "tearful eyes," a "silent sigh," "sweet eye-lids," and a "wan and shivering" anemone with "[g]rief on her cheeks." Courtship and marital images abound, as in these early lines:

What Beaux and Beauties crowd the gaudy groves,
And woo and win their vegetable Loves.
How Snowdrops cold, and blue-eyed Harebels blend
Their tender tears, as o'er the stream they bend;
The lovesick Violet, and the Primrose pale
Bow their sweet heads, and whisper to the gale;
With secret sighs the Virgin Lily droops,
And jealous Cowslips hang their tawny cups,
How the young Rose in beauty's damask pride
Drinks the warm blushes of his bashful bride;
With honey'd lips enamour'd Woodbines meet,
Clasp with fond arms, and mix their kisses sweet.[18]

Sexualized imagery pervades the poem, with references to impregnation, coquetry, wantonness, and passion, for instance. Numerous episodic passages depict a host of male/female arrangements. For instance, crafty females attract multiple males, as in a passage about "five sister-nymphs" who target ten lovers:

> Beneath one roof resides the virgin band,
> Flies the fond swain, and scorns his offer'd hand;
> But when soft hours on breezy pinions move,
> And smiling May attunes her lute to love,
> Each wanton beauty, trick'd in all her grace,
> Shakes the bright dew-drops from her blushing face;
> In gay undress displays her rival charms,
> And calls her wondering lovers to her arms.

The female in another flower, one consisting of one female but six males, lures the potential lovers at two points in her life. In youth, "[p]roud Gloriosa led *three* chosen swains, / The blushing captives of her virgin chains." Later, "[w]hen Time's rude hand a bark of wrinkles spread / Round her weak limbs, and silver'd o'er her head," the female enticed three young males, "[t]he flatter'd victims of her wily age." In a different scenario, three females in a flower, termed "the harlot-band," attract ten males: "The fell Silene and her sisters fair, / Skill'd in destruction, spread the viscous snare." As these and the next examples suggest, sexualized females are often associated with dastardly traits. The "fair Chondrilla," for instance, employs her "charms despotic" to dominate "the soft hearts of *five* fraternal swains." A glowing Galantha, a "playful beauty," draws six competing suitors through floods, hills, and meadows. One "damsel" is drawn "to illicit loves," a virginal water plant has "quivering fins and panting gills," and "the flames of Love" cause "icy bosoms [to] feel the *secret* fire!" To Shteir, the poem's "overriding tone is the lascivious delight of a male-centered sexual fantasy."[19]

As the century that had produced Darwin's encomium to Linnaean taxonomy came to a close, the Swedish system continued its tight hold on the English biological world into the first decades of the next one. After that point, Linnaeus's approach widely gave way to the morphological "natural system," which adopted different criteria than sexual relations for plant categorization. Nonetheless, Linnaean classification maintained its influence to a degree since it was considered appropriate for teaching botany to women after the field was split between its amateur status, which attracted female adherents, and its more professional positioning as males turned to botanical study, Shteir explains.[20]

Not surprisingly, though, the sexualized terminology continued to distress some readers in both the nineteenth century's early and later years. In 1808, one Henrietta Maria Moriarty decried "those ingenious speculations and allusions, which, however suited to the physiologist, are dangerous to the young and ignorant." Also in that year, royal botanist James Edward Smith disputed a name for a particular water lily that was being promulgated by "'an indifferent person'" who wanted to apply a term derived from the word "chaste"; the reasoning for choosing the name, Nicolette Scourse reports in *The Victorians and Their Flowers*, was that "the petals 'chastely fold over and cover the organs of impregnation.'" Jane Loudon, author of the 1846 *British Wild Flowers*, averred that the Linnaean classification method "was unfit for females," advises Jackson-Houlston, but the system was still used, in its "now-bowdlerized artificial" form, for numerous botanical texts. As Fabienne Moine characterizes the situation in writing about Victorian women's nature poetry, Linnaeus's approach, with its perceived unsuitability for consequential botanical work, was either acceptable for "women's limited intellects" or considered "too sexual, and as such an affront to women's decency" in a paradoxical assessment that carried implications for floral verse as well. However, in the waning years of the century, Moine comments, flower poetry offered women writers a vehicle for "re-sexualizing the female body" and "[b]lurring sexual identities."[21]

The Field of Eroticized Flowers

The sexualization of plant life, especially flowers, becomes particularly intensive in the floral poems of Michael Field, many of which appeared in the 1893 *Underneath the Bough*. In an anonymous *Athenaeum* piece, Augusta Webster penned a highly complimentary review of the collection, praising the poems' "intellectual strength and originality," "rich condensed expression," "splendid control of metre," and "beauty of thought and phrase."[22]

The poems in *Underneath the Bough* follow three paths.[23] First, poems with no agential human element—although the speaker may be self-referential—address a flower as an observer or assume an omniscient voice. Second, poems with a greater human presence marginalize an individual so that the flower retains primary standing. Third, poems with more visible and significant human interactions build upon floral sexuality to adumbrate an erotic charge.

The first category offers a good start for investigating the sensuality mapped onto the floral realm because of its preoccupation with botanical actors, beginning with the overdetermined sonnet "Tiger-lilies." Included in an American edition of *Underneath the Bough*, "Tiger-lilies," by virtue of the plant's name alone, communicates the active aspect of nature that carries such strong ecofeminist resonances. The "tiger" portion of the appellation brings forth striking evocations of powerful animality, unrelenting ferocity, and sublime beauty, along with an intertextual gesture toward Blake's "Tyger." The vigorous diction that punctuates the sonnet accentuates such forceful qualities in coupling the distinguishing trait of activity with an overpowering eroticism.

> Lilies, are you come!
>   I quail before you as your buds upswell;
>   It is the miracle
> Of fire and sculpture in your brazen urns
>   That strikes me dumb,—
> Fire of midsummer that burns,
>   And as it passes,
> Flinging rich sparkles on its own clear blaze,
> Wreathes with the wreathing tongues and rays,
> Great tiger-lilies, of your deep-cleft masses!
>   It is the wonder
>   I am laid under
>   By the firm heaves
> And overtumbling edges of your liberal leaves.[24]

The opening line establishes the combined factors of activity and eroticism with the insistent verb "come" and its multiple *Oxford English Dictionary* denotations. The line's literal sense refers to a flowering or blossoming, but "come" captures as well the experience of sexual climax and in that sense is more than worthy of the exclamatory mark. Other predicate choices also underscore the nexus of the two factors since terms that convey eroticism also implicitly include activity. For example, the "upswell" of the buds suggests the amplifying effect created in an impassioned chest as it exaggerates breath. Predicates of movement depict the fire, a traditional emblem of feverish sensuality, as the blaze "burns," "passes," and "fling[s]" its embers upon itself in a self-sustaining act, while the fire "[w]reathes" the lilies in an enclosing move that attests to an encompassing sexuality. Noun choices accentuate the sexual tone. The aforementioned buds suggest virginity through their enclosed form, the urn-like lilies are vessels to be filled, and the "miracle" seemingly overwhelms ("quail[s]") the speaker with sexual connotations so powerful that it "strikes [the speaker] dumb." Moreover, the "sparkles" that feed the "blaze" and the "rays," along with the "firm heaves" that subdue the speaker, mimic the excitement of an erotic encounter. Adjectives perform their service as well. The "brazen" quality of the urns denotes shameless-ness, an appropriate vocabulary choice in heralding unapologetic sexuality. "[T]he wreathing tongues" reiterate the enveloping strength of carnality, with tongues also functioning as participatory organs in ardent activity; "deep-cleft masses" replicate vaginal contours, breasts, and buttocks; the "overtumbling edges" reveal emotion so overwhelming that it cannot be contained as it falls over the edges that would otherwise act as boundaries; and the "liberal" aspect of the leaves takes on the dual *OED* traits of amplitude and licentiousness. In all of these dictional examples, the speaker serves as the object of action and the tiger-lilies are the initiators, further expanding their sexual charge. Contributing to the sense of the lilies' agency is the speaker's supplicatory address to them.

In accord with "Tiger-lilies," the untitled poem "Great violets in the weedy tangle" exudes eroticism but extends the effect by depicting both sexual consummation and a failure to achieve it, with each point developed in one of the paired stanzas. Bridging the stanzas are bees that flit between the violets in seeking successful pollination, the floral world's form of sexuality by which fertilization and subsequent reproduction occur. The process outlined in the poem mimics human sexuality and in so doing disturbs the boundary between humanity and nature, signaling a move that ecofeminists validate to establish a harmonious connection relying, in part, on recognizing agency in the nonhuman world.

A hint of sexuality proceeds from the opening line, with "the weedy tangle" that houses the violets calling to mind the lower part of the female form that must be bypassed for reproductive efforts to unfold. Aggressive bees circle the flowers in hoping to pollinate but meet resistance as they, in sexually redolent terminology, "with the petals wrangle / For their inmost honey." Yet that apparent rejection instead seems like a ritualistic gesture that simply precedes rather than undermines the insects' endeavor. Though the bees "rove / Thieving one and all," they immediately become "welcome thieves." Sexual language mixes with romantic vocabulary as correlations between nature and humanity develop, signaled by the apiarian shadows flitting on the human construction of a wall. Thus, the violets have hearts, engender happiness, and receive "lover-thieves." The phrasing of the encounter suggests contented sexual consummation in citing "[t]he prick that takes its bliss!" The first noun, "prick," not only indicates a piercing but also in *OED* terms is synonymous with a penis, while the second noun, "bliss," relates the *jouissance* of the intimate act. The violets welcome the encounter, so much so that "[n]o heart would miss / A visit that bereaves!" The bereavement, or act of robbing, in an *OED* denotation, continues the idea of a welcome theft, for "[s]o hearts are made" in this reproductive event. The process resembles an ambush, for "[s]weet violets so / Are swift waylaid, / As hive-bees know," the final verb "know" resonating with the denotative meaning of intercourse. Indeed, the intimate meeting between the "lover-thieves" and the desired violets seems like an episode that could appear in *The Loves of the Plants*, which also occasionally features insects seeking their own floral beloveds.[25]

The second stanza presents the scenario of a virginal violet, too young to be enticed by a frustrated bee. The insect, "with gracious triumph drunken" from his successful exploits obtaining honey from the eventually cooperative violets, "[t]aps a bud, unwitting / That its sweets are secret, sunken / From his frenzied hitting." The adjective in this final phrase implies the bee's uncontrolled passion, which subsequent references confirm through "his pain, his fire" as he "encounters early youth / Shut still from desire." As if any doubt of the bee's ardor remains, Cupid enters the poem as a willing accessory prepared to act: "O Love, not yet / Your arrows whet!" The bee's "desire," with the noun's more customary usage in indicating human passion, continues to draw the human-nature link, which is accentuated by further references to unrequited love, irritation at rejection, and an unwanted memory. The stanza ends on a fitting note with eroticized content as the bee will gain sexual acceptance "[a]nd meet for hours / The breath and beck / Of open flowers."

The two main players in the episode—the violets and the bees—are significant in themselves as meaningful images. The violets are reminiscent of Ovid's Proserpina, who had innocently cavorted among violets before being ravaged by Pluto. The violet's connection to modesty in nineteenth-century floral dictionaries provides an intriguing gloss on the Field poem, with the seeming reluctance of the first stanza's violets rapidly succumbing to the bees' ardor and the second stanza's virginal bud unreceptive to the initiatives. Yet the violet connotes a more sexualized flower as well in reference to Proserpina's capture. These antithetical connotations make the violet an apt flower for the poem in insinuating both constraint and passion.

The bee immediately takes on a sexual tint through its pollinating activities, of course. Although the poem's bee in the second stanza carries the masculine pronoun, in actuality the female worker bees collect pollen. In effect, the poem presents a kind of gender bending through the image of the bee intent upon its floral destination and fosters the assumption that the violet is female since the insect lover enters the flower. This gender play points to a significant subtext underlying the poem, for the sexual scenario of female bee and female flower could be read as paralleling and identifying woman-woman desire. Within the constraints of Victorian acceptability, the notion of lesbianism would necessarily require encoding to transmit it to Field readers without immediate condemnation. Flowers present a particularly effective vehicle for quietly disseminating same-sex interactions in a Victorian context, in part through the culture's understanding of the "language of flowers," a familiar contemporaneous designation, as will be described later in this chapter. Indeed, Moore credits *The Loves of the Plants* with having "helped create and circulate a tradition of lesbian landscape arts," which produced "a language" to "express intimacy and desire for other women." The Darwin poem "pervasively represents women . . . who have homoerotic interests," Elizabeth Bernath argues in writing about "queer botany"; "[t]he queer sexualities are suggested," she adds, "but rarely explicitly described."[26]

Despite the homoerotic possibilities, which some of the Field flower poems overtly explore, others evidence an ambiguity as to the speaker's sexual preference, especially since some verses could be read in the more conventional Victorian way of a male rather than female speaker expressing desire. In "Our myrtle is in flower," for example, the speaker refers to a personal romantic relationship without providing detail. Yet the choice of the myrtle itself raises an expansive sexual field, for the plant can reproduce through interactions with different plants or simply with an individual flower. In providing multiple avenues for sexual action, the myrtle heightens erotic potentiality and the robust activity it will usher forth.

> Our myrtle is in flower;
>   Behold Love's power!
> The glorious stamens' crowded force unfurled,
>   Cirque beyond cirque
> At breathing, bee-like, and harmonious work;
> The rose-patched petals backward curled,
>   Falling away
> To let fecundity have perfect play.
>
> O flower, dear to the eyes
>   Of Aphrodite, rise
> As she at once to bare, audacious bliss;
>   And bid us near
> Your prodigal, delicious hemisphere,
> Where thousand kisses breed the kiss
>   That fills the room
> With languor of an acid, dark perfume!

As in "Tiger-lilies," the myrtle poem limits human presence to sharpen focus on the flower, which provides a path that lovers can follow. The myrtle is an appropriate actor in this context, for Venus, under the Greek appellation Aphrodite, venerated it as a sacred flower. In the opening line of the two-stanza poem, the speaker figuratively embraces the flowering myrtle, with the possessive initial pronoun ushering forth a sexual scenario in more obvious terms than in the previous two poems. Like the violets verse, the myrtle poem references Cupid as a mighty influence and incorporates bees, albeit metaphorically, to describe the sexual act but does so in terms of the flower's internal components. Thus, the myrtle's "glorious stamens" are masculinized as a powerful, "crowded force unfurled" that acts in the feminized "cirque," a bowl-shaped vessel, and causes protective petals to surrender; "backward curled" and "[f]alling away," the petals "let fecundity have perfect play."

The second stanza opens with an apostrophe ("O flower") and makes the connection to Aphrodite, for whom the myrtle is "dear to the eyes." As in the violets poem, sexual consummation is signified by the term "bliss," which is deemed "audacious" as the myrtle is urged to "rise," itself a sexualized predicate, in Aphrodite-like fashion to attain pleasure. The speaker implores the myrtle to "bid us near / Your prodigal, delicious hemisphere," a highly sensualized phrase with the adjective "prodigal" amplifying the erotic tone as a synonym for lavish excess and "delicious" relating in one denotation to bodily delight. Within that atmosphere, a "thousand kisses breed the kiss / That fills the room" in a continuation of erotic imagery, which heralds the actual consummation; the next line specifies the influx as the "languor of an acid, dark perfume," the apparent aromatic residue of spent passion.

"Unbosoming" similarly elides the sexual preference of the speaker and references a beloved, but it differs from the myrtle poem by establishing an iris as a model of behavior. The speaker of "Unbosoming" simply serves as a passive observer whose presence the poem barely notes, instead exploring the flower as the central interest. The title of the one-stanza poem certainly establishes an erotic tone in its dual meanings of disclosure and undress, and the opening immediately refers to desire as the speaker announces "[t]he love that breeds / In my heart for thee!" The poem then shifts to the iris, which is described in sexual terminology, for the flower "is full, brimful of seed." With the iris's "thousand vermilion-beads," the flower's agency is accentuated through forceful predicates as the floral components "push, and riot, and squeeze, and clip," with the repeated conjunction providing additional emphasis in prolonging the line's pronunciation. As in consummation, the floral elements "burst," in this case pushing against "the sides of the silver scrip," or wall, in this alliterative phrasing that, with its sibilance, suggests contentment. Vaginal imagery depicts the opened flower through "its tremulous, bowery fold / Of zephyr-petal." As in the myrtle poem, this verse carries resonances to mythological figures, in this case the rainbow goddess Iris, who produced through her union with the west wind Zephyros a son, Pothos, who emblematized passion and desire. The sexual charge attached to the iris is mapped onto the speaker, whose own "breast is rent / With the burthen and strain of its great content." For the speaker, the iris's sexualized experience brings a kind of postcoital demise, reminding again of *le petit mort* in that "the summer of fragrance and sighs is dead." The speaker alludes to personal desire, a "harvest-secret" that "is burning red," which will be presented to the beloved who would receive, "after my kind, / The final issues of heart and mind" in a human version of the iris's carnal journey. This phrasing again obscures the sexual preference of the speaker with the ambiguous "after my kind," which adds to the poem's erotic charge.

Another eroticized flower poem offers a somewhat different twist by presenting a bee as both male and female. In "Butterfly bright," the named insect provides a subtext of transformation through the butterfly's transitions, even though its presence in the poem is minimal; a butterfly begins its life as a cocoon, becomes a caterpillar, and ultimately metamorphoses to its winged form as an adult. The poem's butterfly is immediately thwarted in obtaining nectar by a bee that has successfully plundered some sunflowers. This bee is accorded both the masculine and the feminine pronouns; the bee first "soils himself" and later is "free / From thought of the hive, / That doth never stint her." In obscuring the bee's biological sex, the poem opens up interpretative possibilities, creating a kind of gendered echo of the butterfly's alteration.

The pursuit of the nectar by both the butterfly and the bee takes on a sexual tone, as the first of three stanzas establishes:

> Butterfly bright,
> Thou dost alight
> On the sunflower-bed;
> For the nectar sunny
> Thou div'st, drinking dumb:
> While the bee instead,
> With a laboured hum,
> Clogs and soils himself with the honey.

Eroticism initially inflects the stanza with the reference to the sunflower bed where the butterfly pursues the nectar, which involves a penetrative act as the butterfly dives into the flowers. The butterfly's action is alliteratively mimicked, with the /d/ sounds replicating that of a puncturing motion. The bee's endeavors convey a sensual lushness and excessiveness, as the desired honey saturates the insect.

The second stanza muses upon the "blessèd thing" of an insect that is only pursuing nectar and is devoid of other concerns before switching to a human context, wherein "the busy rout" aims to enrich itself but "[g]rows dull at its task / Of heaping up riches and sorrow." The speaker envies the bee's preoccupation with its task without outside interference and attempts to emulate its experience in asserting, "Oh, let me be / That creature, free / From thought of the hive." Like the insect, the speaker seeks immersion in the sexual act, the human counterpart to clogging with honey and receiving "its fill." The erotic experience gains emphasis through repetition and the effusive effect in the poem's closing lines as the insect, "warm and alive / Feeds, feeding until / The fall of the leaf and winter!"

As in the poems discussed earlier, the speaker is merely a marginal presence in the poem, in this case entering only in the final stanza and taking on significance solely in terms of the insect activity. Other poems, however, fall into the second category of the *Underneath the Bough* verses. This grouping heightens the speaker's importance in describing relations with a beloved, but an interest in flora in particular and landscape in general remains vital for articulating the particularities of the romantic pair's conduct, as in "Cowslip-Gathering." The poem's lovers wander, "hand in hand" and "[y]earning," but nonetheless proceed "divided." Unlike many Field poems, this verse unequivocally identifies the lovers as two females. Considering the contextual framework of the other poems investigated above, the inference is that the two lovers have not engaged in a fully intimate experience. The point is stressed by their status as "*twin* maiden spirits" (emphasis added) and its indication of a degree of separation as distinct entities rather than signifying a couple fully fused together. Moreover, the reference to "maiden" underscores the virginal status of the pair.

Importantly, nature functions as a requisite actor for the pair's movement toward actual unification, since "there must be / In all true marriage perfect trinity"; nature represents the final element of this triad. "[D]ear Nature" serves as the agent for the couple's union as it remarks, "These children I will straight espouse." The statement comes as sexualized terms depict the landscape. The female pair inhabits a thicket "[f]illing with chirps of song," with the verb implying successful consummation. Nature immediately directs the pair "to a tender, marshy nook / Of meadow-verdure" as a "blue cuckoo thrills the alder-boughs." The terrain evokes female sexuality in that the marsh and meadows replicate the lower part of a woman's anatomy. The marsh's moistness brings to mind sexual arousal, and the meadow's grassy expanse replicates the nether hair. The erotic effect expands through the cuckoo's call, which occurs during mating season; the predicate choice as the cuckoo "thrills" its surroundings augurs sexual penetration through its denotation of a piercing or boring movement. As the stanza moves toward its conclusion, so does the sensual impact, for in this locale sexual satisfaction finally occurs. There, where nature has led the pair,

> by twos and threes
> The cowslips grew, down-nodding toward a brook;
> And left us there to pluck them at our ease

> In the moist quiet, till the rich content
> Of the bee humming in the cherry-trees
> Filled us; in one our very being blent.

Erotic references suffuse the lines, beginning with the cowslips "down-nodding," as if protecting their reproductive parts. Despite the poem's interest in the human pair, the cowslips are central to eventual union, for their presence enables sexual satisfaction as they are "pluck[ed]," a highly suggestive predicate that reinforces the site's moistness. The presence of the bee continues the erotic ambience through the insect's pollinating activity, which in this case is figuratively inseminating the lovers with the garnered treasure as it "[f]ill[s]" them. Not insignificantly, the bee is positioned in a cherry tree, which conjures the *OED* meaning of a loss of virginity associated with the suggestive fruit. Ultimately, the two lovers become "one" as the "very being" of each merges with the other's.

Even in a Field poem that barely implies its presence--the third category of the *Underneath the Bough* poems--a flower becomes a crucial image leading to the satisfaction of lovers. In "No beauty born of pride my lady hath," the flowering rowan, an ash tree that produces fruit, provides the important element. Leading to the brief mention of the rowan is the speaker's musing, beginning in the opening line, on "my lady," who is compared thereafter with multiple natural forms. Thus, "[h]er voice is as the path / Of a sweet stream, and where it flows must be / Peace and fertility." The coursing stream and its connection to fertility set up a sensual comparison as the poem continues with its nature imagery, referring first to "[h]er cloudy eyes [that] are full of blessèd rain" and "[a] sky that cherisheth" before turning to "her breast," described as "a soft nook for rest." Immediately an erotic component is inserted, with the suggestion that the lady "hath no varying pleasure / For passion's fitful mood." For the speaker, "[h]er firm, small kisses are my constant food, / As rowan-berries yield their treasure / To starving birds." Since the poem provides little information about the speaker, the voice could be either male or female, an ambiguity that creates a sense of amorphous sexuality by broadening the erotic possibilities.

Such an erotic expansion takes a decidedly different turn in "Ah me, if I grew sweet to man." This unambiguous heterosexual shift builds upon one of the most storied floral images, the rose. The flower's literary heritage spans centuries as an emblem of sexual desire and experience, with both inferences appearing in the Field poem. Eroticism is infused immediately after the poem's opening line, as the speaker reveals somatic signs of arousal through a comparison to the rose, which can "[n]o longer keep the breath that heaves / And swells among its folded leaves." The inference that the enclosed leaves act to protect the rose as well as the speaker from sexual activity is supported thereafter, for "[t]he pressing fragrance would unclose / The flower, and I [become] a rose." The virginal flower initiates an intimate encounter as it "[p]lant[s] an odour in the air." Sexual activity is presented as a natural act, unencumbered by artifice. "No art I [use] men's love to draw," the speaker assures, for "I [live] but by my being's law." Roses are agents in promoting sexuality, for they "are by heaven designed / To bring the honey to the wind." The reference to honey, a by-product of pollination, underscores the erotic insinuation. The final of four stanzas acknowledges consummatory success through physical pain wrought by the loss of virginity, for the speaker "[finds] the blast a riving thing." The closing lines carry an implication that would appear extraordinary to a Victorian audience, for a woman's sexual experience is admirable rather than condemnable: "Yet even ruined roses can / No other than be sweet to man."

The gender uncertainty that pervades several of the poems in *Underneath the Bough* resonates with an earlier Field poem, in the 1889 *Long Ago*. "LII" provides an interesting gloss on the later verse collection in describing the literal shifts between male and female that its main character, Tiresias, experiences. The poem follows a version of the myth wherein Tiresias sees a pair of copulating snakes and "lays the female in the dust," causing Tiresias "to forego / His manhood" as he changes into a woman. For seven years, Tiresias remains a female, until again he encounters a pair of breeding snakes. This time, Tiresias kills the male snake and once more becomes a man. The incidents occur in nature, a logical setting for a Field poem as the site for the serpents' erotic behavior. Amplifying the sensual atmosphere is a passage tracing the sun's effect upon a "young rose's softening leaves" in a mimicry of sexual penetration, for "[h]er plaited petals once undone / The rose herself receives the sun." Another erotic reference appears as Hera demands that Tiresias judge whether a male or a female takes greater delight in "the joys of sex."[27]

The poem also encourages a direct ecofeminist reading. Tiresias's initial act of killing the female snake represents a transgression against nature, especially since the prophet did so with an "idle thrust"; the fact that he killed unthinkingly, in a penetrative way, with the "thrust," serves as a reminder that irresponsible masculine behavior brings environmental damage. In contrast, once Tiresias becomes a female, "the quickening change" alters his outlook, as does "his vision's change." Instead of destruction, Tiresias turns to a "receptivity of soul" as "love [comes]." So consequential is the experience that "[i]t seem[s] that he [has] broken free / Almost from his mortality." The later killing of the male snake suggests a sacrificial offering—wresting "virtue from thy doom"—to atone for the female's death and restore order.

The Polyvalence of Floral "Speech"

The allure of plant sexuality throughout the nineteenth century provides a cultural context for the highly charged eroticism of the Field flower poems in *Underneath the Bough*. Alison Syme states about such perceptions that "[a]ny anatomical fragment, in addition to the more obvious genital apparatus, was susceptible to floral troping and botanical eroticization." Although Syme is primarily investigating the floral ramifications in late-century painting, particularly in John Singer Sargent's work, her observations apply to *fin de siècle* writing as well. Botanical illustration provided an intimate look at the female form, Syme explains, with sexual elements related through such images as folds, petals, buds, calyxes, and grassy areas. As Annette Stott maintains in "Floral Femininity," "[N]ineteenth-century artists used the flower as a versatile sign of female sexuality to represent anything from moral laxity to innocent chastity."[28]

For women poets, states Paula Bennett in assessing sensual floral images, flowers could robustly signal a woman's eroticism. Emily Dickinson, for instance, adopted a "semiprivate code" in her work that provided "a highly nuanced discourse" readers could interpret, and Amy Lowell similarly turned to floral imagery to project an erotic message, Bennett observes. One Dickinson poem that Bennett discusses, "Forbidden Fruit a flavor has," appears merely to portray floral maturation, but the verse also depicts sexual development. Flowers have served for centuries to communicate female physicality and sexuality, Bennett says. "[I]t is inconceivable that [women] poets remained uniformly ignorant of the latent sexual potential of the imagery they used," Bennett maintains, "especially when they themselves used it in such highly suggestive as well as woman-centered ways."[29]

Floral imagery also enabled a woman poet to articulate, in veiled terms, same-sex desire. As Martha Vicinus remarks, *fin de siècle* writers often turned to nature depictions and other means to articulate ideas that had previously been concealed. Indeed, Moore believes that Darwin's plant poem "helped create and circulate a tradition of lesbian landscape arts." Victorian sexologists theorizing about homosexual behavior adopted the word "invert" to describe its practitioners and often turned to botanical analogies of both cross-fertilization and self-pollination, or hermaphroditism, in making their case, Syme comments. "Whether identifying as pollinators or plants," she explains, "invert artists" appropriated the botanical processes "to 'naturalize' sexual inversion."[30]

Michael Field's floral eroticism served, then, as a fitting vehicle for encoding sexuality, especially woman-woman desire, in the *fin de siècle* milieu. Noting that critical commentary has made this point, Jill R. Ehnenn asserts that "Michael Field's poems belong to a long tradition of homoerotically inclined women using flowers to code female sexuality, women's genitalia, and same-sex erotic love." As Moine says, flower poems provided "a much needed outlet for transgressive views on sexuality," allowing the "[b]lurring [of] sexual identities" and the revelation especially of woman-woman eroticism through their concealed messages. Moine cites the Field poem "Cyclamens" as a case in point:

> They are terribly white:
>   There is snow on the ground,
>   And a moon on the snow at night;
>   The sky is cut by the winter light;
>   Yet I, who have all these things in ken,
>   Am struck to the heart by the chiselled white
>   Of this handful of cyclamen.

Moine explains that the cyclamen became a recognizable emblem in lesbian verse appearing at the *fin de siècle*. The exotic cyclamens were "unwelcome interlopers in the (straight) woman's poetic garden." The cyclamen's stooping form conceals reproductive parts as well as eroticism outside Victorian norms, Moine explains. Because the white cyclamens appear against the snow in the Field poem, a traditional reader would not see these plants and thus the message being imparted would be obscured.[31]

The Field floral poetry fits into the nineteenth century's widespread fascination with the "language of flowers." Stemming from ancient times and represented in both pagan and Christian forms, the language of flowers enabled the transmission of messages attributed to different plants as had developed in both previous and contemporary eras. The "language" supposedly reflected a widespread familiarity with its codes, but no decisive dictionary existed to cement floral meanings, which could vary not only diachronically but synchronically as well. Although numerous dictionaries of floral meanings existed—approximately 150 of them appeared, according to Jean Marsh's *Illuminated Language of Flowers*—the symbolic meanings attributed to each flower could be different and inconsistent even within the same dictionary. For example, four nineteenth-century floral dictionaries variously defined a buttercup as representing ingratitude, benevolence, and childishness, Beverly Seaton indicates in *The Language of Flowers*. Color could alter meanings of the same flower, so a lily might suggest rarity, candor, purity, and inquietude, Seaton notes. Not surprisingly in light of such discrepancies, multiple texts included the disclaimer that "a flower is not a flower alone; / a thousand thoughts invest it." Nevertheless, floral discourse did provide a measure of consistency, with some flowers interpreted in the same way from text to text, Molly Engelhardt states in an essay on Victorian floral vocabulary.[32]

The language of flowers rose to prominence in the 1840s, when professional and amateur botany diverged, Shteir observes. As Engelhardt suggests, the schism helped to further women's interest in floral discourse. In the eighteenth century, Lady Mary Wortley Montagu had referenced the discourse, which was presented in Paris the next century in dictionary form, Marsh says. Floral language enabled bashful individuals to communicate in virtual conversations, Marsh reports. As a contemporary book about the discourse comments, "A party walking in a garden, through the means of flowers presented to each other, may carry on a conversation of compliment, wit, and repartee." The gift of a bouquet conveyed a highly detailed commentary, for "every blossom, leaf, and stem was fraught with significance," Marsh explains. Even though floral language declined in popularity near the century's end, books about it arose, with one of the most famous, *Under the Windows*, appearing in 1877 and encouraging numerous imitations. The book, created by Kate Greenaway, was followed in 1884 by her *Language of Flowers*, a text that was highly popular even though the craze had waned by that point, Marsh states.[33]

Yet the ambiguous floral language offered an effective means for poets like Michael Field to transmit their otherwise socially unacceptable messages about female sexuality. With their slippery signifieds, floral signifiers allowed poets to convey sentiments in similar fashion to their predecessors, albeit with very different connotations. Portraying an apparently innocuous scene on a literal level, the Field poetry could speak, though obscurely, about female eroticism to those readers who would decipher the floral codes. The inconsistency in floral language enabled a play with meaning in the verses and allowed the sexual subtext to remain hidden to Victorians who would find it offensive. Through the connotative slippage, as Engelhardt contends, "women could more freely experiment with their feelings, testing them out . . . without paying a stiff penalty" since "the limitations of floral codes for transmitting exact meanings . . . magnified the unreliability of language." Even though a level of "floral literacy" among Victorians was assumed, Engelhardt comments, "practitioners of the language of flowers . . . celebrated uncertainty and relied on floral codes to curtail knowing in order to extend the realm of play." In so doing, floral discourse opened a wide path for Field and other women poets to speak the unspeakable. With the Linnaean system of classification remaining prevalent for amateur women botanists and other nonprofessionals as the century progressed, a familiarity with its sexualized foundation would help prepare Field readers for the erotic content lurking beneath a poem's lines. With this point in mind, Webster's *Athenaeum* review of *Underneath the Bough* seems quite ironic. Praising the "convenient collection of goodly verse," Webster turned to "the fine intensity planned and dominatingly present, *yet skilfully kept half concealed*" (emphasis added).[34]

Ecofeminist Aesthetics

With nature a primary focus in the many Field poems addressed above, a question might arise as to the way this interest fits with the widely acknowledged aestheticism of Michael Field, especially considering the prevalence of ideas in Field poetry that contemporaries Walter Pater and Oscar Wilde also expressed. Aside from their influence on *fin de siècle* aestheticism, Pater and Wilde were well known to Michael Field. Furthermore, for several years Bradley corresponded with John Ruskin, whose perceptions of art were quite antithetical to those of Pater and Wilde.[35] How, then, can Field's aestheticism be appraised in regard to the nature poetry? Field adopted a diverse approach, one that occasionally meshed with these male writers' judgments of nature but far more frequently departed from them. Field's floral approach entails an "ecofeminist aesthetic," wherein the activity of nature, as signified through eroticism, is combined with a perception that nature on its own terms is a worthy subject of art.

Pater's 1874 essay on Wordsworth provides a useful background, with its discussion of the Romantic poet's absorption in natural phenomena. Pater praises Wordsworth's verse for its imaginative as opposed to solely mimetic quality. Wordsworth infused a "sense of a life in natural objects," Pater observes, and "[b]y raising nature to the level of human thought he gives it power and expression." Wordsworth's "moments of profound imaginative power" created "a new nature almost"; that is, through "the prompting of the observant mind, the actual world would, as it were, dissolve and detach itself, flake by flake."[36] To Pater, then, the imagination was responsible for the significance of Wordsworth's poetry. Field's verse, however, departs from this prioritization in that a far more mimetic approach dominates the presentation of natural elements.

Pater imparts a similar judgment of art to the preface of his book *The Renaissance: Studies in Art and Poetry*, published the same year as *Underneath the Bough*, 1893. Pater argues that an "aesthetic critic" expresses interest in the "fairer forms of nature" as items worthy of praise, implying a selection process rather than including the natural world as a whole. Field's poetry seems to adopt the *Renaissance* concept that "the aim of the true student of aesthetics" is "[t]o define beauty, not in the most abstract but in the most concrete terms possible"; the verse, however, does not accommodate Pater's interest in "the formula which expresses most adequately this or that special manifestation of [beauty]." Thus, the fascination with beauty provides an intersection of Paterian and Field philosophies. The Field nature poetry aligns with Pater's praise in his conclusion to *The Renaissance* of "the desire of beauty" that "give[s] nothing but the highest quality to your moments as they pass." The poetry adheres as well to Pater's famous comment about the importance of "burn[ing] always with this hard, gem-like flame" and his conviction that sustaining ecstasy amounts to "success in life." A discerning Field reader can certainly assess their erotic nature poetry as producing such effects. Indeed, Field's *Works and Days* includes the approving remark that "the whole problem of life turns on pleasure"; "Pater," the journal continues, "shows that the hedonist—the perfected hedonist—is the saint."[37]

The correlations between Wilde and Field seem illusory at best in view of his insistently negative statements about the natural world. In *The Decay of Lying*, first published in 1889, Vivian presumably serves as Wilde's mouthpiece in unambiguously favoring art over nature. "[T]he more we study Art, the less we care for Nature," Vivian avers, noting "Nature's lack of design, her curious crudities, her extraordinary monotony, her absolutely unfinished condition." It is art, Wilde insists, that confers value upon nature, and he praises imagination as the key determinant. Art and nature are antithetical, Wilde believed. *The Decay of Lying* rejects mimesis, arguing that art should be free of comparisons to the actual world. Thus, art provides "a veil, rather than a mirror," says Vivian in quoting Iago. Underscoring the crucial factor of imagination, Wilde states that nature's role is to supply, in some situations, "Art's rough material." Wilde also contends that art "has flowers that no forests know of, birds that no woodland possesses." In sum, nature is a human invention, given life through the mind, Wilde maintains. In contrast, "[a]ll bad art comes from returning to Life and Nature, and elevating them into ideal." With such sentiments, any intersection with Field's poetry seems unlikely, yet the preface to *The Picture of Dorian Gray* does reveal some commonalities. The Field poets fit the criterion presented in the 1890 novel that "[t]he artist is the creator of beautiful things," and Wilde's rejections of judgments on morality or immorality could accord with the poetry's marked eroticism despite Victorian conservatism.[38]

The Field link to ecofeminist aesthetics partly counters the Pater and Wilde assumptions that nature needs to be infused with the imaginative process to become a worthy subject of art. As Field explains in the preface to *Sight and Song*, the goal with poetic descriptions of paintings is to convey "what poetry they *objectively incarnate*" (emphasis added). To do so requires "patient, continuous sight as pure as the gazer can refine it of theory, fancies, or his mere subjective enjoyment." These statements apply equally well to the natural elements that other Field poetry highlights. As Ana I. Parejo Vadillo remarks about the *Sight and Song* poems, and as equally applies to the nature poetry, "Field projects a theory of visuality that values the autonomy of the object."[39]

Michael Field more closely follows Ruskin's views of nature outlined in *Modern Painters*, though not his belief that art should carry a moral message. Ruskin argues that the term "beautiful" applies to "[a]ny material object which can give us pleasure in the simple contemplation of its outward qualities without any direct and definite exertion of the intellect." Nature, of course, fits this definition, and Ruskin addresses the point directly in asserting that "everything in nature is more or less beautiful." In fact, "there is not one single object in nature which is not capable of conveying" an "exalting and purifying" effect.[40] Unlike Pater and Wilde, then, Ruskin is contending that nature, without the intercession of the imagination, carries value on its own.

These comments offer insight in assessing the Field nature poetry, for it is through the observation of natural elements that their energy and activity become apparent. Ruskin considers this idea as well in describing plant life, upon which he, too, confers these attributes. The pleasure provided by plant life "is in proportion to its appearance of healthy vital energy," Ruskin comments. A plant's indication of "signs of life and enjoyment" brings delight, he says, and "the amount of pleasure we receive is in exact proportion to the appearance of vigor and sensibility." Ruskin contends that a plant's health, symmetry, smoothness, and color reflect "the plant's own happiness and perfection." Despite these multiple similarities to the Field perspective revealed in the nature poems, Ruskin's moralistic grounding departs from it. Beauty, Ruskin maintains, is dependent on the plant's (or other object's) serving as a symbol of "Divine attributes in matter."[41] The sensual component of nature that Field so insistently presents, then, would oppose Ruskin's focus on conventional Victorian morality.

Perhaps a closer example of an aesthetic influence is Immanuel Kant, through the arguments he crafts in *The Critique of Judgement*, which appeared in the late eighteenth century. Although Kant theorizes a moral role for art, he avoids the grounding in divine representation that Ruskin applies in articulating nature's claim to the designation of the beautiful. Compared to the ideas of Pater and Wilde, Kant's views present an oppositional perspective to those Victorians' disdain for nature, mimetic art, and the implicit judgment that nature on its own terms does not provide an appropriate subject for art. Kant contends, however, that aestheticism's focus on beauty should mainly be directed to nature, with art taking a secondary role. In fact, Kant cites "our admiration of nature which in her beautiful products *displays herself as art*" (emphasis added), a statement that attests to the concept that nature alone provides a suitable subject for art. Moreover, in defense of mimesis, Kant avers that "the indispensable requisite" for being deemed beautiful is "that the beauty should be that of nature, and it vanishes completely as soon as we are conscious of having been deceived, and that it is only the work of art." Kant also claims in accentuating the importance of mimesis that "art can only be termed beautiful, where we are conscious of its being art, while yet it has the appearance of nature."[42]

The aesthetic judgments of Kant and Ruskin, with their validation of nature as a vital interest, conform smoothly with ecofeminism's own approbation.

Although configured generations later, environmental aesthetics offers useful ideas that can be productively applied to the Field poetry. Indeed, environmental aesthetics developed from the aesthetic theories that came to prominence during the 1700s and 1800s, Allen Carlson contends in *Nature and Landscape*. The modern environmental approach stemmed from Kant's formulation that favored nature over art in terms of beauty and the idea that nature is "an exemplary object of aesthetic experience," Carlson indicates. In another work, "Aesthetics of the Environment," Carlson observes that in the modern theorization, "the 'object' of appreciation, the 'aesthetic object,' is our environment."[43]

As Carlson explains, different approaches to environmental aesthetics exist, each attracting proponents, with the two primary threads identified as "subjectivist" and "objectivist" (also called "cognitivist") in promoting ways of aesthetically assessing the environment. The first argues that a designation of appropriateness cannot be conferred upon environmental valuation in the same way as humanly created works of art. The second approach asserts that resources do exist for aesthetic consideration of the environment. In a particular setting, "an environment itself . . . can bring us to appreciate it 'as what it is' and 'on its own terms.'" Thus, "the environment offers the necessary guidance in terms of which we, the appreciators, by our selecting and framing, can answer the questions of what and how to appreciate." As a general statement of environmental aesthetics, a natural setting can match human art in potential for aesthetic appreciation, Carlson adds.[44]

Like the environmental version, feminist aesthetics advances ideas helpful in considering the ecofeminist aesthetics that characterizes the Field poetry. In fact, in the Victorian era, Pater "debarred women from possessing the artistic conscience," observes Angela Leighton. Although no single conception of feminist aesthetics exists today, the approach in general questions the gender aspects of aesthetic judgments produced in a male-dominated society. The valuation of beauty is especially problematic because the female body has been an integral component of male-directed aesthetics. As Kathy Alexis Psomiades maintains, "Aesthetic ideology . . . is grounded in the logic of aestheticism's iconic feminine images." Mary Devereaux explains in "Feminist Aesthetics" that its practitioners believe that gender aspects must be part of a viable theory. In a comment that applies especially well to the *fin de siècle*, Devereaux states about gender considerations that "feminist critics have demonstrated that what are presented as 'purely formal' aesthetic criteria actually reflect local, historically specific attitudes and assumptions."[45]

Also significant when considering *fin de siècle* aestheticism from a feminist perspective are the workings of homoerotic desire. Attention has focused mainly on male-male desire in this connection, revealed in a variety of fictional and

nonfictional venues of the time. Yet as Talia Schaffer and Kathy Alexis Psomiades assert, aestheticism can also reflect woman-woman desire, and they add that
female writers, like their male counterparts, may wish to code homoeroticism in
their work. Through the combination of "the aesthetic and the erotic," Schaffer
and Psomiades maintain, "aestheticism could provide women, as well as men,
with a language in which to celebrate and value desire." Like their contemporary
Vernon Lee (the pseudonym of Violet Paget), Psomiades comments, Field saw
female-female desire as aesthetically pleasing. With Field's ecofeminist aestheticism derived from the eroticism of nature, Vadillo's characterization of the poets'
work is especially suitable in that the aesthetic approach "includes both the beautiful object and the sexual subject that experiences it, but both as autonomous
entities." Distinguishing between the aesthetics of Field and of Pater, Vadillo adds
that "Field offers a two-phased aesthetic, one in which objective enjoyment is
followed by subjective *jouissance*."[46]

For ecofeminism, though, it is the active component identified in nature that
is especially significant. Both in building on nature's erotic connections formu-
lated in the past and in reflecting contemporary endeavors to address sexuality
in the Victorian *fin de siècle*, Michael Field brought a complex and intriguing
approach to a presentation of nature as an active force. With the sexual inferences
and associations made in their poetic oeuvre, Field undermined long-standing
perceptions that nature is merely a passive entity that can be acted upon unproblematically. Like the ecofeminists who decried such an assumption many decades
later, Michael Field presented a very different construction of nature, one that
recognizes agency and empowers the nonhuman world.

CHAPTER FOUR

Alice Meynell
Unsettling the Nature/Culture Dichotomy

THE POETRY OF ALICE MEYNELL reveals an intriguing contestation of the nature/culture split assumed by Victorians. Indeed, the verse echoes the agency Michael Field attributed to nature by positioning the nonhuman world not as inferior to culture but as an integral participant actually enabling it. In seeking to reevaluate the "definition of nature and its relationship to culture," Luce Irigaray states, "[w]e need to start again from cosmic nature . . . since it is a resource for life, culture," and human relationships.[1] Meynell recuperated nature through her own form of ecopoetics, the parameters of which can be readily derived from her verse. This chapter will explore numerous components of Meynell's ecopoetics, but a brief summary will provide key aspects by way of introduction.

The most important concept in Meynell's ecopoetics is the conviction that nature is a vibrant entity on its own terms and is not to be marginalized as a vehicle for human interests. Nature must receive the esteem and reverence that it so deservedly requires. An admirable poet is immersed in nature—at one with the nonhuman world—rather than attempting to describe it from a detached standpoint. Therefore, the poet aims to overcome to the greatest extent possible a culturally perceived division between human self and environmental other. Nevertheless, the poet must recognize that nature maintains its own secrets beyond human understanding, which necessitates respect rather than aggressive intrusion. The natural world exhibits its own integrity and its own voice, which the poet needs to hear as well as its silence. Thus, nature is a presence with its own materiality. Nature represents a necessary guide for the poet, who becomes an emissary for that world. The poet effectually becomes an instrument of nature, which always remains a robust presence as an inspirational creative body. As such, nature takes on the role of the collective unconscious, an ultimate poetic source that spans generations. Indeed, nature acts as a poet itself. These ecopoetical concepts frequently emerge in Meynell's verse, and many of her incisive views also underlie the work of the other poets featured in this study.

The Nature of Ecopoetics

Meynell's version of ecopoetics, though not contemporaneously labeled with the term, of course, fittingly anticipates modern theorists of such writing. The term "ecopoetics" reflects the current situation, in the twenty-first century, with its myriad environmental challenges but acknowledges as well the predecessors who believed that societal assessments of nature created their own set of concerns. "Ecopoetics" is an unfixed label lacking a concrete denotation, with an array of views put forth about its putative meaning. As Lynn Keller explains in an essay about modern ecopoetry, the term has stood for any verse, regardless of the era, that deals with environmental concerns. Others use "ecopoetry" strictly to differentiate past poetry about nature from modern experimental verse, Keller points out. A third approach sees "ecopoetry" as specifically addressing environmental problems and written after 1960, Keller says. In their anthology of ecopoetry, editors Ann Fisher-Wirth and Laura-Gray Street say of this third position that the term "is shaped by and responds specifically to [the environmental] crisis." Although "ecopoetry" does not have a rigid definition, it does have certain characteristics, the editors assert: ecopoetry focuses on modern concerns, opposes the presumption that humans are entitled to dominate the environment, and contests the "hyperrationality" that creates a schism between rationality and physicality, which also separates human from nonhuman life. Perceptions about ecopoetry have evolved in recent decades to encompass a host of poetic approaches, the editors say. In brief, though, they comment, "Ecopoetry enacts through language the manifold relationship between the human and the other-than-human world."[2]

Such explanations of ecopoetry certainly apply in general to Meynell's nature poetry, and other assertions raise more specific issues that fit her work especially well. To Forrest Gander, writing in *Redstart: An Ecological Poetics*, the term "ecopoetics" includes among its multiple meanings the various methods of responding in poetry to environmental challenges. The approaches resemble those of the past, Gander says, and one strategy mentioned is particularly evident in Meynell's work: a recognition that a poem stems from nature rather than simply from the writer. Gander cites the supposition that ecopoetics could influence opinions and by so doing could decrease environmental damage through "less dogmatically binary perspectives of interaction between human and nonhuman realms." Also pertinent to Meynell's verse is the contention of Jed Purdy in an essay about "losing nature" during the modern era of the Anthropocene. Purdy unsettles the belief that nature and culture are discrete entities, a point raised in previous decades within the humanities, noting that "the nature we are concerned with has always been partly a cultural thing, a product of the hopes and anxieties of the time."[3]

Other appraisals of ecopoetry also offer a useful context for considering Meynell's nature poetry. Even though no definitive explanation exists, J. Scott Bryson comments in the appropriately named *Ecopoetry*, the approach "differs in many ways from the traditional romantic nature poetry produced by writers like Wordsworth or Whitman." Bryson cites various attempts to define works of "eco-poetics," which include poetry sharply focused on the environment itself, on the need for a sound human-nature relationship, and on perceiving the environment in a more positive way. Bryson offers his own definition, incorporating other ecopoetical convictions, which states in part, "Ecopoetry is a subset of nature poetry that, while adhering to certain conventions of romanticism, also advances beyond that tradition." Bryson's definition goes on to identify the modern condition as the focus of ecopoetry, but two of the factors he identifies relate as well to verse by Meynell and like-minded Victorian contemporaries: the realization that humanity and nature are intertwined as a community and the necessity for humility in dealing with the natural world.[4]

Describing ecopoetry in *Sustainable Poetry*, Leonard M. Scigaj remarks that its practitioners "present nature in their poems as a separate and equal other . . . and offer exemplary models of biocentric perception and behavior." In *The Environmental Imagination*, Lawrence Buell sets out four criteria for environmental literature, which can be applied to late Victorian poetry. To Buell, nature must not be evaluated simply as a background for human activity but as an active agent itself; nature must be recognized as having its own history and integrity, apart from specifically human interests; nature must be accorded respect, with "human accountability" made a priority; and nature must be recognized not as an immutable entity but as one that is in "process." As Scott Knickerbocker maintains in *Ecopoetics*, "[A]ll aesthetic experience occurs within nature, in the broadest sense of the term," and poetry could not exist "without the physical, nonhuman world that precedes, exceeds, and environs it." In a related vein, Irigaray speaks of "man" as "believ[ing] himself to be the creator of language, of poetry, of reason, but, in fact, he has only imitated the strength of the universe which surrounds him."[5]

Meynell's own focus on a tight human linkage with nature in its materiality resonates with Stacy Alaimo's identification of trans-corporeality, defined as "the time-space where human corporeality, in all its material fleshiness, is inseparable from 'nature' or 'environment.'" Such a recognition, Alaimo argues, points to the indivisibility of humanity and nature; thus, nature is not appraised as a background against which humanity acts but instead is recognized as a vibrant place filled with active entities, Alaimo explains. Referring to Karen Barad's theorization of "agential realism," which steps away from a customary belief in human prominence, Alaimo quotes Barad's assertion that "[a]gency is not aligned with human intentionality or subjectivity" but is "a matter of intra-acting." Barad additionally comments that nature cannot be reduced to an inscribable, inactive tablet upon which humanity writes, nor is matter immutable. Humans, Barad notes, live within, not outside of, the active realm of nature. If linkages between the materiality of humans and of nonhumans are recognized, Alaimo contends, a division between humanity and nature would not prevail. As Laird Christensen remarks in an essay in an ecopoetry criticism anthology, "Despite the fact that language necessarily diminishes presences to objects, . . . poetry can call attention to the fact that we dwell in a world of presences."[6]

Most of the Meynell poems in this chapter appeared in the 1875 *Preludes*, in which nature and the role of the poet are dominant themes. *Preludes* was Meynell's first collection, and in later years she was to dismiss it as unworthy. "My first book of verse was accepted by a publisher only because my elder sister, who had just made a great reputation as a battle-painter, was kind enough to illustrate it," Meynell claimed. The volume received tepid or poor reviews, and Meynell would later write about "the long discouragement which has followed the enthusiasm and hope of my publication of *Preludes*." She added, "So disappointed had I been at the reception of a book to which I had intended to enclose much feeling and some thought" that the project would "become a sore memory, and I never thought of my little volume and never opened it." Her daughter, Viola, would write that the poet was "thorough" in "her own repudiation" of the poems in later times. Nevertheless, such notable figures as Tennyson and Ruskin admired *Preludes*, June Badeni notes in a Meynell biography. Meynell would later speak disparagingly of her *Preludes* poetry in referring to certain verses as "*dreadfully early works*." However, the poems in *Preludes* offer a revelatory adumbration of Meynell's ecopoetics.[7]

Modern critics analyzing Meynell's *Preludes* and other poetic works have touched upon a significant gender component, drawing a connection to the challenges facing a woman seeking to craft nature poetry in light of the existing male oeuvre.[8] Although such scholarship is valuable in its gender investigations, this chapter considers Meynell's approach in quite a different light, for the nature poetry addressed seems to bracket off gender almost entirely; Meynell was attempting to speak to all nature poets, with gender elided in this connection. The poems examined almost entirely avoid assigning gendered pronouns to poet figures. Meynell's ecopoetics communicates a particular philosophy for creating admirable nature poetry that applies to anyone desiring to do so. In effect, Meynell establishes parameters that guide, shape, and determine a praiseworthy nature poet. This figure dominates Meynell's nature poetry, with relatively few verses appraising the flawed counterpart.

Immersion in Nature

Meynell's iterative and approbatory perspective on nature, which is so ubiquitous in her ecopoetic work, means that a thoughtful individual seeks absorption within the nonhuman world to the utmost extent possible. In this way, a division between humanity and nature is almost entirely elided, so that contrary societal perceptions of a definitive and exclusionary separation between self and other cannot endure. Indeed, Michael Field's 1908 verse "Poets" suggests this relationship in fusing nature and versifiers together: "Consider them thy poets, how they grow, / Thy lilies of the field!" With such a bond, as Irigaray muses in speaking of the earth, "nothing separates us." Although Irigaray problematically feminizes nature in her work, the point she is making is an important one: "Immersed in her," Irigaray says, "I share colors and light. I become her, becoming also myself. . . . She is with me and outside of me. . . . She surrounds me, radiates in me, illuminates me, comforts me."[9]

Meynell's "The Visiting Sea" demonstrates the intense connection achievable between humanity and nature. Although at first glance the poem may seem to depict a human-to-human romance, the speaker more convincingly is addressing the natural world. Advancing tidal waters infuse the speaker, establishing an intimate link between them, as the poem opens.

> As the inhastening tide doth roll,
> Home from the deep, along the whole
>   Wide shining strand, and floods the caves,
>   —Your love comes filling with happy waves
> The open sea-shore of my soul.

The language of romance appears in the stanza, and the atmosphere of robust affection intensifies through an image of breadth, with the adjectival selection of "wide." Moreover, the sea erotically suffuses the speaker as it travels across a strand that evokes a prone body, "floods" the hidden places of the caves, and saturates the speaker's very being as it enters the individual's "open" inner core. This sexualized terminology underscores the speaker's deep union with nature, presented here synecdochically in its characterization as the sea, especially since images such as the caves and seashore describe the speaker's own self.

The poem imparts as well the notion that a closeness with nature produces vast but subtle effects upon an individual, as the second stanza presents in continuing demonstrative imagery.

> But inland from the seaward spaces,
> None knows, not even you, the places

> Brimmed, at your coming, out of sight,
> —The little solitudes of delight
> This tide constrains in dim embraces.

Nature, the speaker advises the personified sea, affects an individual far beyond an apparent influence. The sea shapes a subject as it "constrains in dim embraces," with the adjective intimating nature's almost unrecognized impact. The concept continues into the third stanza, with a repetition of a dimmed or nearly unidentified force, yet one that nevertheless overwhelmingly affects the individual who adopts a welcoming response to it.

> You see the happy shore, wave-rimmed,
> But know not of the quiet dimmed
>   Rivers your coming floods and fills,
>   The little pools 'mid happier hills,
> My silent rivulets, over-brimmed.

Again, sexualized vocabulary infuses the stanza, with the flooding and the filling sea able to reconfigure the speaker's "silent rivulets." The blending of nature's language in reference both to the sea and to the speaker continues the impression of a union between them and of a speaker transformed by nature's life-altering presence. In this stanza, as in the first one, references to happiness appear in reinforcing nature's positive role in human consciousness.

Despite the seeming fusion of nature with the speaker stressed throughout the poem, the closing stanza carries the recognition that humanity is both part of and distinct from nature. After all, a Victorian reader might ponder, only humans have the ability to disrespect, dominate, and destroy the natural world they inhabit. The stanza's opening line alludes to a separation in referring to secrets that the speaker withholds from nature, but once that admission is made, the emphasis returns to the realization that nature must be embraced to achieve a lasting sense of fulfillment.

> What! I have secrets from you? Yes.
> But, visiting Sea, your love doth press
>   And reach in further than you know,
>   And fills all these; and when you go,
> There's loneliness in loneliness.

Nature's ineluctable importance is signaled by the capitalization of "Sea," the first such honorific in the poem, in closing the speaker's argument. Indeed, if one is not attuned to nature, the stanza reminds the reader in fulsome terms, a crushing feeling of lack and emptiness undoubtedly ensues.

A true understanding of nature requires an astute attentiveness to its constituents and diligent study over time, as the speaker of "In Early Spring" articulates. With its opening apostrophe, the poem addresses the nascent season like a close acquaintance in asserting, "O Spring, I know thee!" As Jonathan Culler comments, apostrophes "serve as intensifiers, as images of invested passion." In Meynell's poem, apostrophes amplify the intimate relationship between speaker and environment while according as well with Culler's remark that "[t]he apostrophizing poet identifies his universe as a world of sentient forces." Meynell turns to the apostrophe in multiple nature poems to establish a sense of closeness, which conforms to other Culler appraisals of the apostrophe. It enables the "visionary poet" to "engage in dialogue with the universe" and "takes the crucial step of constituting the object as another subject" with which "the poetic subject might hope to strike up a harmonious relationship."[10]

"In Early Spring" proceeds from the apostrophe to describe the development of the bond with nature. The verse contrasts the speaker's lengthy study with the "sweet surprise" that nature immediately registers "[i]n the young children's eyes"; the speaker has "learnt the years" and can anticipate nature's response to seasonal change in "know[ing] the yet / Leaf-folded violet." The speaker reveals extensive knowledge of the natural realm through anticipatory musings about the avian songs indicative of spring along with a sensitivity to nature in its muted form: "Mine ear, awake to silence, can foretell / The cuckoo's fitful bell," the speaker avers, as well as understand "how, in kindling Spring, the cuckoo shall / Alter his interval." The speaker's perspicacious insights earlier appear in a direct address presenting the alliance with nature:

> And all you wild birds silent yet, I know
>   The notes that stir you so,
> Your songs yet half devised in the dim dear
>   Beginnings of the year.
> In these young days you meditate your part;
>   I have it all by heart.

Moreover, the speaker is literally immersed in nature while walking through the landscape. Temporal passage accentuates the sustained effort required to comprehend this world, in that "[a] year's procession of the flowers doth pass / My feet, along the grass." Interestingly, the latter phrasing resonates with a notation in Meynell's essay "The Foot" that recognizes and validates the materiality of nature. "[T]he feet should have more of the acquaintance of earth," Meynell writes. "If our feet are now so severed from the natural ground," she adds, "they have inevitably lost life and strength by the separation."[11]

The speaker's comments in the poem become more particularized, progressing to "know[ing] the secrets of the seeds of flowers / Hidden and warm with showers." Yet the speaker recognizes that the accumulated knowledge does not represent a superiority over nature conferred through a human understanding of its inhabitants and its workings. Instead, the speaker bestows respect to and reveals awe of the surroundings in a humbled voice, crediting nature rather than a dominating self for the wonders revealed. Therefore, "not a flower or song I ponder is / My own," the speaker asserts, "but memory's," and this recollection stems from the lessons nature has provided over time. In a further submissive act, the speaker's own voice quiets to experience the exaltation the natural world provides: "I shall be silent in those days desired / Before a world inspired." The lengthy stanza concludes as it began with an apostrophe to nature, coupled with an ardent request that the elements presaged by the early spring unfailingly appear.

Even though the praiseworthy poet achieves a deep intimacy with nature, Meynell's ecopoetics repeatedly suggests that the nonhuman world holds secrets that humanity will never have the capacity to tap. This realization emanates particularly from "To Any Poet," which repeatedly advises that access to all of nature's secrets and a fulsome comprehension of its world will remain unachievable objectives. The opening stanza immediately imparts the point in telling poets that "[a]ll the earth's wild creatures fly thee," "they defy thee," and "[t]here is something they deny thee." The addressed poets are depicted as interlopers who "marrest mirth," and the negative portrayal continues as the poem progresses. Thus, nature "shuns thy long endeavour," even when a poet seeks to be steeped so deeply in nature—identified with one of the nature poems' few gendered references—that "her flowers and wheat / Throng and press thy pausing feet." Even if a poet can befriend a bird or literally become immersed within plant life, nature nevertheless retains "[s]ecrets in the bowers, / Secrets in the sun and showers." Regardless of poetic efforts, nature's "truth is not for thee." A poet presents "fictions" that are greeted with nature's "distrust," which will cease only when flowers "blossom from thy dust." Only with death, and the resultant termination of artistic efforts—that is, when nature is "set free from thy fair fancies / And the art thou shalt resign"—can a poet achieve true union with the natural world. At that time, "[t]hings thou longest for / Will not fear or shun thee more," and "[a]ll things shy and wild" will "[t]ell thee secrets." With death will come "[s]ilence, the completest / Of thy poems, last and sweetest."

Nevertheless, the admirable nature poet, Meynell suggests in numerous references, adopts the zealous appreciation of nature that "The Visiting Sea" and "In Early Spring" depict. The true poet of nature, Meynell argues, responds to its rhythms and accords with its time. Nature poetry, *Preludes* especially stresses, must be firmly grounded in the world it describes, paralleling the speaker's articulations in the verses previously addressed. "In February" offers a pertinent example in accord with the lengthier "In Early Spring," for the sonnet situates a poet-speaker figuratively within nature's cycle. In the octave's first three lines, February serves as a harbinger of the capitalized "Spring," with multiple references to a world in waiting, with its "colourless sky of folded showers," "folded winds," and "no blossom in the bowers." Nestled within that prefatory space, "[a] poet's face" rests "asleep in this grey morn." Like the barren terrain, the poet has not yet awakened, as if subsisting in a kind of winter hibernation that the surroundings similarly are undergoing. As such, the poet is participating in nature's own temporality, a situation that the octave stresses more overtly when the speaker comments, "I keep this time." Moreover, the poet's work, like the landscape, will respond to the forthcoming spring, the sestet indicates. Indeed, the reference to the poetry that will eventually arise immediately follows nature images in the same syntax and initial preposition ("to"), all of which are allied with nature's own temporal progression: "To all the miles and miles of unsprung wheat, / And to the Spring waiting beyond the portal, / And to the future of my own young art." The sestet's final lines directly address February with the personal terms "my sweet" and "[m]y friend," which punctuates the profound bond between the speaker and the "immortal / Child" of spring that the month portends.

The monumental importance of the poet's being in tune with nature's cycles emerges as well in "To One Poem in a Silent Time." Although not wholly concentrating on that topic, since the verse mainly relates the speaker's musings as to whether the addressed poem entails a final effort or merely another instance of the speaker's art, the poem itself seemingly derives from nature. In fact, the poem is directly depicted as a product of nature with the image of a cold-weather bloom, as the octave relates:

> Who looked for thee, thou little song of mine?
>   This winter of a silent poet's heart
>   Is suddenly sweet with thee. But what thou art,
> Mid-winter flower, I would I could divine.

The final two lines of the passage even play on the dual meaning of "art" through the denotation of this verb that identifies the poem as a figurative flower and through the connotation of "art" in its noun form to credit nature, in effect, for the speaker's creation.

Not only the poem itself but also the speaker's own state of mind is expressed with natural images, as if the bond they share enables the artistic process to move forth. Furthermore, the speaker both is positioned within nature and absorbs it within the self, obviating a clear boundary between the two entities.

> Art thou a last one, orphan of thy line?
> Did the dead summer's last warmth foster thee?
> Or is Spring folded up unguessed in me,
> And stirring out of sight,—and thou the sign?

The sestet continues to merge nature and poetry, with the flower's aroma linked to the poetic endeavor ("thy fragrance") and the poem specifically addressed as a particularized flower ("December violet").

> Where shall I look—backwards or to the morrow
> For others of thy fragrance, secret child?
>   Who knows if last things or if first things claim thee?
> —Whether thou be the last smile of my sorrow,
> Or else a joy too sweet, a joy too wild.
>   How, my December violet, shall I name thee?

As the final line suggests, the poem and the natural world from which it derives confound nomination, since the two appear inseparable.

The nature-poetry connection is especially pronounced in "The Poet to Nature," a formally odd sonnet in *Preludes* that inserts stanza breaks within the octave and the sestet. In a direct address to nature, the speaker terms it a "lyre," the traditional symbol of poetry, and credits nature for the speaker's own verse.

> I have no secrets from thee, lyre sublime,
> My lyre whereof I make my melody.
> I sing one way like the west wind through thee,
> With my whole heart, and hear thy sweet strings chime.

The lines offer a forceful message to the aspiring poet of nature: the writer must be utterly attuned to nature's workings to produce authentic art. The speaker's lack of secrets from nature reveals a connection so definitive that it resembles the intimate relationship depicted in "The Visiting Sea." The sonnet's third and fourth lines continue that closeness, for the speaker's poetry is sung in the same way as is nature's own version. Fully committed to that methodology, the speaker can discern nature's metaphoric strings, stressing in the fifth line, "[T]hou, who soundest in my tune and rhyme." In view of the unequivocal respect the speaker accords nature, the use of "thou," like the earlier "thee," seems entirely fitting, as if a deity is being saluted.

The Appreciative Gaze

For the genuine nature poet, an acute power of observation underlies a true appreciation of the environment, Meynell suggests. As the preceding poems have shown, keen observation becomes an essential component of understanding the natural world better. Several poems refer specifically to this sense experience through inclusion of the predicate to "look," and in others the quiet directive comes simply through the manner in which the natural elements are portrayed. In effect, Meynell argues for an appreciative gaze—in the traditional sense of the noun as attentive observation—to be directed to the environment, but this vision is far different from the penetrative form employed to objectify, subdue, or dominate an observed entity. A distinction exists here between an invasive gaze, as theorized in a literary register, and its antithesis of a valorized appreciative gaze, which refuses to assign inferior status to the surroundings. The dissimilarity between the appreciative and the invasive gaze serves as one crucial measure that differentiates the esteemed from the imperfect nature poet. The appreciative gaze recognizes the multifarious aspects of the natural realm and applauds its diverse components. In sharp contrast, the flawed nature poet adopts an aggressive and controlling gaze.

Several of Meynell's landscape essays helpfully demonstrate the necessity of the appreciative gaze for the authentic poet. These commentaries reveal an adept observational approach whereby natural elements are perceived with such care that their myriad aspects can be detected. As the essay "Grass" notes, for instance, "an inattentive eye" might fail to realize a change in landscape that dramatically alters one's impression, presenting a view that assumes a "new look of humility and dignity" and causes the surroundings to "seem suddenly gentle, gay and rather shy." Through the appreciative gaze, the landscape not only escapes negative designation as an other but also may be somewhat personified, as in the cited phrases. To a mindful observer, seemingly insignificant vegetation takes on the contours of beauty, evidenced in one example by a blade of grass that an unconcerned man will slash before it reaches fruition. Of special interest in the phrases is not just the discerning observation that recognizes the complexity of the seemingly mundane grass, but also the condemnation of an ungrateful human inhabiting the natural world, as in this example as well:

> His ideal of grass is growth that shall never be allowed to come to its flower and completion. . . . Not only does he cut the coming grass-flower off by

the stalk, but he does not allow the mere leaf—the blade—to perfect itself. He will not have it a "blade" at all; he cuts its top away as never sword or sabre was shaped. All the beauty of a blade of grass is that the organic shape has the intention of ending in a point. Surely no one at all aware of the beauty of lines ought to be ignorant of the significance and grace of manifest intention, which rules a living line from its beginning, even though the intention be towards a point while the first spring of the line is towards an opening curve.

In its indictment of human indifference to and interference with the beautiful waves of grassy plots, the essay remarks on "the gracious grass of the summer [that had] not been content within enclosures" but instead preferred to "[cheer] up and [sweeten] everything," decided "to live and let live," demonstrated "respect [for] everybody's views," and secured "what nobody wanted." A disturbing lack of regard for nature's verdant gift dominates the essay, and human destruction of the grass derives from an invasive gaze that has run amok and metamorphosed to an unbearable extreme.[12]

"In July" also provides a powerful example of the appreciative gaze, this essay demonstrating such acuity as to "perceiv[e] all the differences of the green of leaves." As in the above quotations from "Grass," nature takes on the trappings of a sentient creature in the essay's personifying descriptions, such as trees that "stand in their differences of character." Other references abound. For instance, there is "[n]o lurking" for some trees, oaks "wait to be found," poplars show themselves to be "alert" with "an alarum aloft" that prevents their sleep, and the trees "are salient everywhere, and full of replies." Before examining individual varieties and characteristics of trees, the narrator details the nuances of the summer hue detected by an observant eye. "Almost all the green is grave, not sad and not dull," the essay observes. "It has a darkened and a daily colour, in majestic but not obvious harmony with dark gray skies, and might look, to inconstant eyes, as prosaic after spring as eleven o'clock looks after the dawn." In another example, referring to a Keats description of "fingers cool as aspen leaves," the essay elaborates with more precise detail: "It is a coolness of colour, as well as of a leaf which the breeze takes on both sides—the greenish and the grayish," the narrator explains. "The poplar green has no glows, no gold; it is an austere colour, as little rich as the colour of willows, and less silvery than theirs." Moreover, "[t]he sun can hardly gild it; but he can shine between."[13]

Not surprisingly, in view of these examples, "In July" is interspersed with references to observation. In speaking of poplars, for instance, "[t]he eyes do gather them," and "[n]ot one is unperceived, even though . . . hill-sides [are] dense and deep with trees." As a result, "the poplars everywhere reply to the glance." Different types of trees "shake themselves perpetually free of the motionless forest," and "[g]lances sent into the far distance pay them a flash of recognition of their gentle flashes." In addition, "[l]ight and the breezes are as quick as the eyes of a poplar-lover to find the willing tree that dances to be seen." A drought alters the green tone, but "fresh and simple eyes" are required "to recognize their unfaded life."[14]

Several other essays similarly turn to descriptive phraseology and pertinent modifiers in delineating an aspect of nature recognized through careful vision. "Rushes and Reeds" is a noteworthy example, for it closely examines the particularities of sedges. The essay speaks of these plants that "etch their sharp lines upon the sky," and the "grey, soft, cloudy darkness of the sedge" benefits the countryside with "the distinction of its points, its needles, and its resolute right lines." The essay's mellifluous phrasing continues, as in this passage:

> Ours is a summer full of voices, and therefore it does not so need the sound of rushes; but they are most sensitive to the stealthy breezes, and betray the passing of a wind that even the tree-tops knew not of. Sometimes it is a breeze unfelt, but the stiff sedges whisper it along a mile of marsh. To the strong wind they bend, showing the silver of their sombre little tassels as fish show the silver of their sides turning in the pathless sea. . . . A field of tall flowers tosses many ways in one warm gale, like the many lovers of a poet who have a thousand reasons for their love; but the rushes, more strongly tethered, are swept into a single attitude, again and again, at every renewal of the storm.

Perhaps most attentive to the need for astute observation is "Rain," which intersperses copious references to vision in its depictions. Aside from the unadorned noun "eyes" are several examples of amplified phrasing. For instance, the essay mentions "our unready eyes," "gentle eyes of man," "inexpert eyes, delicately baffled," "man's eyes," and "meditative eyes," along with the related "clinging sight" and "exquisite game of visibility." The essay is replete with its literal reminders of the importance of careful vision, and Meynell's nature poetry also transmits this idea, albeit often in a quiet way.[15]

Meynell's essays fit with a particular tradition of nature writing, exemplified by Richard Jefferies, that is "rich in its literary skill," as Linda H. Peterson observes. Identifying Jefferies as the nineteenth century's preferred writer about the natural world, Peterson explains that to Jefferies, the defining characteristic of "great nature writing is to have 'sympathy' and 'an artist's eye for landscape.'" Excerpts from one of Jefferies's essays, "On the Downs," provide an idea of his technique.

> Stoop and touch the earth, and receive its influence; touch the flower, and feel its life; face the wind, and have its meaning; let the sunlight fall on the open hand as if you could hold it. Something may be grasped from them all, invisible yet strong. . . . Now, at this moment, the blue dome of the sky, immense as it is, is but a span to the soul. The eye-glance travels to the horizon in an instant—the soul-glance travels over all matter also in a moment.

A subsequent passage conveys a similar sentiment.

> The delicate odour of the violet cannot be written; it is material yet it cannot be expressed. So there is an immaterial influence flowing from it which escapes language. Touching the greensward, there is a feeling as if the great earth sent a mystic influence through the frame. . . . This sense of absorbing something from earth, and flower, and sunlight is like hovering on the verge of a great truth.

Jefferies's approach, Peterson maintains, "came to fruition" in Meynell's essays.[16]

Peterson also relates that Meynell's essays accord as well with the enduring style of Gilbert White, the eighteenth-century writer of the popular *Natural History of Selborne*, an edition of which Jefferies handled. The later writer admired White for "the spirit in which [he] look[ed] at nature" and mentioned White's "sympathy" with nature, which "enabled him to see much farther than the hedges by which he walked." White's book is notable for its detailed observation of wildlife in the Hampshire village, with references such as the following: a yellow wren "mak[ing] a sibilous shivering noise in the tops of tall woods"; a bat moving "with more dispatch than I was aware of; but in a most ridiculous and grotesque manner"; a "grand rendezvous" of harvest-mice; and the surprising presence of "a *locusta* whispering in the bushes."[17]

Even though Meynell's landscape essays demonstrate a high degree of particularization, the poetry does not elaborate to such an extent in its references to nature. Although the difference in methodology may seem paradoxical, Meynell's essay on Tennyson provides illumination. In making an argument about Tennyson's validated approach to poetic description, Meynell says of a pair of exemplifying paradigmatic lines that they evidence "no taint of manner, no pretty posture or habit, but the simplicity of poetry and the simplicity of Nature, something on the yonder side of imagery." Meynell expands on Tennysonian technique after chiding, "We are apt to judge a poet too exclusively by his imagery." In contrast, she maintains, "Tennyson is hardly a great master of imagery." Offering another telling clue to her own poetic approach, Meynell declares that Tennyson "sees the thing, with so luminous a mind's eye, that it is sufficient to him; he needs not to see it more beautifully by a similitude." Moreover, she asserts, Tennyson represents "the poet of landscape" so much so that "this he is more dearly than pen can describe him." Meynell credits Tennyson with "a new apprehension of nature" and a talent to depict "the perpetually transfigured landscape in transfiguring words." She closes her analysis in designating Tennyson "our wild poet," repeating the adjectival judgment in stating, "Wild flowers are his—great poet—wild winds, wild lights, wild heart, wild eyes!" Interestingly, Meynell adopts the same adjective in her own poetry, and in the context of the Tennyson essay, the term serves as an assuredly positive reference to the natural world.[18]

Meynell's admiration of Tennyson's style does not mean that her poetry lacks a descriptive quality, however, for frequent adjectival turns in her verse bring forth noteworthy effects. Generally, though, the adjectival verbiage seems stripped to an almost skeletal form. Meynell's customary technique presents sparsely phrased depictions with merely a sprinkling of adjectival descriptors that seem rather quotidian and restrained. The 1902 "West Wind in Winter," for instance, remarks on a "sudden tryst," a "gentler light," a "tossing park," and a "softened street" with no more elaborative modifiers included. The poetry frequently conveys a mental impression through an almost prose-like format of straightforward, unembellished lines that read like narrative statements. "West Wind in Winter," for example, includes such comments, phrased in typical sentential form and ending with a full stop. Nouns and pronouns rather than adjectives tend to carry a poem's weight, as in the opening lines: "Another day awakes. And who— / Changing the world—is this? / He comes at whiles, the winter through, / West Wind!"

With her often terse phrasing, Meynell was participating in Tennyson's practice of simple, unadorned imagery, which enables the reader to gain immediate access, as it were, to the natural element being referenced. The approach is a materialist one, for the reader's focus is concentrated directly on the element, barely adorned, if at all, to minimize vocabularic distractions. In addition, the narrative-like sentences tend to follow a basic linear structure of subject, verb, and object, perhaps strewn with prepositional phrases, which mimics syntactically the simplicity that Meynell admired in Tennyson's work. In "West Wind in Winter," a few lines from the third stanza illustrate both practices, revealing merely a nod to elaborative adjectives along with a conventional syntactic progression: "My window waits; at dawn I hark / His call; at morn I meet / His haste around the tossing park / And down the softened street." As in other Meynell poems, the materialist aspect of nature, accentuated by unencumbered verbiage, carries a significant underlying message: nature must be valued on its own terms. Indeed, the stylistic method contributes to her ecopoetics and its emphasis on the importance of grounding poetry in nature.

Nature as a Collective Unconscious

Another consequential feature of Meynell's ecopoetics relates not only to the conviction that verse emanates from nature but also to the desire for poetic extension far beyond the contemporaneous moment. To the latter end, several poems intimate that nature provides a kind of collective unconscious from which multiple generations of estimable poets necessarily must draw, presenting a similitude of an immortal fount. As the poetic source as well as an avatar of a poet itself, nature acts as origin, stimulus, and objective of authentic verse, regardless of the era in which a writer lives. Meynell's version of a collective unconscious intersects with the Jungian version only obliquely, but adoption of the term coined in 1916 is nevertheless fitting, even though anachronistically applied and certainly never used by Meynell. Both notions of the collective unconscious convey the idea that a reservoir of sorts enables the sharing of knowledge, which in Meynell's case involves a repository residing in nature. This tacit receptacle supposes a seemingly endless span of temporality sweeping across generations both ancestral and descendant. In Meynell's ecopoetics, a versifier's location in the span of time matters little, for an adept nature poet, in a sense, draws from an anticipated future as well as from the ongoing present and the enduring past.

A fitting poem to begin exploring Meynell's concept of a collective unconscious is "A Song of Derivations" (1893), which melds multiple generations. The first of the five stanzas establishes the guiding presence:

> I come from nothing; but from where
> Come the undying thoughts I bear?
>   Down, through long links of death and birth,
>   From the past poets of the earth,
> My immortality is there.

The opening phrase suggests that a void exists for the poet in not realizing the creative heritage implied by the concept of a collective unconscious. Yet the misapprehension is immediately corrected as the speaker recognizes the extended line of previous poets. Of crucial consequence, though, is the stanza's final pair of lines specifically acknowledging that the admirable nature poet is "of the earth," and it is through that immersion in nature, the speaker realizes, that artistic immortality derives.

In the second and third stanzas, which open identically ("I am like") except for the addition of a conjunction, the speaker situates the self as part of nature, with the fruition of poetic art linked to the workings of nature in expected ecopoetical fashion.

> I am like the blossom of an hour,
> But long, long vanished sun and shower
>   Awoke my breath i' the young world's air;
>   I track the past back everywhere
> Through seed and flower and seed and flower.
>
> Or I am like a stream that flows
> Full of the cold springs that arose
>   In morning lands, in distant hills;
>   And down the plain my channel fills
> With melting of forgotten snows.

Along with the insertion in nature, the stanzas attest to the influence of previous poetic generations. The second stanza signals their effect with the "long, long vanished" natural elements that, like poetic predecessors, caused the speaker's awakening. Buttressing the contention is the comment that the past exists wholly in the present as "I track the past back everywhere." The third stanza builds from this idea and employs the image of a rivulet filled by the thoughts of artistic ancestry. Especially important in these stanzas is the notion that the earlier poets were themselves shaped by a bond with nature, since the references to the ancestors are entwined with the many natural images presented. Also recognizable in the stanzas is a sense of ubiquity, for these images extend throughout the contours of the visible world, proceeding from the sun, shower, and air existing above the ground to the flowers, seeds, streams, hills, and melted snow found upon the ground. The featured poet--all three stanzas stress, in accordance with Meynell's ecopoetics--recognizes, however, that complete erasure of the boundary between human and nonhuman cannot be accomplished, as indicated by the designation "I am like" rather than "I am."

The final two stanzas accentuate the influence of earlier poets on the speaker's work and reiterate the viability of the collective unconscious stemming from nature's presence. "Voices, I have not heard," the speaker comments, have "possessed" the current verse and shaped it "[w]ith relics of the far unknown." The collective unconscious enables a blending of "memories not my own" that infuse the speaker with "sweet streams" that "throng into my breast." In the final stanza, the speaker recognizes the poetic heritage—that is, "[t]he happy songs" that "[w]oke long ago" and that now "wake in me"—and the need to follow in the literary steps made by the admirable poets of nature. The speaker feels a responsibility to embrace this poetic practice, as "[h]eavily on this little heart / Presses this immortality." Unspoken but implied is that following this valorized tradition offers a path toward making the speaker's own voice an immortal one.

An inheritance of the tradition also serves as the theme of "The Moon to the Sun" (1893), wherein the speaker functions as the moon to a predecessor's sun. Multiple references situate the earlier poet as the source of inspiration, lighting the way as a "glory-giver" to the speaker, who is "unto thee for ever."[19] As in "A Song of Derivations," the previous poet has bonded with nature, as suggested by the speaker's comment to that versifier, "Shine, Earth loves thee!" The speaker seeks to benefit from the poet-model's influence—"And then shine / And be loved through thoughts of mine"—but the speaker will not function merely as a conduit mimicking the mind of another. Instead, the later poet will build upon that inspiration to make an individual contribution as well.

> All thy secrets that I treasure
> I translate them at my pleasure.
> I am crowned with glory of thine,
>   Thine, not thine.

The "translation" that the speaker imagines attests to a new voice and presentation of the natural world that the ancestral articulation valued. The repetition of "thine" communicates this point. Although the speaker inherits the predecessor's appreciation of nature in the penultimate line, the distinctive emerging voice will chart a personal path; in the final line, the speaker's work will be "thine" through the poetic inheritance and "not thine" through the speaker's own creative endeavors. This double effect gains further weight in the final stanza, for the speaker will transform "thy strong gold" into "silver-white," marking the speaker's own contribution, but it is through the earlier poet's appropriate influence that "all beauty of mine thou makest." The poem's closing lines represent a movement forward from the past; the speaker is branching into a new avenue, indicated by the interaction between the sun and the moon. As the representation of the speaker, the moon has exerted its own power in shaping the sun, or predecessor poet, into a new voice: "I have made thee fair all night," the speaker informs the sun, "[d]ay all night." With that closing phrase, the speaker marks the transformative moment from the past to the present that enables the speaker's own voice to issue forth.

The idea of a collective unconscious proceeds from a divergent angle in a related poem, "The Day to the Night," a *Preludes* poem, which plays on imagery of light and darkness as did "The Moon to the Sun." The difference between the two verses comes in generational terms, for the speaker of "The Day to the Night" is projecting the address to a future rather than an ancestral poet. Conforming with Meynell's ecopoetics, the effective poet is steeped in nature, and the successful descendant is so as well. The idea of nature figuratively serving as a collective unconscious emerges in the first stanza, which emphasizes the disjunction between the two poets based on their existence in disparate eras, characterized by daybreak and twilight. "From dawn to dusk, and from dusk to dawn," the speaker begins, "[w]e two are sundered always." Nature's implicit function as a collective unconscious brings the two generations together, for they intellectually meet upon a shoreline beneath a scattering of stars. This joining becomes explicit in the second stanza, as the speaker insists that the two poets "are not day and night, . . . [b]ut one." So momentous is the conjunction of the pair that its origin is marked as "an hour of hours." Only through nature's inspirational effect, the speaker suggests, can praiseworthy poetry proceed, for "thoughts that are not otherwhere / Are thought here 'mid the blown sea-flowers." The separation indicated in the poem's first line, with its temporal division of dawn and dusk, dissolves through the imaginative "meeting" in nature whereby the individuals both exist in "this dusk of ours." As in "The Moon to the Sun," the next generation will build from the past one, as creativity—designated by a "wild wind"—produces "a new song to the olive trees." Appropriately, the poem concludes with a reiteration of the pair's eventful cognitive juncture within nature, as the two poets "meet by the sounding pine." The elder's realization of a new generation that will supplant the earlier one comes as the younger poet's "sweet eyes answer mine" while "Hope and Weariness kiss each other."

The thematic thrust of "The Day to the Night" similarly guides "The Spring to the Summer," another *Preludes* poem, with the two generations of poets designated as participating in nature's cycle. In "The Spring to the Summer," the speaker remarks somewhat regretfully that a later poet will assume the creative role, identifying the "poet of the time to be" as "[m]y conqueror." Nevertheless, the speaker urges the descendant to stay true to nature—that is, to "take the riches of the rain"—and to "keep the promise of my lays" by becoming grounded in the nonhuman realm. The poem invokes the concept of the collective unconscious as the speaker comments on the later poet's own power to influence the earlier one. Thus, the relationship is twofold as each poet affects the other;[20] "if thy thoughts unfold from me," the speaker opines, "[k]now that I too have hints of thee." Nature again provides the setting where such exchanges take place, within "the rare days of warmer wind, / And tones of summer in the sea." The speaker enjoins the follower to be immersed in nature, situating the directive in relevant imagery, and to continue the poetic work the speaker has set forth: "And I have set thy paths, I guide / Thy blossoms on the wild hillside." As the poem closes, it reinforces the instruction, in this case through a literal grounding in nature. "And I, thy bygone poet, share / The flowers that throng thy feet where'er / I led thy feet before I died."

Analogous thematic strands wind through "The Poet to Nature," discussed above briefly, but it carries a more definitive realization that future poets will develop verse that the speaker cannot even imagine. Descendant poets, the speaker anticipates, will demonstrate an even greater closeness to and comprehension of nature. Addressing the "lyre sublime" of nature, the speaker recognizes that "thou, who soundest in my tune and rhyme, / Hast tones I wake not, in thy land and sea." This degree of "[l]oveliness [is] not for me," the speaker acknowledges, and "secrets [will be kept] from me" but will become "[t]houghts for another, and another time." A kind of poetic evolution will occur in understanding natural wonders; whereas the speaker's verse "falters" in comprehension, a subsequent poet will bring forth from nature "other songs than mine."

Another poem takes a markedly different stance in questioning whether unborn poets will recognize the environment's indispensable importance for the creative process. Fittingly, the speaker of the 1893 "Singers to Come" is placed within nature, "lift[ing] mine eyes to hill and field," while questioning the direction an "unrevealed" poet, with an as "yet dumb lyre," will take. The poem stresses the role of nature for writing authentic poetry, a point compounded by the notion that the environs are anticipating the future work. The speaker wonders, "What words of yours [will] be sent / Through man's soul, and with earth be blent?" The phrasing itself specifically intermingles the unborn poet's words with nature, and the intertwined relationship deepens as the poem proceeds. Words become parts of the nonhuman world themselves as avian forms, and they interact with other natural elements, the trees and the seas.

> Who knows what musical flocks of words
>   Upon these pine-trees tops will light,
>   And crown these towers in circling flight,
> And cross these seas like summer birds,
>   And give a voice to the day and night?

In a sense, the stanza suggests, the poet serves as an instrument of nature, for through verse its voice can be heard. The idea of the versifier as nature's medium heightens the level of respect that must be accorded to the environment. The collective unconscious again plays a role in bringing together the poets of different times, with nature serving as the shared site of artistic fecundity. "Something of you already is ours," the speaker muses, and "[s]ome mystic part of you belongs / To us whose dreams your future throngs." The requisite connection to nature is reiterated, as the speaker's generation is identified as those "[w]ho look on hills, and trees, and flowers, / Which will mean so much in your songs." Nature is all-encompassing, extending from soil to firmament, as in "A Song of Derivations," and the speaker is steeped within it: "I, i' the world of land and seas, / The sky of wind and rain and fire."

In the 1893 "Unlinked," the collective unconscious assumes a different cast from its appearances in the poems addressed above as this speaker ponders eventual death and the fate of verse that has been penned. In the octave, the speaker adopts powerful nature imagery—winds, streams, and rain—that could sweep away the speaker's work, suggesting it is a transient endeavor belying immortality. At first glance, the octave seems to reject nature in this argument, but in fact the images depict the permanence of art that reflects environmental influence. A claim of potential immortality arises in the sestet, for the speaker contends that "[f]rom me, my art, thou canst not pass away," nor can the linkage between artist and work be undone. Rather, the speaker "[s]hall own" the poetry, albeit unaware in death of any pleasure or regret such possession would bring. Yet "Unlinked" implies that after death the speaker's thoughts will be lodged in the collective unconscious, and poems will emerge seemingly on their own as if wrought through an alliance with immortal nature. Thus, as in "Singers to Come," nature shapes the poet as its instrument, a situation that demands veneration of the nonhuman world.

A correlative message characterizes the previously discussed "West Wind in Winter." In this case, the wind, as a signifier of nature, is definitively identified as a versifier, which the speaker designates as "[m]y poet." The speaker reiterates the point in asserting, "I know his note, his lay." Through this "poet's" direction, as it were, the speaker can craft worthy verse; indeed, the speaker remarks that the wind "finds me 'twixt his wings." These images call to mind those of Shelley that are suggestive of poetic inspiration. Firstly, in "Ode to a Skylark," as Yopie Prins comments, "the bird is invoked as a figure for the poetry that the poet has projected into nature." Secondly, Shelley similarly presents the wind as a poetic progenitor, which carries the implicit reminders of "wind" as a synonym for "breath," "spirit," and "life." In the 1820 "Ode to the West Wind," Shelley urges the wind to "[m]ake me thy lyre, even as the forest is," and proclaims, "Be thou, Spirit fierce, / My spirit! Be thou me, impetuous one!" Shelley's speaker proceeds to ask the wind to "[d]rive my dead thoughts over the universe" and thereby "quicken a new birth." With poetry and the wind inseparably bound together, the speaker seeks "by the incantation of this verse" to spread "my words among mankind" and to "[b]e through my lips to unawaken'd earth / The trumpet of a prophecy!" Meynell's essay "Winds of the World" also draws the connection between verse and the titular force in claiming, "Every wind is, or ought to be, a poet."[21]

As the masculine pronoun in Meynell's "West Wind in Winter" indicates, the poem personifies the wind, which even literally seems to speak, its onomatopoeic moniker mimicking the sound of a robust breeze. Personification continues through the deployment of sexual imagery in the poem, as in "A Visiting Sea." The erotic references included in the first stanza of "West Wind in Winter" further the close association that the accomplished poet experiences with the natural world as well as imply the need to appreciate that realm in full while endeavoring to understand it. The poem's opening additionally suggests that the speaker has been unaware of the dramatic effects wrought by a bond with nature but upon that recognition undergoes a transformation in crafting verse, an idea that the reference to being beneath the wind's "wings" ultimately will confirm.

> Another day awakes. And who—
>   Changing the world—is this?
> He comes at whiles, the winter through,
>   West Wind! I would not miss
> His sudden tryst: the long, the new
>   Surprises of his kiss.

Nature serves as guide as the poem continues, with agential references to the speaker tending simply to record reactions of a dedicated follower. The speaker states, for example, "I make haste to close / With him who comes my way," "go to meet him as he goes," "hark / His call," and "meet / His haste." By the poem's penultimate line, the speaker seemingly has absorbed nature within the self in asserting, "I feel, I know, him."

The Flawed Poet

The speaker's concluding thoughts in "West Wind in Winter," that nature is felt and recognized, provide insight in examining Meynell's ecopoetics and her belief that a closeness with the nonhuman world leads the admirable nature poet toward worthy work. The obverse of such an approach, the ecopoetic philosophy admonishes, comes from the versifier whose primary concern is manipulation, whereby the poet perceives nature as merely a vehicle providing access to a desired objective. Thus, nature is marginalized to the position of an other, while the poet is concerned with self-aggrandizement and elevation beyond a materialist entity.

Meynell's *Preludes* poem "The Love of Narcissus" provides a telling analogy to the undesirable poet figure, with the sonnet's title signaling a disturbing comparison. As the beginning of the octave manifests with mirror imagery, all of nature is simply a self-reflexive tool to such an individual.

> Like him who met his own eyes in the river,
>   The poet trembles at his own long gaze
>   That meets him through the changing nights and days
> From out great Nature; all her waters quiver
> With his fair image facing him for ever;
>   The music that he listens to betrays
>   His own heart to his ears; by trackless ways
> His wild thoughts tend to him in long endeavour.

The homonymic pun of the initial line, with "eyes" connoting "I's" as well as the literal organs, sets a congruous tone for the following line, with its emphasis on this poet's vision. The second line accentuates the poet's self-absorption, with him as a Narcissus analogue so overcome with a vaunted sense of self that he is even shaking at his reflection.[22] With his extended "gaze" wholly self-directed, the poet cannot seem to wrest himself away from the spectacle. The comment in the third line that the gaze "meets him" continually, regardless of time's passing, becomes especially troubling in the fourth line because of the contextualization within nature. As such, this poet is utterly oblivious of nature—a condition signaled in the verse's opening line, when he completely ignores the river in which his face is reflected. Nature, in effect, is invisible to this poet. Instead, the river serves as a perpetual mirror that blocks out all sights besides his image. The river's own trembling suggests through this personifying gesture that nature itself holds no interest but instead the poet can simply exploit it as desired to enhance his sense of self. As the octave continues, the poet appropriates nature's own voice, its music, and considers the sound as an auditory reflection of himself since he hears only "[h]is own heart"; this poet, then, is also deaf to nature.

As the octave imparts, nature serves as the poet's other, providing the reflection that cements his own identity, and through the process nature becomes a specular tool. Irigaray's theorization of the speculum is pertinent here, with nature assuming the role of a woman in providing an obverse mirror for the poet's sense of identity. As with the speculum envisioned by Irigaray, this version involves a penetrative gaze, which in the poem appraises the natural world as an object to be appropriated for the poet's own purposes. Nature becomes the poet's other, his negative reflection that enables him to craft a picture of himself as master of the environment. Mapping Irigaray's scenario for women onto nature, the similarity is evident in that nature "serves as reflection, as image of and for man, but lacks specific qualities of her own," as do the surroundings of the narcissistic poet. Moreover, nature's "value-invested form amounts to what man inscribes in and on its matter."[23]

The marginalization of nature continues in the sestet, wherein several parts of the surroundings, like the octave's river, become reflections of the poet rather than truly being seen as valued material entities.

> His dreams are far among the silent hills;
>   His vague voice calls him from the darkened plain
> With winds at night; strange recognition thrills
>   His lonely heart with piercing love and pain;
> He knows again his mirth in mountain rills,
>   His weary tears that touch him with the rain.

With each image of nature, the poet self-reflexively transforms it. Thus, the hills—silenced since the poet does not hear them, as he did not listen to nature's other sounds—represent, along with the surrounding plain, merely surfaces to echo his own voice and enable it to rebound to him. Perhaps the vagueness of his voice attests to a lack of direction in his poetry since he has rejected the guidance that nature can provide. The "strange recognition" that excites the poet again stems from his egocentric approach to nature as the wind helps to carry his voice back to him. Brooks proceeding from lofty peaks and a rainy sky carry meaning to the poet only through their reminders of personal contentment or desolation. Like Narcissus, this poet is consumed with love of himself, and nature becomes his Echo, returning him back to himself and repeating only his voice.

A similar picture of the self-absorbed poet for whom nature is merely an instrument to be manipulated appears in the *Preludes* verse "A Poet of One Mood." At first glance, the sonnet may seem to be an encomium, with the poet's sole objective being to heap praise upon nature, but the verse instead carries an unsettling tone. The octave conveys the apparent message of approbation in the opening pair of lines before undercutting it in the two lines that follow.

> A poet of one mood in all my lays,
>   Ranging all life to sing one only love.
>   Like a west wind across the world I move,
> Sweeping my harp of floods mine own wild ways.

The third line may seem to be a positive one, for it invokes the wind imagery that elsewhere can signal glorious poetic inspiration, but the word "like" brings pause. The speaker's verbiage suggests a mimicking of a noteworthy poetic voice, but being "like" is not equivalent to "I am." The fourth line's negative implications will teleologically confer a troubling cast on the speaker's movements since their breadth engenders a widespread result. "Sweeping" in the fourth line implies an overpowering and comprehensive effect, which the "floods" reinforce. However, a flood conjures a lack of control, inundation, and destruction, and the remainder of the line maintains the dark tone through the speaker's "own wild ways"—with "wild" used derogatorily—bringing forth a similar sense of danger.

The octave repeats the idea that the speaker's verse issues forth from a single mood, in that "[t]he countries change, but not the west-wind days / Which are my songs." The idea of sameness takes on an ominous aspect in its self-congratulation that the speaker's influence seemingly extends everywhere—from sky, upon seas, and across ground—as the rest of the stanza conveys with its opening possessive: "My soft skies shine above, / And on all seas the colours of a dove, / And on all fields a flash of silver greys." The stanza's coloration underscores the idea of sameness that the poet's one mood carries, with the grey hues indicative of the dove and of the fields imparting an unpleasant dullness.

It is in the sestet, though, that the dreary flatness of the verse assumes an especially disheartening aspect. The poet announces, "I make the whole world answer to my art / And sweet monotonous meanings," revealing that nature is considered in self-aggrandizing terms; through the speaker's manipulations, nature becomes simply an instrument to be wielded as desired to accomplish the poet's ends. As in "The Love of Narcissus," nature carries value for its contributions to self-interest. Unlike that poem, though, a modicum of regret appears in the closing lines of "A Poet of One Mood," as the speaker acknowledges "[a] small cloud full of rain upon my heart / And in mine arms, clasped, like a child in tears." That regret, however, alters nothing that the poet has done.

A much later poem, "The Poet to the Birds," deserves mention even though it appeared in 1923, well past the Victorian period that this study covers. The verse assails the flawed poet in a different manner than the pair of poems just discussed by causing the titular birds to fall silent or to flee upon hearing the speaker's words. The defective poet refuses to nurture a connection with nature, as the frightened reaction of the birds communicates, but spreads the poetry nevertheless, with self-serving motivation. The avian reaction reveals that the speaker's poetry is so distanced from an understanding of the natural realm that it presents danger. The belief that a poet is justified in concentrating on the self without regard to the nonhuman world, this verse implies, constitutes an attitude that when projected to the culture at large carries menacing repercussions. In an imaginary dialogue with the birds, the speaker even recognizes the deleterious effect that the verses, with their troubling images, are having on these inhabitants of the environment.

> You bid me hold my peace,
>   Or so I think, you birds; you'll not forgive
> My kill-joy song that makes the wild song cease,
>   Silent or fugitive.

Indeed, an element of violence is even insinuated through the adjectival choice of "kill-joy."

As the poem progresses, it elaborates on the effects brought by the speaker's presence. "Yon thrush stopt in mid-phrase / At my mere footfall," the poet recalls, "and a longer note / Took wing and fled afield." The auditory references carry a scornful tone in that the speaker's own deafness to the environs leads to the muteness of the birds. In the concluding stanza, the speaker even seems defiant in insisting that his message be projected, telling the birds to "[b]e patient till 'tis done," for "I shall not hold my little peace." The hostile attitude, to some extent, may have arisen in an envious view of the birds' seeming immortality in existing "the ages long" so that "[t]herefore you do not die," whereas the mortal speaker is facing the prospect of "my adieu." As "Builders of Ruins" in *Preludes* avers, nature will endure while human creations crumble as "Time to come" will be "[u]ndoing our work." Adds the speaker, "O years that certainly will bless / Our flowers with fruits, our seeds with flowers" will, for humans, "ruin all our perfectness."

The self-absorption presented in "The Love of Narcissus," "A Poet of One Mood," and "The Poet to the Birds" becomes clearer when Meynell's work is contextualized within literary history and the movement that had prevailed in earlier decades. As is evident in Romantic poetry, particularly Wordsworth's verse, the speaker's tone is egocentrically focused. For Wordsworth, the poet represented a special individual able to gain access to an elevated cognitive level by utilizing nature as an intermediary instrument. As Scott Hess puts it, "Wordsworth stores . . . internalized images as resources for the construction of an autonomous self." Although Wordsworth's poetry extensively details, ardently praises, and abundantly appreciates nature, such sentiments are not endpoints in themselves. Instead, the valued aspect is ultimately nature's ability to function as an effective stimulus to exalt the imagination. The progression charted in "Lines Composed a Few Miles above Tintern Abbey" provides a telling example. The poem proceeds from appreciation of nature's wonders in boyhood to fading enthusiasm in later years, favoring the imaginative prospects that nature has opened. The speaker feels no regret that the passage of time has altered his perception of nature from the passionate "appetite" when he "had no need of a remoter charm, / By thought supplied, nor any interest / Unborrowed from the eye." Rather than a sense of loss, the speaker instead has attained "[a]bundant recompense" and experienced "[a] presence that disturbs me with the joy / Of elevated thoughts." Similarly, the speaker comments in the conclusion of Wordsworth's *Prelude* that he hopes other individuals can learn "how the mind of Man becomes / A thousand times more beautiful than the earth / On which he dwells." In *The Prelude*, Hess says, "Wordsworth's imagination in . . . moments does not so much harmonize with as consume nature, in order to assert its own autonomy."[24]

As Margaret Homans argues, "Wordsworth's imagination at its strongest shuts out the natural world," and nature's "function is to serve." Homans additionally comments that a "sense of difference between the self and nature" enables domination over the latter.[25] The relationship between the two is equivalent to the self/other distinction that undergirds the key difference between the genuine and the defective nature poet in Meynell's ecopoetics, with the former type of poet seeking to narrow the division as much as possible and the latter poet endeavoring to broaden the separation. A Lacanian analogy helps to illustrate the dissimilarity between the two types of nature poets. The desirable poet is figuratively poised near the boundary between the imaginary stage and the symbolic order, where the division between self and other barely exists. Thus, this poet perceives merely an inkling of difference between the self and nature, analogously to a child on the brink of fully recognizing that the self and the other are not wholly the same. The imperfect poet, by contrast, has passed the imaginary/symbolic border and developed a full recognition of difference between self and other, with an eventual abjection of the other as part of the maturation process. This analogy applies in somewhat different terms to the poet who focuses on the materiality of nature as the valorized endpoint of the creative endeavor, in contrast to the poet ultimately concerned with elevating the imagination.

The self-interested approach of the undesirable poet is evidenced in two verses with the same subject matter, one by Meynell and one by Wordsworth.[26] In Meynell's *Preludes* version, "To a Daisy," the flawed poet takes an aggressive stance toward nature in attempting to probe its secrets, with the phrase "penetrate all things and thee" directed to the daisy exemplifying the invasive approach. A resentful tone underlies the verse, with the speaker's recognition that nature's mysteries cannot be entirely understood. The speaker complains that the daisy, despite its fragile demeanor and its "little veil for so great mystery," nevertheless is "enough to hide / Like all created things, secrets from me / And stand a barrier to eternity." The speaker couches the desire to probe the daisy's enigmas within the claim that the motivation is merely to "praise thee well and wide." As the poem unfolds, however, the rationale appears to be simply a yearning for unattainable knowledge and power, which separates "the hither side," where the speaker exists, from the desired locale of "God's side." Yet through the imagination, the speaker implies, a higher state of understanding can be achieved. The daisy will be situated "[l]iterally between me and the world," as if providing the stimulus for the speaker to attain imaginative prowess. Once accomplished, the speaker "from a poet's side shall read his book."

Considering Wordsworth's conception of the relationship between nature and imagination, Meynell's poem appears to be addressing his work directly in the concluding stanza with the reference to the male poet's book. Through the avenue of imagination, Meynell's speaker apparently now is capable of achieving a Wordsworthian level of comprehension that had formerly been elusive in contemplating nature. Such understanding comes from an act of appropriation that enables the speaker, like the poetic model, to consider nature as a possession in articulating, "O daisy mine."

The assumption that Meynell's poem is directed at Wordsworth's poetics is supported by the fact that his counterpart poem is titled "To the Daisy," differing from Meynell's verse only by an article. In Wordsworth's version, nature becomes a preliminary step, as in "Tintern Abbey," and the idealized progression is depicted in much the same terms. The opening stanza of "To the Daisy" recalls the speaker's youthful "pleasure high and turbulent" when bounding across rocky hills, resembling the experience of the speaker in "Tintern Abbey." From the speaker's present stance, however, "now my own delights I make." As is typical of Wordsworth's work, the poem includes extensive and detailed descriptions of nature but unequivocally proclaims the superior power of the imagination. An early clue to that stance comes, for instance, when the speaker advises a rose that it deserves to be proud as it is bedecked with dew, yet "[t]hou liv'st with less ambitious aim." Later, the speaker recalls that from nature, a "sweet power," comes

> Some apprehension;
> Some steady love; some brief delight;
> Some memory that had taken flight;
> Some chime of fancy wrong or right;
> Or stray invention.

The poem reinforces the privileging of imagination over nature as the speaker compares nature to a lesser object: "If stately passions in me burn, / And one chance look to Thee should turn, / I drink out of a humbler urn / A lowlier pleasure."[27]

Meynell's distaste for the misguided nature poet gains further credence with Wordsworth's definitions of imagination and its presumed lesser counterpart, fancy. In the 1815 preface to his *Poems*, Wordsworth begins by acknowledging the importance of observation for the poet but considers it a practice to follow only temporarily; "its exercise," Wordsworth says, "supposes all the higher qualities of the mind to be passive, and in a state of subjection to external objects," resembling a translator's activity. Invention—noted in the quote from his "To the Daisy" given above—enables the poet to engage in creative activity using the information attained through observation that is "most impressive to the imagination." Wordsworth clarifies the distinction between imagination and fancy in this way: "Imagination is the power of depicting, and fancy of evoking and combining." Imagination, Wordsworth maintains, "has no reference to images that are merely a faithful copy." Rather, it "is a word of higher import, denoting operations of the mind upon those [observed] objects, and processes of creation or of composition." Wordsworth continues his clarification between the higher faculty of imagination and the designated lesser one of fancy,

> Fancy does not require that the materials which she makes use of should be susceptible of change in their constitution, from her touch; and, where they admit of modification, it is enough for her purpose if it be slight, limited, and evanescent. Directly the reverse of these, are the desires and demands of the Imagination. She recoils from everything but the plastic, the pliant, and the indefinite.

Wordsworth subsequently adds, "Fancy is given to quicken and to beguile the temporal part of our Nature, Imagination to incite and to support the eternal."[28]

These definitions offer valuable insights into Meynell's ecopoetics. Unlike Wordsworth's philosophy, her ecopoetics privileges the fancy; that is, the emphasis is on valuing nature for itself, rather than for the instrumental role it can play. Meynell's ecopoetics marginalizes imagination, for it draws attention away from the materiality of the natural world from which it springs. In light of Meynell's appraisal of the two terms, the title she adopted for a later grouping of her verses, selected from the 1875 *Preludes* and 1893 *Poems*, is especially fitting. In a volume of Meynell's work, *Later Poems*, published well after the turn of the century, this subset carries the designation "A Poet's Fancies."

In a way, Meynell's "The Two Poets" of 1902 presents the choice of validating fancy or imagination that faces a budding poet. In this complex and opaque poem, the opening stanza questions which type of poet is preferable in presenting nature's voice.

> Whose is the speech
> That moves the voices of this lonely beech?
> Out of the long west did this wild wind come—

> O strong and silent! And the tree was dumb,
>   Ready and dumb, until
> The dumb gale struck it on the darkened hill.

The narrative shifts dramatically in the second stanza, wherein two distinct avenues are pondered: "Two memories, / Two powers, two promises, two silences." Nature, the stanza explains, has been presented by both types of poet in the past within "these thousand leaves / Articulate." At the moment when a nascent poet is wondering as to the appropriate approach—at "[t]his sudden hour"—the potential approaches to nature poetry are given; in one, nature and the poet are "[s]eparate, apart," while in the other, the two "embraced, embraced at last," with the latter phrasing intimating the effort required to speak for nature in an authentic voice.

The final stanza consists of a conversation that includes three voices: those of nature, the admirable poet, and the flawed poet.

>   "Whose is the word?
> Is it I that spake? Is it thou? Is it I that heard?"
> "Thine earth was solitary, yet I found thee!"
> "Thy sky was pathless, but I caught, I bound thee,
>   Thou visitant divine."
> "O thou my Voice, the word was thine." "Was thine."

Nature speaks in the first two lines, wondering if the poetic voice addressing it provides a genuine representation of the nonhuman world or if the voice instead is self-oriented. The admirable nature poet speaks in the third line, expressing delight at discovering nature's offerings. Subsequently, the disingenuous poet gives a dismaying response marked by aggressive verbiage praising this speaker's seizure and restraint of nature, with the "visitant divine" reference signaling the view that nature's primary role is to stimulate the imagination, a quasi-divine creation, to elevate the poet. The final line brings nature's reply, in the first sentence crediting the praiseworthy poet with providing a genuine voice that strove to express nature's "word" and in the second sentence giving the good poet's response reiterating that the verse created indeed aimed to reflect nature in honest terms.

Such a representation, Meynell's work advises, is the proper path for the true nature poet to follow. As seen in the poems analyzed in this chapter, Meynell's ecopoetics requires a full appreciation for nature as it exists, not as it is distorted in flawed poetry seeking merely to aggrandize the writer. Seeking an immersion within the natural world is utterly essential for crafting authentic poetry, which recognizes nature as its own entity, Meynell maintained. In so doing, the poet unsettled the deleterious distinction between nature and culture, causing it to fall by the wayside.

CHAPTER FIVE

Constance Naden
Embodying Spirituality, Making Matter Matter

CONSTANCE NADEN BROKE APART CONVENTIONAL ideas about religion, moving away from Christianity's belief in God as a detached, celestial entity to elevate matter instead, including nature and humanity, as a kind of embodied spirituality. The poet-philosopher pursued the iconoclastic theory of Hylo-Idealism, which proceeded from the tenet that dualistic presumptions of body and spirit, the core of Christian belief, are inherently and irretrievably flawed. The approach negates "all distinction between body and soul, between God and world," Naden believed, so that mind and spirit are inseparably bound, in this annihilation of dualism in favor of an unwavering monism. Through the identification of matter as the ultimate truth, the Christian concept of a discrete spirit dissolves, being instead fused within matter, in Naden's formulation. "Spirit" is "the very equivocal term . . . irrevocably committed to Dualistic associations," Naden argued; spirit "really is itself material, as it means nothing but 'breath' or 'wind.'" As Luce Irigaray comments, "Spirituality is already situated in nature itself."[1]

Premises of Hylo-Idealism

Naden's Hylo-Idealism stems from the hylozoism championed by her intellectual guide, Robert Lewins. Hylo-Idealism has ancient roots through its hylozoist provenance, for early Greek philosophers embraced a form of the theory. A 1911 *Encyclopaedia Britannica* entry traces the origins to proponent Thales and the Ionian philosophical school. The early thinkers believed that elemental forces—air, water, and fire—carry life and animate the earth; the medieval and Renaissance eras brought alterations to the long-enduring theory, which extended into the nineteenth century, according to the 1911 entry. The ideas of Herbert Spencer, whom Naden knew, greatly affected her conception of Hylo-Idealism, Nour Alarabi indicates about Naden's philosophical grounding. Philip E. Smith II explains in his account of the Lewins-Naden theory that Hylo-Idealism grew from "nineteenth-century materialism," and he identifies as substantive influences such prominent individuals as Epicurus, Berkeley, and Hume.[2]

Naden explains Hylo-Idealism, which is so significant for her nature poetry, in various texts. The theory takes as its starting point, she posits, the conviction that "man can know nothing but phenomena"; that is, individuals are wholly dependent on their senses. Thus, cognition itself depends on sensation, for "[a]ll thought begins with physical phenomena." As a result, "the universe, as known to us, exists only in our sense-perception," thereafter to be "synthesised by the intellect." Naden deems as "false conceptions" the belief systems that "treat man's psychical nature as separable from his physical." Instead, Naden emphasizes, "the world is made inside, and not outside, the cerebrum." Consequently, in Naden's Hylo-Idealist view, "the only Cosmos known to man, or in any way concerning him, is manufactured in his own brain-cells."

> What we know as the external world is composed of colours, sounds, tastes, touches, and odours; and, since these can have no existence prior to their birth in the sensory ganglia, we see clearly that every man is the maker of his own cosmos. It comes into embryonic existence with his very first gleam of conscious life . . . and developes with his development, as he gradually learns to combine its lights and shades into symbols of form, size, and distance, and to indue its varying tones with relation and significance.[3]

The ramifications of this stance are enormous, since "[t]he ideas to which the brain gives birth cannot, of course, represent any but subjective truth," which entails "the highest certitude within our reach." Through its reliance on "subjective truth," then, Hylo-Idealism undermines traditional religious thought and its foundational belief in God as an actual being existing independently of human cognition. Rather than create individual truths about God, Christianity advises that humanity instead must search for absolute meaning outside of the self and embrace inviolable verities. In Hylo-Idealism, however, such objective meaning cannot exist, for "we cannot transcend the range of our own being." As Naden clarifies, "The creative power of man is not limited to the sphere of intellect, but extends to that of religion." Therefore, "if we will have deities, [we] are forced to create them ourselves." Through "hours of introspection and stern self-analysis," Naden concludes as follows:

> Though . . . forced to assume the real existence of some proplasmic substance, generating all those images of which our consciousness is composed, we shall not clothe this proplasm with divine attributes and bow in worship of the Absolute and Unknowable. Having traced our intellectual and moral faculties to their seat in the brain, we shall cease to inquire for the noumenon of this ultimate phenomenon, and shall find ample scope for

ideal aspirations in the sublime generalization, that "the sun, the moon, the stars, the seas, the hills, and the plains" are but products of our own *finitely infinite* personality.[4]

Naden connects her philosophy to Darwinian evolutionary theory, as does Mathilde Blind in her work. Naden argues for a continuum from lower organisms to humanity that proceeds without divine involvement. Emotion and memory appear in nonhuman species, she points out, so the presence of these traits in humans follows a logical progression. Since the development of intelligence is an evolutionary process marked by increasing intricacy, "we cannot invoke a supernatural agent to complete the process." Instead, "in these grey thought-cells lives the God who says, 'Let there be light,' and there is light." In Naden's thinking, "the God within" translates "simply [to] the energy stored up in the thought cells; and this energy is no separable spiritual being, but a specialized form of that cosmic vitality which is inherent in matter." Naden asserts that "cosmic energy is inseparable from the material cosmos," stressing that "we have obviously no right to invoke a spiritual agent for its production." Curiously alluding to St. Paul, Naden maintains that through the self "are all things created," including both the observable and the unseen.[5]

In place of a supernatural being, Naden inserted matter, with its innate energy, as the crucial element in Hylo-Idealism. "Matter" is a broad term that incorporates not only nature and humanity but the universe as well. Naden's theory coincides with Lewins's view regarding hylozoism. The approach, Lewins contends, "means that energy is inherent in matter itself, and not dependent on any influx from outside . . . or on extranatural influence." To Naden, "God is no longer without, but within; no longer transcendent, but immanent," with matter being the "sentient garment of incarnate Deity." This assumption leads Naden to confer a kind of divinity upon both nature and humanity; "the dust of the earth, and therefore the body of man is divine," she asserts, obviating the need and undermining the logic for a soul. In short, matter "is the *fons et origo* of all entities" and "the ultimate reality beyond which it is impossible to penetrate." Matter thus constitutes the divinity that Christianity instead attributes to a separate, celestial being:

> [T]he vain search for final causes, to which all religion may be referred, should be renounced by those whom reason must teach to behold in the orderly arrangements of the Cosmos only a supreme glorification of Matter, the Universal Mother, and of Man, her child. In the grey cells of the cerebral cortex are generated . . . the visible Heaven . . . and even the conditions of time and space which correspond to the revolution of its spheres.

Naden not only designates matter as "the Universal Mother" here, she clarifies elsewhere that the term is equivalent to "'mater,' the mother or producer." The feminization of matter as the Latin *mater* and its identification as the ultimate truth, as it were, reverses the traditional privileging of masculine spirit when forming a binary relationship with materiality. Indeed, Naden's dismissal of the masculine spirit and validation of feminine force is similar to Blind's supposition in "Nûît" and its presumption of a female creative power. By both overturning the customary valuation to favor feminized matter and obviating conventional religious ideas about divinity, Naden rejects the concept of a male, disembodied God and the hierarchies established by this view in "a long chain of assumptions, increasing as it proceeds in complexity, difficulty, and inconsistency."[6]

Humans, as themselves bodies, Naden argues, help comprise matter as a part of the whole and function as "an integral part of cosmic physiology." She uses a biological analogy of a constituent cell in a larger organism to underscore the point: "Man is to the circumambient world as a blood-corpuscle to the organism of which it forms a part." As a result, humanity "possesses no vitality distinct from that of its Cosmos, the body, where its life as an individual cell begins and ends," though an individual "moves with apparent freedom." Thus, "man is distinct from his environment only as a cell may be said to be distinct from the matrix, or intercellular matter, which forms its home, and supplies it with nutriment." By extension, since humanity is integrally a component of the surrounding world, causing damage to nature would represent a kind of self-destructive act.[7]

Nature, like the other entities Hylo-Idealism describes, is thought to be a creation of the mind. "[E]very one of us creates Nature herself," Naden maintains, "in a tiny cerebral studio, without pencil and without pigment." Thus, "[w]e make the mountains, and the sea, and the sun himself." In effect, Naden argues that human perceptions of nature represent constructions rather than objective observations. Without human cognition, matter would exist as simply "a void and formless chaos" and would remain that way "until the first living eye gives it shape and colour, the first living organ of touch endows it with tangible solidity, the first living ear wakes the dumb to speech and song." Quoting Schiller, Naden stresses that "[w]e see in [nature] only what we ourselves have written"; Hylo-Idealism changes the terms of "[m]an see[ing] himself mirrored in nature" to "man feel[ing] and know[ing] that nature is mirrored in himself, being the image of his Ego, and not vice versa."[8]

Poetic Explanations

Naden's rejection of traditional Christian beliefs about God emerges forcefully in "The Nebular Theory," a poem that appeared in 1887, after nearly all of her prose writings on Hylo-Idealism. The currents of Hylo-Idealism are abundantly evident in "The Nebular Theory," for it represents a dramatic revision of the creation story; indeed, as James Moore observes, the poem reshapes the opening of Genesis. Naden's version entirely omits God from the story, which instead is crafted as a kind of scientific genesis based on the workings of cosmic energy and the progression to materiality. Naden's account begins with an appropriation and paraphrasing of the initial verses of Genesis, with its well-known statement "In the beginning God created the heaven and the earth, and the earth was without form, and void":

> This is the genesis of Heaven and Earth.
>   In the beginning was a formless mist
>   Of atoms isolate, void of life.

The language of Genesis is signaled by the inclusion of "genesis" as a common noun. The reference comes from the second chapter of Genesis, which proclaims that "there went up a mist from the earth" and God provided "the breath of life" for Adam (2:6, 7). There is a quasi-homonymic resonance in Naden's rendering, with "atom" replacing "Adam" to mark both a similarity and a difference from the biblical story. Thus, in Naden's depiction, "a cosmic motion breathed and hissed / And blazed through the black silence." The blazing referenced here evokes the opening of Genesis again, in which "God said, Let there be light: and there was light" (1:3).[9]

"The Nebular Theory" subsequently offers a poetic summary of the nebular hypothesis of creation, popularized especially by Robert Chambers in *Vestiges of the Natural History of Creation*. The text appeared anonymously in 1844 and underwent a dozen editions, in some cases extensively revised, through 1884, as Marilyn Bailey Ogilvie explains in an essay on the theory. The hypothesis describes cosmic energy as initiating the formation of the smallest known components of matter at that time, atoms, which subsequently agglomerated to produce more complex entities. Although the scientific community widely criticized the hypothesis for conclusions lacking evidence and for factual misstatements, Chambers's work nevertheless attained widespread approbation. Even Spencer was intrigued by the theory, writing about it in an 1858 *Westminster Review* essay. Chambers perceived cosmic development as following three phases: the joining of isolated atoms, the onset of a rotating motion, and the dispersal of rings that would create planets as well as their moons. Chambers also adopted the concept of the whirlpool to explain the rotation, although that analogy was later dropped, as well as an originary "universal Fire Mist." After the nebular matter formed, it underwent a cooling period. As an 1872 *Appleton's Journal* essay by Rush Emery comments, the process began with "one illimitable mass of nebular or gaseous matter," followed by "the formation of fiery, liquid globes," the "hurl[ing]" of nascent planets and their satellites into orbit, and the eventual cooling of the matter, which ultimately led to the development of plant and animal life. Naden's poem follows Chambers's multipart sequence, even alluding to his whirlpool imagery through the term "gyres," with its denotation of a circling oceanic current.

>   atoms kissed,
>   Clinging and clustering, with fierce throbs of birth,
>   And raptures of keen torment, such as stings
>   Demons who wed in Tophet; the night swarmed
>   With ringèd fiery clouds, in glowing gyres
>   Rotating: aeons passed: the encircling rings
>   Split into satellites; the central fires
>   Froze into suns; and thus the world was formed.[10]

As in the poem's opening lines, Naden inserts religious language amid the scientific verbiage here. The effect is analogous in that the Genesis narrative is again wholly rejected, in this case through the notion of "raptures." To a devout Christian, the concept of rapture evokes ecstasy, mysticism, and exaltation in conjunction with a soul's journey to heaven. Naden's poem, however, undermines the sanctified presentation of creation in Genesis with the substitution of a hellish scenario whereby rapture is yoked to excruciating agony. Even more dismissive of the Christian creation account is the reference to Tophet, which is associated with the destruction of false gods through fire, implicitly suggesting that the divinity portrayed in Genesis is such a fallacious god. The poem's final phrase, "thus the world was formed," accentuates the point that the scientific hypothesis replaces the biblical account since it echoes the first verse of chapter 2 in Genesis, "Thus the heavens and the earth were finished, and all the host of them."

Branching from ideas related in "The Nebular Theory," Naden's "Starlight II" even more overtly substitutes matter for religion to explain the development of life, immediately dismissing the Christian deity as the creative source in its opening line and inserting astronomic principles instead in the sonnet's octave.

>   Man needs no dread unwonted Avatar
>   The secrets of the heavenly host to show;
>   From waves of light, their lustrous founts we know,
>   For every gleaming band and shadowed bar
>   Is fraught with homelike tidings from afar;
>   Each ripple, starting long decades ago,

> Pulsing to earth its blue or golden glow,
> Beats with the life of some immortal star.

The first line characterizes religious belief in harsh tones, affixing an adjectival "dread" onto the "Avatar," which is capitalized as a deity would be but refers to an incarnation in human form that unequivocally repudiates the Christian God. The subsequent pair of lines follows an interlacing pattern, whereby religious terminology fuses with scientific discourse and the divisions between them fade. Thus, knowledge of the universe will be attained not through the biblical "heavenly host," but through the light waves explored through scientific study. The waves themselves are mixed with baptismal imagery in their equation with the "lustrous founts" crafted in gold for the vital ceremony indicating one's initiation into Christian faith. As the octave continues, stellar beams transmitted to Earth generate life, and the immortality accorded to a deity is transferred onto starlight of "blue or golden glow," the hues of heaven and sacred accoutrements, respectively. In the process, the concept of deity and the existence of matter are united, which accords with the Hylo-Idealist denial of dualism.[11]

Further attesting to this unification is the sestet's reference to atoms, which compose humanity, Earth, and the cosmos.

> A life to each minutest atom given—
>> Whether it find in Man's own heart a place,
>> Or past the suns, in unimagined space—
> That Earth may know herself a part of Heaven,
>> And see, wherever sun or spark is lit,
>> One Law, one Life, one Substance infinite.

The final three lines not only reinforce the idea of unity but again blend together the material Earth and the spiritual Heaven into a single phenomenon. Light imagery suffuses the sestet as it did the octave, again blurring distinctions between materiality and spirituality. The final line serves as an emphatic exclamation of Hylo-Idealist monism in nullifying any division suggestive of dualism. All three nouns of the line, with their stress on oneness and infinitude, can be read from either a scientific or a religious perspective: the natural *law* governing the cosmos versus the common biblical phrase "Law of the Lord"; the scientific determination that all *life* proceeds from the cosmos versus the common reference to both God and the soul; and the materiality of a *substance* versus the biblical injunction to recognize "that ye have in heaven a better and an enduring substance" and that "faith is the substance of things" (Heb. 10:34, 11:1). With all three nouns capitalized and with all three carrying such strong scientific and religious valences, the two realms are so inseparably bound that dualism necessarily disappears and monism incisively consolidates in an affirmation of the Hylo-Idealist principle of one force infusing the universe, Earth, and humanity.

Not only does "Starlight II" provide, like "The Nebular Theory," an all-encompassing materialist view, the poem also identifies Earth as female through the feminizing pronoun in the sestet. Naden's pronominal usage taps into the centuries-old concept of Gaia, a vital goddess in Greek mythology viewed as the mother not only of Earth but also of the universe as a whole. Gaia was believed to have given birth to all of creation, including Zeus, through her pairings (sexual or otherwise) with the god of the sky, Uranus, as well as with the god of the sea, Pontus. Appropriately, Gaia was termed Terra in the Roman version of the mythological story.

As the preceding discussion of Hylo-Idealism has demonstrated, Naden in a general sense creates a kind of equation in her various writings: nature equals matter, and matter equals divinity. With nature as a form of matter replacing the divine father, a dualistic order is reduced to a monistic paradigm that validates the body of the earth, and a feminized one at that, instead of a detached deity. As Hylo-Idealism amply demonstrates, Naden's position is an atheistic one. Even with the overwhelming prevalence of Christianity in nineteenth-century England, however, Naden's embrace of atheism was not wholly anomalous, of course. The presence of "avowed atheism" there has been dated to 1782, which marked the year in which Matthew Turner published an atheistic text, George Landow indicates. Indeed, in 1811 Shelley wrote "The Necessity of Atheism," in which he maintained that "the mind cannot believe in the existence of a creative God." Identifying himself as an atheist, "thro' deficiency of proof," Shelley claimed that "[t]here is no God" in terms of "a creative Deity," though he did assert that "[t]he hypothesis of a pervading Spirit co-eternal with the universe remains unshaken."[12]

Following the Romantics, a prolific and especially influential Victorian atheist, Charles Bradlaugh, remarked that "the gradual and growing rejection of Christianity . . . has in fact added, and will add, to man's happiness and well being." Bradlaugh also averred that "general progress is impossible without skepticism on matters of religion." Atheism garnered an array of prominent Victorian adherents, either with long-term or temporary enthusiasm for the antireligious position; they included such luminaries as John Ruskin, Robert Louis Stevenson, Thomas Carlyle, George MacDonald, and James Thomson, as well as Mathilde Blind. Even George Eliot registered disbelief in various writings. "I could not without vile hypocrisy and a miserable truckling to the smile of the world . . . profess to join in worship which I wholly disapprove," Eliot claimed in an 1842 letter to her father. Elsewhere, she wrote, "God, immortality, duty—how inconceivable the first, how unbelievable the second, how peremptory and absolute the third." Annie Besant observed in *My Path to Atheism* that a "tiny seed . . . was slowly to germinate and to grow up, later, into the full-blown flower of Atheism."[13]

Despite Naden's own bona fides as a determined atheist, the poet, quite surprisingly, inserted religious imagery into various verses that specifically describe observable nature, as did Blind. The seeming paradox gains a plausible explanation, however, from the very prevalence of Christianity in Victorian England. By incorporating abundant religious images, Naden provided a bridge to further an understanding of her position, as if leading readers to her views through references to their own. Naden's poems present a panoply of religious allusions, including variations on biblical language and themes, descriptions of the sacred accoutrements of church services, and references to the ingrained beliefs of the devout, as will be seen. Naden's poetic maneuvers and Hylo-Idealist approach also resonate with ecofeminist configurations of embodied spirituality that would arise in the next century; this similarity offers another informative and compelling lens through which to read her verse in productive ways. The correspondences between the ecofeminist model and Naden's writings are evident in assuming a diffuse, life-generating energy instead of a disembodied spirituality; in emphasizing vital importance of matter; and in conferring a kind of divinity upon nature as part of a reconceived universe.[14]

Ecofeminism and Embodied Spirituality

Although multiple permutations exist in examining ecofeminist spirituality, certain threads offer the most productive and relevant avenues for a discussion of Naden's poetry, intersecting with it in correlative ways. Granted, Naden moves well beyond the positions of various ecofeminist theorists in her utter rejection of a Christian divinity. Nevertheless, perceptions of the vexed notion of the spiritual often take similar paths, proceeding from the idea that a disembodied, male God existing apart from humanity and nature is an erroneous assumption.

Ecofeminists arguing against such a view of a disembodied divinity call for a reassessment of traditional conceptions of a detached, patriarchal being far removed from the universe in general and from the natural world in particular. This long-standing scenario, as ecofeminist theologian Rosemary Radford Ruether observes, "model[s] God after alienated male consciousness, outside of and ruling over nature." Ecofeminist theology opposes the presumed separation between divinity and nature along with the attendant rationalization of dominion. As Ursula King asserts, the "disconnection between our selves, the earth, and the Divine" represents "a deep split that must be healed." In opposition to the separation of divinity from nature, Ruether explains, "[t]he concept of God is deconstructed" and recast "as a matrix of life-giving energy that is in, through, and under all things," including nature.[15]

Another answer to the schismatic problem, most notably advanced by ecofeminist theologian Sallie McFague, derives from a very different model. As mentioned in this study's introduction, McFague calls for the recognition of the universe as a physical manifestation of God rather than the disembodied version of divinity that has for so long driven Western thought. God is interpreted as a body in McFague's postulation, one that incorporates the universe, humanity, and nature. "[W]e and all others belong together in a cosmos," McFague states. Furthermore, she asserts that all earthly elements should be appraised as being bound together in a unified way that promotes and requires harmonious relationships. As Ruether also comments, nature is recognized as "a living matrix of interconnection."[16]

With the corporeal model, McFague maintains, the natural world is no longer a terrain that can be dominated and exploited but instead is perceived as part of an "intricate web of life" in which all entities become "interdependent parts." The concept of embodiment, she adds, brings humanity and the rest of the world together. McFague's body model not only includes life forms but can be broadened to cover all forms of matter. In McFague's thinking, "if God is embodied, then matter, the natural world, is not only 'good' but in some sense sacred—a place where God is present." In a relevant comment, Irigaray remarks that "the sacred consists in honoring nature, not immolating it." The ecofeminist depictions of embodiment and the divine body distinctly resonate with Naden's perception of matter as incorporating a kind of divinity and its central role in the workings of the universe. In Ruether's appraisal, "God is the font from which the variety of plants and animals well up in each new generation, the matrix that sustains their life-giving interdependency." This view accords with Naden's concept of energy as a life force that replaces the Christian deity.[17]

Such postulations demonstrate another intersection between ecofeminist spirituality and Hylo-Idealism. In Naden's theorization of cosmic energy, alluded to earlier, she avers that an inseparable bond exists between this force and materiality. Naden's formulation resonates with modern ideas of the relationship between matter and energy whereby they participate in a process of exchange enabling each to change into the other. "Just as the forces which operate in a living cell cannot be essentially different from those which sustain the entire body," Naden argues, "so the identity of vital and cosmical energy is conclusively proved by the constant interchange of matter—and consequently of material force— which takes place between that body and its environment." In ecofeminist terms, this interchangeability undermines the notion of dualism, with its presumption of impermeable boundaries between spirituality and materiality. As Gillian McCulloch observes in *The Deconstruction of Dualism in Theology*, "[I]f matter is energy, then the Cartesian dualist view of mind (spirit) and matter as two distinct categories could be abandoned," with the result that energy would be the origin of both. McCulloch notes an equivalence between energy and divinity in that God is considered the animating source in nature. To McFague, if "matter is not inanimate substance but throbs of energy, [it is] essentially in continuity with spirit." McFague thus sees a "continuum between matter and energy" that dissolves various dualisms, such as that of the body and the spirit. Other ecofeminist theologians also draw a relationship of equivalence. Ruether, for one, states that "[m]atter dissolves into energy," with the latter serving as the formative foundation of the former. This relationship precludes the possibility of separating the energy associated with divinity and that associated with materiality, for "spiritual energy" functions as "life energy," Ruether affirms.[18]

An additional correspondence between Naden's work and ecofeminist spirituality centers on the idea of nature as a construct. As indicated earlier, Naden argues that through cognition, each individual creates a particular picture of nature rather than everyone seeing the exact same one. McFague takes up the issue in her own analysis of constructed nature. "There is no *one* view of nature," McFague says in rejecting the perception that nature can be essentialized. Instead, nature "is never 'natural,'" for a person's idea of nature depends upon a variety of influences. "[W]e live *within* our personal, cultural, historical, geographical, economic, racial, class, and gender understandings of the natural world," she points out. Denying that any interpretations of nature are fixed or ingenuous, despite exclamations to the contrary, McFague asserts in quoting Yaakov Jerome Garb, "We see in Nature what we have been taught to look for, what we feel we have been prepared to feel." Of course, nature has been feminized as inferior, which has served as a rationale for oppression. Built on a hierarchical platform, ecofeminists point out, Christianity implicitly privileges male authority and assumes male superiority. Under conventional dualisms existing over centuries, Christianity associates men with spirituality and the mind, whereas it links women to the earth and the body. The supposition develops through this scenario that men, as the privileged entity, have an innate right to dominate the supposedly inferior women as well as nature. As Carol J. Adams comments in *Ecofeminism and the Sacred*, repression is sanctified when corporeality, females, and the natural world are connected and eclipsed. When such a model is invalidated, as in ecofeminist spirituality, the female body and feminized nature are not only recuperated but elevated. Hierarchies validating domination, as Ruether remarks, need to be discarded in favor of a "mutual interdependency" among individuals, regardless of gender differences, and among humans and other species.[19]

Some ecofeminists have unproblematically turned to Gaia lore in developing an essentialist construction of nature and women. Such positions undoubtedly are flawed, and the rejection of the construct by other feminists is certainly justified. Yet there are aspects of the Gaia legend that provide a useful perspective on Naden's version of embodied spirituality. In a general comment about "feminine spiritual traditions," Irigaray makes the point that these traditions "respect and celebrate nature" and "have allowed the union of nature and grace, of the cosmic universe, the body and the word." In the Gaia story, Riane Eisler explains of its ecofeminist connection, ancient societies worshipped the goddess and understood that they must venerate, not exploit, the earth. Additionally, these long-ago cultures did not have a structure wherein men dominated women, Eisler relates, but instead embraced the compassionate qualities associated with femininity and rejected the aggressive behavior attributed to masculinity. To Gaia disciples, unlike advocates of Western religious views long thereafter, Eisler indicates, spirituality was inseparable from nature, with "no need for the artificial distinction" that would later prevail. Because of Naden's advocacy of women as well as her high valuation of a feminized nature, the Gaia legend, despite its shortcomings from a modern standpoint, can offer a helpful vehicle for understanding Naden's Hylo-Idealist presumptions.[20]

Epiphanic Moment

With Naden's Hylo-Idealism and ecofeminist spirituality providing an instructive background, it is fitting to examine several of her nature poems. "January 28th, 1880" offers a helpful beginning in that it repeatedly reinforces Naden's monist idea that in the terms of embodied spirituality, divinity exists in the material realm of nature rather than as a detached supreme being. At first glance, the poem's title seems an odd choice, for its precise calendar date sharply contrasts with the poem's far more general musings that could arise in any winter moment. The title thus seems to mark an arbitrary day, the meaning of which is never specified in the stanzas. Yet on extended consideration, the title suggests that it is citing a day of epiphany whereby the speaker came to realize the divinity within matter that Naden's prose works explore so prominently. Adding to that assumption, the particularized date reminds of a religious holy day, in this case not commemorating a special person or event vital to Christian believers but signaling a very different moment generating inspiration.

The opening stanza of "January 28th, 1880" points to such a transformation, for the speaker calls attention to a dramatic shift in thought that altered the customary appraisal of the winter, imparted in terms evoking a religious revelation.

No more I long for April's fitful sheen,
    For little fluttering lives, that passed in June,
      For leaves and flowers, by sad October lost;
Since now in ecstasy mine eyes have seen
    The rich blue heaven of a summer noon
      O'er dazzling trees, thick-robed, with mossy frost.

The initial line suggests a definitive break in time ("No more") marking a transformative moment, which in the context of Naden's prose implies that the speaker has risen to a higher plane of thought. The speaker is not praising and preferring the natural world in warmer months, as is commonly done, but is recognizing great significance in the winter scene, which is permeated with Naden's customary religious imagery. In fact, references to the warmer months in the first three lines carry a dismissive and censorious tone in the speaker's recollection of the perfunctory manner in which nature had been appraised before the epiphany occurred. The "fitful sheen" conveys a restlessness in its adjective, which would be far removed from the tranquility experienced by a devout believer, and the noun signals insubstantiality with its connotation of a superficial effulgence. The following two lines continue the impression of impermanence, with the brief lifespan of the natural elements listed, as if the speaker assesses nature on a temporal level rather than considering the seasons as part of a cyclical continuum suggestive of eternity. The brief spans of the "fluttering lives" and the fading vegetation designate transience and the finite linear time demarking death.

The stanza's concluding tercet shifts to an abundance of religious language. The "ecstasy" elicits the mystic transcendence of a pious zealot, with the line's subsequent phrase recalling the four words beginning the Anglican hymn "Mine Eyes Have Seen the Glory."[21] The next line more apparently makes the religious connection, with its celestial terminology, but the heaven referenced here is not the one in Christian thought but rather is one linked to nature. The "summer noon," which identifies the most intense light of both the day and the year, is mapped onto winter elements in the stanza's final line to resonate with the idea of a divine illumination through nature instead of a supreme being. Vocabulary choices in this closing line reinforce the connection; the arboreal "dazzl[e]" reminds of divine light and also of the shining golden vessels on an altar, and the shimmering frost coating the tree is depicted as a robe, a synonym for a vestment.

The religious elements continue in the next stanza, subtly interwoven into a depiction of massive trees framed by shrub-like vegetation.

Amid the leafless hedge-rows jewel-twined,
    Great trunks and boughs, not crystal-clad as they,

Like black majestic arches I behold;
All wreathed and crowned with woven sprays, defined
In every tender shade of pearly grey,
And radiant white, that glitters into gold.

The splendor of religious vessels suggested in the first stanza surfaces here as well in the opening line, with the gem-like appearance of frost in the hedge-row enclosure. The curvature of the stately trees calls forth the arches of a grand cathedral, and the speaker's comment "I behold" echoes a frequent biblical interjection. The noun choice "sprays" brings to mind the decorative floral arrangements upon an altar, the reference to wreaths signals the conferment of honor, and the crown alludes to Christ's diadem of interlaced thorns. The coloration of the bedecked trees enhances the religious connections: the pearly grey characterizes not only a gem highly valued in biblical contexts but also the heavenly gates in the biblical Revelation; the bright white and the glittering gold create a sparkling brilliance so pronounced that it mirrors the blinding luminosity associated with a celestial being. The fact that every tree is so adorned suggests an omnipresence connected with divinity, and the denotation of the verb indicating that the trees are "defined" provides a determination of meaning. The image of death ("leafless") in the first line contributes to the stanza's religious tone, in contrast to the sense of vibrant splendor emerging as the stanza unfolds, paralleling the salvational act of Christ that opened for sinful humanity the way toward eternal life. The frost's dual significations of death and life further support the impression of Christ's salvation. The multiple images of enclosure in the stanza—hedge-rows, arches, wreaths, and crowns—create an omniscient effect, as if all elements are subject to the enveloping quality of the frost. All of these descriptive elements position the trees as a kind of church, celebrating nature in Naden's version of embodied spirituality.

The inference that the trees form such a place of worship is reinforced in the third stanza, which adopts and extends various images of the previous lines.

Around the mighty limbs all gnarled and bowed,
    The oak-tree twigs are finely interlaced;
        The willows droop in bright cascades of foam,
Each distant tree, a white and feathery cloud,
    The nearer branches, delicately traced,
        And gleaming pure against the azure dome.

In this stanza, the accoutrements of a church again appear, as if the trees are forming a lattice-like structure mimicking the contours of the religious edifice. The intertwining of the twigs creates an enclosure-like impression of omnipresence, supported by the indication that "all" the tree limbs are involved, and the "mighty limbs" imply omnipotence as well. Yet the stanza differs from its predecessors in that the trees perform a double function, which heightens the atmosphere of religiosity. Not only are they creating a cathedral-like setting, they are also taking on the role of a supplicant, for they are adopting the postures of a devout believer. Thus, the limbs of the massive oak trees are "bowed," while the willows "droop." This dual role as a place of worship and as the worshippers themselves coincides with Naden's suggestion that individuals construct their own images of a supreme being and cannot step outside of themselves in the search for objective truth; devotion, faith, and the very site in which worship is performed are inextricably bound together. That is, if the self devises all religious "truth," then the divisions among individual, deity, and church are blurred and unstable. As in the poem's first stanza, death and life are intermingled, quietly suggested by the presence of an oak, which is customarily associated with strength, and the willow, which is linked with death in arboreal symbolism.[22] The trees' resemblance to luminous downpours of foam, appearing as clouds, hints at resurrection through Christ's ascension to heaven. The religious connection expands through the description of branches that are "gleaming pure," as if projecting divine illumination and the stainlessness wrought by Christ's sacrifice. Appropriately, the branches touch the "azure dome," with the coloration reminding of heaven and the dome marking the apex of a religious structure.

The connection to worship becomes more definitive in the final stanza, for the depiction resembles a church service, with its silent atmosphere.

> The winds are hushed—there comes no murmuring breeze
>   To stir the poplar's lofty sun-lit cone,
>   Or myriad branchlets of the wide-spread beech:
> Through this all-glorious temple of the trees,
>   As through the house of God, I walk alone;
>   A silence, as of worship, is their speech.

Again, a worshipper, church, and nature are blended in the stanza, further erasing the boundaries between them and conforming to Naden's assumption that the individual constructs religious belief rather than its existing through a detached deity. The opening line resembles a quiet church in which worshippers are absorbed in prayer. The inclusion of the poplar provides a biblical link to life (Gen. 30:37–38). In the context of Hylo-Idealism, these associations intimate that viewing nature as its own divine presence brings forth an intellectual rebirth and expanded comprehension ("wide-spread"). The Hylo-Idealist conviction that matter itself is inherently divine is further implied by the "lofty sun-lit cone" of the poplar, as if a signifier of sacred illumination and heavenly elevation. The stanza's second tercet connects nature to divinity in more straightforward fashion, in that the trees are specifically identified as an "all-glorious temple," which is subsequently likened to "the house of God." In "walk[ing] alone," the speaker calls forth the notion that the self, not an exterior being, innately creates religious belief. The stanza's final depiction of the tree's silence as a form of worship, considered with the tercet's other lines, again positions matter, the individual, and divinity as a blended whole.

The poem's prosodic elements accentuate its thematic constituents, beginning with the stately iambic pentameter that well suits the majestic trees described. Every stanza contains two tercets, and each of them forms a trinity, which underscores the idea that nature, divinity, and the individual merge into a unified order like the Christian triad. Each tercet follows an *abc* pattern, and with the identical rhyme sequence continuously repeating, a sense of infinity associated with divinity emerges even as that idea of order is reinforced. Through these prosodic moves, the poem adds another layer of emphasis to the Hylo-Idealist perceptions of matter and spirituality.

Creation Rewritten

Another Naden poem titled with a date, "December, 1879," incorporates aspects of "January, 28th, 1880" but follows a decidedly different trajectory in its approbation of embodied spirituality. Like "The Nebular Theory," the verse entails a reworking of the creation story, but in this case religious references are not only deconstructed but also jumbled and then reconstructed in a nature-oriented depiction of divinity. The sonnet's titular month prepares for the religious undertone as the time of Christ's birth, while the year marks the end of a decade and the onset of a new beginning, mimicking the poem's departure from traditional Christian thought and emphatic movement to a nature-based paradigm of embodied spirituality.

The octave sets out several important points:

> Now is the Earth at rest from sun and storm;
>> And stripped of all her gems and vestures gay,
>> Gives thanks to Heaven, while weaklings can but pray:
> In germs of life, uncouth of hue and form,
> She feels the glory of the summer swarm,
>> And knows December not less rich than May;
>> For she is young as on her primal day,
> And still beneath the snow her heart is warm.

The stanza initiates the breakdown of conventional religious belief by echoing the second chapter of Genesis, which proclaims that "on the seventh day God ended his work which he had made; and he rested on the seventh day from all his work which he had made" (2:2). In Naden's telling of the narrative, biblical divinity is replaced by materiality in the form of Earth, with the word capitalized in the opening line as would be the word for a deity. As the poem proceeds, the deconstructive process begins through images of divestiture, as Earth is "stripped of all her gems and vestures gay." The shedding of vestures, synonymous with vestments, implies the dismissal of conventional religious practice in this removal of priestly garb. The line provides a curious parallel to the biblical telling of Jesus's own removal of clothing, described in the book of Matthew, by a band of soldiers who denounced Christ and "stripped him." Yet in Matthew's account, the soldiers "put on him a scarlet robe" prefatory to setting upon his head the injurious crown of thorns (27:28). Since a crown typically is decorated with jewels, the poem's reference to the wresting of gems presents a seeming inversion of Christ's experience. Additionally, the poem recounts only the elimination, not the replacement, of clothing, to rupture further the parallel to Christian lore. Accentuating the divergence from the biblical story is the presence of the feminine pronoun in the poem's second line, which replaces the familiar male divinity with a female alternative in this breakdown of Christian patriarchal presumption through the subversive effect.

Religious references continue to appear in the poem's third line as Earth expresses gratitude to the heavenly kingdom while "weaklings can but pray." The Bible carries multiple references to Christ's giving thanks, to provide another curious parallel with the poem. In Christ's case, he is addressing another entity of the divine trinity, the Father; thus, one deity is communicating with another. In the poem, Earth's gratitude suggests an analogous correspondence between divinities and again serves to deify materiality. The second phrase of the line draws a definitive contrast between the immanent power of the material deity and the "weaklings" who pray. The phrasing undercuts traditional Christian belief through the implication that those who accept dualism, evidenced by their participation in religious ritual, and ignore the integral divinity of monistic materiality are preventing themselves from recognizing their own immanent divinity as presented in the Hylo-Idealist philosophy.

In the remainder of the octave, the materialist version of the creation story covers Earth's early appearance following the process that formed the celestial version outlined in "The Nebular Theory." "December, 1879" also includes the resonances to Genesis and the description that "the earth was without form, and void" (1:2) through the sonnet's development of life from another kind of void, in this case winter, where "germs of life" are merely "uncouth of hue and form."

Yet through Earth's ministrations, reminiscent of God's own distinctive "glory," a term that abundantly appears in the Bible, the planet "feels the glory of the summer swarm" that will arise with the change of the seasons. The noun choice "swarm" is especially relevant in this context, for it includes teeming life among its denotations and points to Earth's agency in creating animate and inanimate entities. The final lines of the octave convey multifarious linkages to divinity: a sense of omniscience through Earth's unfettered comprehension of the cycle of life, represented by seasonal change; a sense of immortality conferred through the existence of an eternal present that leaves Earth unmarked by aging; and a sense of invulnerability through the unproblematic coexistence of death (December, snow) and life (May, warmth) that entails a form of resurrection.

The sestet amplifies the existence of embodied spirituality, particularly in the opening line:

> All flowers and fruits are folded in her breast,
>> Waiting but fuller radiance from above;
>>> And she lies dreaming of her destined hour,
> All white and still, most like a soul at rest,
>> Rich in hid wealth, and strong in secret power,
>>> Silent with joy, and pure with perfect love.

With such overt maternal imagery, the connection between matter, *mater*, and mother traced in Naden's Hylo-Idealist prose is certainly foregrounded, and it is compounded as well through the conspicuous /f/ alliteration, which requires a definitive pronunciation that demands attention. The effect of the feminine pronouns in the octave reaches a crescendo here in presenting an empowered mother figure upon whom life depends as it rests within her protective envelopment of its nascent forms.

The sestet's second line relates Earth's anticipation of additional celestial splendor, suggestive of the cosmic energy that Naden identifies in "The Nebular Theory" as well as in essays, energy that replaces God as the giver of life, in similar fashion to the octave. Rather than implying a lack of agency through Earth's "waiting" for the vital event, the line instead recalls Naden's prose commentary that all matter is interfused with cosmic energy as part of a unified whole. Naden's notion of the cycle of life reverberates with the octave's harbinger of resurrection, again evoking religious belief: Christ rose from the dead on the third day through God's will, and mortals ultimately will live eternally in heaven or in hell. In Naden's terms, however, energy is the decisive force as matter continuously recirculates. As Irigaray frames a similar notion, "Life whispers. The earth, like a great nest, houses us, nurses our rebirth."[23]

Resurrection Explored

Naden's particular view of resurrection through the cycle of life is more openly explained in "The Pantheist's Song of Immortality," and a brief aside provides a gloss of sorts to "December, 1879." In "The Pantheist's Song of Immortality," a ten-stanza sequence of quatrains, the narrative voice comments upon a woman's death while observing the body awaiting burial. Chiding a listener not to regret death, the speaker points to the cycle of life as ample compensation:

> Canst thou repine that sentient days are numbered?
>   Death is unconscious Life, that waits for birth:
> So didst thou live, while yet thy embryo slumbered,
>   Senseless, unbreathing, e'en as heaven and earth.

As the poem develops, the speaker assures that one's life is not in vain, for even in death one leaves an "enduring token," and "earth is not as though thou ne'er hadst been." The final two stanzas more overtly relate Naden's perception that all exists within a harmonious whole, again blending Hylo-Idealist thought with religious imagery.

> Yes, thou shalt die: but these almighty forces,
>   That meet to form thee, live for evermore:
> They hold the suns in their eternal courses,
>   And shape the tiny sand-grains on the shore.

> Be calmly glad, thine own true kindred seeing
>   In fire and storm, in flowers with dew impearled;
> Rejoice in thine imperishable being,
>   One with the Essence of the boundless world.

Thus, despite death, existence continues on a different plane through inclusion in the ongoing cycle of life.

Returning to "December, 1879," one sees that the remainder of the sestet proceeds from the resurrection allusions to develop further the embodied spirituality that the matter/*mater* of Earth represents. In the third line, "she lies dreaming of her destined hour" is reminiscent of biblical references to God's relating his will to his subjects through dreams, while the prospect of destiny recalls the statement in Matthew about the fulfillment of scriptures (26:54) and in Luke that "all things must be fulfilled" (24:44). In the sestet's final three lines, religious imagery expands in the description of Earth: "All white and still, most like a soul at rest,

/ Rich in hid wealth, and strong in secret power, / Silent with joy, and pure with perfect love." The color reference in the first of these lines provides an obvious religious connection to purity, which is heightened through the biblical description in Matthew citing the "angel of the lord['s] . . . raiment white as snow" (28:2–3). Underlying the remainder of the line, especially in the context of the two following lines, is another suggestion of resurrection. The stillness suggests death, which provides an additional layer of meaning to the whiteness that could also signify the sepulchral hue of a corpse. The line's continuation noting the resting soul not only conjures a subsequent journey to eternal existence but also reinforces the resurrection imagery through the implicitly intertwined states of death and life. In the next line, the richness seen in the initial phrase stresses the glorification of nature that the poem as a whole is depicting, reminding as well of an altar's accoutrements, such as a chalice, crafted in gold. The line's final phrase intimates a godlike force within nature along with the idea of the empowered mother/*mater* figure and life force that Naden equated with nature. A similar force is noted in the Bible, wherein God is designated as "the greatness, and the power, and the glory" (1 Chron. 29:11). The poem's final line accentuates the religious connection with the godly qualities of ecstasy, purity, and "perfect love," while the opening reference to silence makes another divine connection, as Revelation tells that "there was silence in heaven" heralding the presence of an angelic host (8:1).

The sonnet's dignified iambic pentameter provides an apt meter for a majestic entity, and its rhyme scheme signifies both similarity and difference appropriate to a rewritten creation story. In no way does the poem veer from the idea that nature is neither inferior nor dominated, which compounds the Hylo-Idealist premise of nature both as *mater* and master, in the sense of its embodiment of cosmic force. The plethora of feminine pronouns creates a subversive effect in that the poem not only is undermining a patriarchal deity that is both detached and distanced but also is replacing it with feminized matter as the site of embodied spirituality.

Fluid Thematic

The poem "Springtide" follows a somewhat divergent path to develop the concept of embodied spirituality, although religious references also suffuse this verse steeped in nature imagery, as do various Hylo-Idealist precepts. A key metaphoric strain in "Springtide" is fluidity, which carries multifarious associations to movement, circulation, alteration, and the female body. In the latter connection, Irigaray observes that "historically the properties of fluids have been abandoned to the feminine." The poem's title signals the importance of fluidity through its second syllable. Among its denotations, "tide" indicates the diurnal motions of the waves, a flowing body of water, a fluctuating oceanic force, and an overflowing stream. These varied meanings accord with the poem's messages in that all of these fluidic permutations—fluid being "by nature, unstable," as Irigaray points out[24]—are themselves part of matter. Additionally, a tide is generated by the influence of the moon, which in turn has traditionally served as a symbol of women through the monthly cycles of the body, the most apparent connection to matter among a tide's many linkages. Fluidity also serves to promote the tenets of Hylo-Idealism, for the circulatory aspect of movement connoted by fluidity accentuates the cyclic process underlying the ongoing exchange of energy and matter.

Composed of twenty-two lines, "Springtide" can be divided into its three "sentences" for analytic purposes. The first "sentence" is itself formed from three parts, separated by pauses inserted through punctuation. This section blends nature, fluidal, and religious imagery, with nature given the privileged position of opening the poem and emphasizing the notion of embodied spirituality in this significant representation of matter.

> The silver birch, with pure-green flickering leaves,
> Flooded by morn with golden light, rejoices,
> And mingles with the kindred merriment
> Of perfume-laden winds and happy voices . . .

The birch, with its vigorous leaves a vibrant symbol of life, carries a religious intimation through its "pure" appendages; the hyphenated joining of this adjective with the paradigmatic color of nature, "pure-green," accentuates the religious connection to the material world. The flickering of the leaves is a form of movement as well as a signifier of agency, points that will be developed further in this poetic segment. The flooding of the second line overtly brings fluidity into the poem, and the "golden light" that "rejoices" provides an overdetermined depiction of religiosity, the adjective indicative of sacred implements, the noun a common synonym of "God," and the verb alluding to the worshipping faithful. Fluidity is implied in the third line as well through the verb's denotation of intermixture and the adjectival "kindred" further conveying the joining of entities, in harmonious fashion. The winds of the final line also suggest fluidity by carrying and dispersing scented air. The personification references suffusing the four lines—rejoicing and mingling, kindred merriment, and delighted voices—counter Victorian suppositions of nature as passive and inert.

The personification continues in the next segment of the first "sentence," in this case equating nature with humanity, conferring feelings upon nature, and enabling natural entities to bind together in close communion.

> No child of spring is lonely, but receives
> Some subtle charm, by diverse beauty lent,
> And with another life its own inweaves . . .

Fluidity also is intimated, in that inweaving, or interweaving, brings together disparate elements, altering them in the process as they assume a new form. As the poem continues to complete its first "sentence," another kind of interweaving occurs, in this case through the Hylo-Idealist view that humans are themselves part of matter and that matter gains its existence, in effect, through human cognition. Religious vocabulary—"light" and "glory"—situates matter on an elevated plane: "E'en man's creative eyes win all their gain / From light, whose glory, but for him, were vain." Yet the light here is not identifying divine presence but instead is part of the sunlight referenced in the poem's second line that initiates the activity of nature and thereby gives the verse its substance.

In the second "sentence" of the poem, consisting of seven lines, the workings of cosmic energy constitute the focus.

> While bud the flowers, while May-tide sunshine beams,
> Through all the world of mind and body streams
> One constant rapture of melodious thought,
> One fragrant joy, with summer promise fraught,
> And one eternal love illumes the whole;
> For odour, light, and sound are truthful dreams,
> Inspired by Nature in the human soul.

The first line's "beams" provide an understated link to fluidity in that this beam of light travels from its solar source to the earthly vegetation. The next line conspicuously presents the idea of fluidity through the verb "streams," stressing the importance of fluidity in an investigation of cosmic energy. The conjunction of "mind" and "body" within a single "world" accords with Hylo-Idealism's dissolution of the conventional Victorian division between spirit and matter. Accentuating this unification are the single entities of the next three lines—rapture, joy, and eternal love. Not surprisingly, each of these three entities is also part of religious vocabulary and imparts such a connotation to nature as well. The trio of lines further develops the harmonious union of spirit and matter through the "melodious" aspect and the definitive reference to "the whole," appropriately illuminated in another fluidic image of a sunlight beam. In addition, the joining of thought and fragrance provides an exemplar of spirit and matter coming together in this overdetermined triadic segment of the poem. The penultimate line itemizes three illustrations of matter that foreground sense experience—a crucial process in Hylo-Idealism of indicating how meaning is derived—through the functions of smell, sight, and hearing. The line's phrase "truthful dreams" echoes the biblical recognition of God communicating through dreams, and in the context of Hylo-Idealism raises sense experience to a deified plane. The linkage between sensation and cognition posited by Naden's approach is intimated in the concluding line of the "sentence" through the juncture of nature and humanity. The line again incorporates a religious component through the capitalization of "Nature" and the inclusion of the "soul," which additionally serves to remind that under Hylo-Idealism, religion is conceived from within the human mind rather than proceeding from a detached exterior being. Furthermore, the line reflects Naden's view that humanity is not isolated from nature but instead is part of it. Overall, the "sentence" repeatedly stresses unity, presents nature as a kind of divinity, and erodes conventional religious belief.

The thematic emphases of the second "sentence" resonate in the third as well. In the final "sentence," humanity is firmly incorporated within nature rather than existing apart from it, religious vocabulary abounds, fluidity appears, and monism rather than dualism prevails.

> This fresh young life, whereof my own is part,
> With boundless hope all earth and heaven fills;
> The birds are waking music in my heart,
> A voiceless chant, more sweet than they can sing;
> My thoughts are sunbeams; all my being thrills
> With that exultant joy whose name is Spring.

The first line of this final segment presents the only designated inclusion thus far of a first-person speaker, which to this point has effectually served to foreground nature as an enveloping and authoritative presence. Through the marginalization of a human voice, the line relegates human existence to merely one facet of nature rather than a dominant or superior force. In a way, the poem seems to be presenting a logical progression of Hylo-Idealism's key components that in the final "sentence" are recognized and accepted by the speaker. In considering oneself part of nature, an individual would be recognizing humanity as a component of matter and part of a cosmic unity. The seeming infinitude of circulating energy emerges in the second line of the "sentence" in the "boundless" reference, which is heightened through the linkage once again of earth and heaven, or matter and spirit. The effect of the avian song on the speaker in initiating a kind of internal music resounds with the vital role of the senses in human understanding of the world; even though the speaker proclaims that the "voiceless chant" exceeds the beauty of the birds' song, no human superiority is responsible, in that nature began the whole process. Moreover, the theological association of a chant continues the poem's abundant characterizations of Hylo-Idealism's status as a kind of religion itself and a viable substitute for traditional belief. The penultimate line's characterization of thoughts as sunbeams returns the poem to its opening image of flooding light, creating in the process a Coleridgean impression of an organic whole that accords seamlessly with the notion of cosmic energy as an all-encompassing presence. Indeed, the poem's structure itself—unbroken by individual stanzas—subtly reinforces such unification. The fact that the speaker's "thoughts are sunbeams" serves as a recognition that sense experience stimulates cognition and also provides a metaphor for cosmic energy. In the concluding line, religion is again folded into the poem, not only through the speaker's "exultant joy" but also through the capitalization of "Spring" as a kind of divinity. In the final analysis, with the positioning of nature as a simulacrum of divinity, "Springtide" continuously puts forth a powerful depiction of embodied spirituality. One of Irigaray's musings on springtime provides an interesting gloss: "One . . . imagines angels whispering, souls quivering, while leaves and flowers grow."[25]

Privileging Nature

The sonnet "Sunshine" works with several of the thematic components of "Springtide," but it privileges nature over humanity to a greater degree, thereby reinforcing that humanity is merely a part of nature rather than a separate and superior entity. The similarity between the two poems is signaled by the title of "Sunshine" in its incorporation of the multiple resonances that sunlight also conveyed in "Springtide," as well as the inclusion of spring imagery, religious references, and the workings of cosmic energy. "Sunshine," however, immediately presents nature as privileged over humanity in that the speaker beseeches the sunlight to provide instruction and guidance, as the octave indicates:

> Come, tender sunlight of the spring, and shine
>> Through all my thoughts; my inmost being fill,
>> Teaching my heart to glow, and yet be still,
> With that victorious quiet which is thine.
> Oh that my hand had cunning to combine

> The tints wherewith thou robest copse and hill!
> But I, so rich in love, am poor in skill,
> And praise fair Truth, yet may not build her shrine.

Each pair of the octave's lines stresses nature's preeminence by tracing sunlight's actions upon the speaker: it enters, occupies, instructs, exceeds, and overmatches. Additionally, in suffusing the speaker's thoughts, the sunshine illustrates the Hylo-Idealist principle that all cognition derives from sense experience, as well as the idea that the psychical and physical realms are inseparable. After all, the physical presence of sunshine—part of the cosmic energy—blends with the speaker's inner being to the extent that the division between the two cannot be delineated. Indeed, the structure of the initial quatrain underscores the point with the pattern of indented lines. The second and third lines, which ask for tutelage, are subsumed within the sunlight that is dominating the opening line.

Furthermore, Hylo-Idealist tenets mix with religious forms of address ("thine," "thou") and other deific terminology ("Truth," shrine") to place Naden's philosophy upon a similarly lofty level. Religious verbiage is even heightened in the sestet, marked by "spirit," "worshipping," and "glory," along with more occluded references, such as to seekers of light.

> But every spirit, worshipping aright,
> Must glory in the gifts that others bring;
> So would I triumph—not as one apart,
> But with the kindred throng who love the light,
> Joying in beauty that transcends my art,
> And mutely dreaming notes I cannot sing.

As in the octave, the speaker humbly recognizes the limits of human efforts, paralleled by the power of nature. These realizations bracket the sestet, for they appear in both the opening and concluding pairs of lines. Poised between them and providing the central focus is the idea of unity, which quietly alludes to the presence of the cosmic whole that Naden averred so emphatically. The sestet's indentation pattern accentuates unification; the unindented lines, which overshadow the pairs beneath them, encompass "every spirit" in the first case and "the kindred throng" in the second. The lines with the greatest indentation, and therefore the least dominance, are self-referential. The remaining two lines, with intermediate indentation, again point to human subservience, with an injunction to the speaker ("[m]ust glory") and an obviation of agency ("mutely," "cannot sing").

A Different Eden

In seeming contrast to the poems discussed above, "In the Garden," by its very title, implies an element of ostensible human superiority in that a garden is a confining place that orders and controls nature. To a devout Victorian, the title also could signal the garden of Genesis, which would implicitly insert Christianity's dualistic format, with its presumption of a detached divinity, into a reading of the poem. Yet when filtered through Hylo-Idealism, the sonnet instead displaces conventional religion by situating nature as the source of an embodied spirituality, following several maneuvers also detected in the other poems discussed. The title leads to a very different depiction of an Edenic paradise, one that is devoid of the traditional Christian deity and wholly marked with nature's presence. By situating its message in a cognitive space removed from Christian teleology, "In the Garden" suggests an origin commensurate with the workings of cosmic energy, operating through a universe that follows its rhythms in a seamless unity. Indeed, the poem invokes a kind of pre-prelapsarian world that predates and preempts the Christian narrative to articulate an embodied spirituality derived from the material realm.

The sonnet immediately sets forth a series of sensations that in Hylo-Idealist terms initiate human thought and the resultant individual perceptions of the exterior world. The process is a pleasant one, as the octave's opening line prefaces with its trio of smooth sibilants.

> Sweet sounds, and scents, and colours join to woo
>   My musing heart to love and reverence;
>   A tender and a subtle influence
> Comes from each graceful form, each brilliant hue;
> Strange power have they, my spirit to imbue
>   With thoughts above themselves; for e'en while sense
>   Adores the Beautiful with joy intense,
> The soul, far gazing, only seeks the True.

Embodied spirituality replaces the Christian form in the second line as the speaker adopts terms, "love" and "reverence," associated with God. The line thus establishes nature as a divinity worthy of such homage, thereby undermining cultural presumptions of human superiority that are further upset by the "musing heart." This phrase quietly situates the speaker in an auxiliary rather than dominant position through the adjectival resonance to a muse and its capacity as passive inspiration rather than active agent. As the octave continues, another indirect reference to divinity appears through the phrase "graceful form," with the adjective's first syllable evoking the sanctifying power and assistance of a deity to characterize the "tender" and "subtle influence" of nature's own manifestations. The subsequent line attests to that force in recognizing the "[s]trange power" of nature's grace to infuse the speaker and elevate thought. Religious verbiage punctuates the rest of the octave ("adores," "the Beautiful," "joy intense," "soul," "the True") to accentuate the divine quality of nature and its ability to elevate human cognition. The octave's messages parallel the Hylo-Idealist process in establishing the poem's conception of embodied spirituality: sense experience is the basis of human thought, individuals cannot transcend themselves or the material world to seek an absolute external meaning, and the self creates a deity. With divinity situated in both nature and the human body, then, spirituality is utterly bound to materiality.

In this poem as well as other Naden sonnets about nature, structural components replicate the poetic thematics in oblique ways, even in meter pattern. Iambic pentameter buttresses the idea of embodied spirituality replacing Christianity's detached spirituality; this point becomes clear when one examines the meter's numerical parts. The ten-syllable format brings to mind the Ten Commandments, and the iamb's indication of two parts links to Christ's explanation that on one pair of commandments—loving God and one's neighbor—"hang[s] all the law" (Matt. 22:40). Even the "pent" syllable of "pentameter" applies, as part of "Pentecostal" and its denotation of sects prioritizing individual experience and worship, which in turn fits as well into Hylo-Idealism's emphasis on these self-driven activities. Moreover, a Petrarchan sonnet suggests both origin, as a pattern frequently copied, and variation, as a change from the standard rhyming pattern of the sestet. In these features, a Petrarchan sonnet is a fitting form for "In the Garden"; the embodied spirituality of Hylo-Idealism incorporates originary acts, through the presence of cosmic energy, and variation, with this sonnet's departure from Christian belief.

The sestet shifts focus to cosmic energy as the cycle of life unfolds.

> And ye, fair flowers, translating to my sight,
>> In gold or blue the pure uncoloured beams,
> Are poets and revealers of the light;
> Soon is your message told, your life-work done,
>> For all your tints are only passing dreams
> Of the eternal splendour of the sun.

As in the octave, nature is the active entity here, instructing humanity in the workings of cosmic energy and its return to the source, "the eternal splendour of the sun," once the "fair flowers" perish. Appropriately, in Hylo-Idealist terms, the lesson is transmitted through sensation—the source of all human knowledge—in this case, by means of the speaker's vision. Terminology again creates a religious context for Hylo-Idealism and embodied spirituality, particularly through light imagery. It is evidenced in the specific reference not only to the sun but also to the "pure uncoloured beams" through which the flowers are "revealers of the light." Since light in its unmediated form is colorless, nature acts as a kind of prism to unveil its mysteries to humanity, much as nature does in teaching about the complexities of cosmic energy.[26] As the sestet continues, the agency of nature is reiterated, for it imparts its lesson and completes its mission. Ultimately, the sestet imparts the "True" that the speaker sought in the octave. The sestet does so through the recognition that material nature, as a mortal entity with its ephemeral "tints" and "passing dreams," participates in the rhythms of cosmic energy: the quasi-religious life force in the Hylo-Idealist schematic and the origin of embodied spirituality.

The structure of "In the Garden," like that of "Sunshine," helps to articulate the poem's thematic paths through indentation. The unindented lines subsume the indented ones not only by physical placement but by level of significance. The unindented lines of the octave privilege sense experience, the magnificence of grace imparted by nature, the power of nature to elevate thought, and the soul's imperative to discover truth. The structural format applies to the sestet as well: nature provides a vital translation to convey the crucial "light" to humanity, and the transience of nature evidences its participation in the circulation of energy. With the final line's *s* sibilance, the poem returns to its fluidal opening line and reiterates energy's circulatory operation.

As these multiple analyses of the poetry demonstrate, Hylo-Idealism acted as a foundation for Naden's original conception of embodied spirituality. Reworking Christian imagery and precepts allows matter to take on the trappings of divinity, thereby eliding distinctions between materiality and spirituality. The implication is inescapable: nature, like the divinity worshipped by Christians, deserves the utmost respect and reverence.

CHAPTER SIX

L. S. Bevington
Seeking a Harmonious Relationship

L. S. BEVINGTON's *Key-Notes* FROM 1879 provides an apt subject for the closing chapter of this study as many of the important concepts addressed by the five poets previously discussed come together in her volume. Thus, one can find within its leaves an assimilation within nature, a rejection of domination, a recognition of agency, a disavowal of essentialism, an embrace of embodied spirituality, and a respect for nature's teachings. Overall, *Key-Notes* presents an argument for seeking a harmonious relationship between nature and humanity, which depends upon the acceptance of these tenets as well as others, such as the necessity of understanding humanity's place in the ecosystem, listening to nature's voice, and heeding the lessons of the nonhuman world.

In broad terms, the trajectories of the chapters intersect here to reveal important commonalities in the poetic approaches to the natural realm. The priorities of the writers all proceed from the same underlying convictions, and the particular concerns of each author also permeate the work of the other poets, whether expressed directly or conveyed implicitly. Most evidently, the poets demonstrate a deep respect for and a high valuation of nature, which joins with an unmistakable recognition of its overwhelming beauty and splendor. The poems begin with the assumption that nature is a living and active body, not a tool to be dominated, exploited, essentialized, marginalized, ignored, or underestimated. In sum, these crucial intellectual and emotional currents have surfaced throughout *Reconceiving Nature*, regardless of an individual poet's religious outlook, sexual preference, aesthetic approach, personal causes, educational background, or other factors. Bevington's *Key-Notes* seemingly gathers together the multifarious thematic threads and weaves them into an intricate fabric that illuminates the profound ecofeminist ideas these poets articulated so eloquently. The twelve primary poems of *Key-Notes*, named for the months and accompanied by numerous complementary verses, provide a manifesto of sorts adumbrating significant strains of ecofeminist belief that proponents would articulate many generations later.[1]

Key-Notes opens with an epigraph from Ralph Waldo Emerson, which provided the title for Bevington's text: "Melodious poets shall be hoarse as street ballads when once the penetrating Key-Note of nature and spirit is sounded—the earth-beat, sea-beat, heart-beat which makes the tune to which the sun rolls, and the globule of blood, and the sap of trees." The choice of epigraph not only intimates the British poet's fascination with the natural world, it also reveals her familiarity with the eminent transcendentalist's work. In many respects, *Key-Notes* responds to precepts that Emerson articulated in his 1836 *Nature*, for Bevington's poetry quietly identifies and compellingly interrogates unsettling ideas that are expressed either overtly or obliquely in his occasionally ambiguous first text. Lurking in *Nature*'s interest in the environment and its relation to civilization are problematic issues, primarily concerning the role of humanity, which Bevington's poetry assiduously undercuts in its ecofeminist defense. Serving as both a corrective and a correlative to Emerson's thought, which was extensively disseminated and embraced, *Key-Notes* counters misguided assumptions, erroneous beliefs, and flawed conclusions of *Nature* while evidencing a profound valuation of the natural world.[2]

An early version of *Key-Notes* appeared in 1876, privately printed under the pseudonym "Arbor Leigh." The collection lacked the Emerson epigraph but included religious poetry that the 1879 volume would exclude. Intrigued by nature from childhood, with the environment providing subject matter for her juvenile verse, Bevington would proceed to champion evolutionary interests among other causes in her maturity. Reared in a Quaker atmosphere, though likely not raised in the religion, as Jackie Dees Domingue comments in introducing a collection of the poet's essays, Bevington would dramatically depart from Christianity and turn to atheism. The shift apparently occurred in the timeframe leading to the publication of the later *Key-Notes* edition; previously, while her father was alive, Bevington may have been reluctant to reveal her views, Domingue says. Yet Bevington's assault on religious ideas becomes quite curious when considered in light of the spiritual tone imparted in various *Key-Notes* poems, a point that will be addressed later in this chapter. In this regard, Bevington followed the strategies of Blind and Naden. Ultimately, Bevington became an ardent anarchist, and her writing turned especially to the British movement's causes in efforts to oppose exploitation and protect individual rights. Though supportive of women's issues, Bevington focused instead on problems she saw facing the working class that affected both males and females, Domingue indicates.[3]

In its correspondences to ecofeminism, *Key-Notes* calls for a reconceptualization of nature on a number of "fronts," as it were. First, Bevington's poetry envisions an altered relationship whereby humanity respectfully acknowledges its placement within the natural world, as opposed to viewing itself as separate and superior. As Mary Mellor observes in *Feminism & Ecology*, ecofeminism links nature and humanity within "an interconnected and interdependent whole."

Second, *Key-Notes* rejects a philosophy of domination that privileges human desires over the natural world. Third, *Key-Notes* urges individuals to attend to the voice of nature rather than dismissing it as illusory. Fourth, Bevington's work challenges essentialist conceptions of nature. "To be defined as 'nature,'" as Val Plumwood argues in *Feminism and the Mastery of Nature*, "is to be defined as passive, as non-agent and non-subject." Fifth, *Key-Notes* presents an embodied spirituality that departs from traditional Christian perceptions of a disembodied, detached divinity. The Christian model, comments theologian Sallie McFague, poses harm, "for it encourages a sense of distance from the world, is concerned only with human beings, and supports attitudes of either domination of the world or passivity toward it." Sixth, in accordance with an ecofeminist respect for nature, *Key-Notes* urges a recognition of and an embrasure of the sagacious lessons on improving the human condition to be gleaned from the natural world.[4]

Humanity Integrated within Nature

In the first "front," Bevington's reconceptualization of nature involves the human relationship to that world, and in *Key-Notes*, humanity is subsumed within nature as one of its myriad components, not a distinct entity existing apart from the natural world. As Ynestra King notes in a discussion of feminism and ecology, one ecofeminist tenet holds that "[l]ife on earth is an interconnected web." In "Ecofeminist Literary Criticism," Gretchen Legler remarks on the ecofeminist "effort to reimagine nature and human relationships with the natural world" as involving, in part, "an ethic of caring friendship, or 'a loving eye,' as a principle for relationships with nature." At first glance, Emerson appears to promote an analogous perception that smoothly coincides with Bevington's view. Defining "[t]he lover of nature" as one "whose inward and outward senses are . . . truly adjusted to each other," Emerson asserts that for such an individual, "[h]is intercourse with heaven and earth, becomes part of his daily food." Indeed, nature avers that "he is my creature, and . . . he shall be glad with me." Additionally, Emerson contends that "no disgrace, no calamity" exists that "nature cannot repair." Through nature's influence, "I see all," Emerson states, and he describes experiencing as well a spiritual uplifting whereby "[t]he currents of the Universal Being circulate through me; I am part or particle of God."[5]

Yet further exploration of Emerson's philosophy reveals a sense of separation from nature; humanity exists outside of it, distinguished by exclusionary traits that unequivocally privilege humanity in a comparison. His position surfaces as early as *Nature*'s epigraph, quoting Plotinus that "Nature is but an image or imitation of wisdom, the last thing of the soul; nature being a thing which doth only do, but not know," in an unspoken contrast to human cognition. Emerson underscores the rupture thereafter in arguing that nature can be identified as "the

NOT ME," in emphatic capitals, or "all that is separate from us." Further relegating nature to an inferior stance, although offering the conciliatory comment that "[n]ature never became a toy to a wise spirit," Emerson maintains that nature's diverse components "*reflected* all the wisdom of [the wise spirit's] best hour" (emphasis added). In effect, only through humanity's conferment of significance upon it does nature attain substantive value. Turning to the analogy of an ant, Emerson indicates its unimportance until "a ray of relation is seen to extend from it to man," at which moment the insect "become[s] sublime." Moreover, nature performs a mediating role, serving as "an interpreter, by whose means man converses with his fellow men."[6]

In *Key-Notes*, however, nature suffuses and shapes individuals, as it does the multitude of entities that an Emersonian would consider so dissimilar to humanity. Bevington's speakers recognize that becoming an integral part of nature entails a vital step in the ongoing process of self-development within an imperfect world. Barriers complicating such a perspective prevent growth rather than allow nature to infuse a person's being and illuminate the way to a higher form of consciousness. In "May," for instance, the speaker urges, "Flow May-time into me / And set my soul from its own vision free." In "October," an encomium on death, the speaker intimates that a true path to a meaningful existence stems from participation in the cycles of nature. "January" establishes the tone, as the calendar time that titles each of the twelve major *Key-Notes* poems rapidly dissolves into the ongoing time of nature, rarely appearing within the verse itself, to underscore the objective of absorption in nature. Although the sonnet could be read literally as simply the progression from December to January and the start of a new year, the verse more compellingly reveals a movement to become one with nature. Intimating the vast expanse of geological temporality and perceiving calendar time to be folded within it, the speaker asserts, "Away into the past the minutes slide, / Dies the old year and dies my old distress," as if being subsumed within the time of nature provides a wholly restorative effect. The temporal and resultant psychological transformation is subtly signaled through reference to "the new year," with a "new blessedness" heralded by the workings of nature's elements. Hourly time signified by night's endpoint merges with nature's time in sidereal ambience, as the speaker proceeds to a loftier realm during "frost-bound midnight," when "I will rise, and go / Out in the herald hush where stars move slow, / And wait the new year's calm birth-moment there."[7]

Harmony Replacing Domination

Achieving a sensation of oneness with nature, the *Key-Notes* poems abundantly suggest, requires an unencumbered respect for and an inalterable recognition of shared community rather than an injurious fixation on dominance. With this second "front," Bevington's poetry communicates a consequential facet of the ecofeminist position that decries inappropriate mastery of the environment and urges a reimagining of nature whereby it exists in harmony with humanity. Ecofeminists repeatedly emphasize the necessity for dismantling a domination paradigm, but Emerson disturbingly presumes that outright domination is a human prerogative. Citing nature's "ministry to man," Emerson contends, "All the parts incessantly work . . . for the profit of man." Moreover, "the universe is the property of every individual in it," so that "[e]very rational creature has all nature for his dowry and estate." Thus, "[i]t is his, if he will." Emerson subsequently expands on this philosophy of use value:

> Nature is thoroughly mediate. It is made to serve. It receives the domin-
> ion of man as meekly as the ass on which the Saviour rode. It offers all its
> kingdoms to man as the raw material which he may mould into what is
> useful. Man is never weary of working it up. . . . More and more, with every
> thought, does his kingdom stretch over things, until the world becomes, at
> last, only a realized will,—the double of the man.

Nature's final sentence, in fact, leaves the reader with a disquieting thought in speaking of "[t]he kingdom of man over nature."[8]

Bevington's "April" serves as a harsh indictment of the Emersonian position justifying domination of nature. The structure of the poem itself amplifies the condemnatory content. The first two stanzas suggest a fragmented sonnet and a corresponding annihilation of a harmonious locale. Comprised of fourteen lines, the quasi-sonnet that begins the poem first departs from convention in situating the thematic turn in the midst of the seventh line rather than the customary eighth, which disrupts the typical Petrarchan format of octave and sestet.

In the opening lines, the quasi-sonnet presents a vivid picture of the natural world existing without human interference.

> O sights, and scents, and sounds of this fair earth,
> When Nature has her way unmarred by man!
> From the arched beauty of the rainbow span
> That sheds its lustre through an April hour,
> To yonder lark's intensity of mirth,
> Or the mysterious fragrance of a flower,
> There is no imperfection. It is strange
> That man alone has power to disarrange,
> And, when he will, can mar. Who dare suspect
> This creature, called a "crowning work," with hands

Working the meddling will of intellect,
The more he can do the more he understands

To dim the face of Nature's loveliness,
Or make the sum of all her beauties less!

The sibilance of the first line replicates a peaceful environment, and the triad of sensory experiences conveys its vibrancy. In fact, the apostrophe introducing the line elevates nature to an almost divine level, supplemented on the second line through honorific capitalization and a later indication of perfection. The descriptive phrases situate nature on a comprehensive scale, with its extension to the firmament ("rainbow span") and its origin on the earthen surface ("mysterious fragrance of a flower").

This idyllic picture immediately dissolves into a realm under attack, with the assailant unambiguously identified as "man." The thematic turn positions humanity as a vicious, relentless, and devastating opponent bent on exploiting the natural world and shaping it to brutish human will, fully cognizant of the harmful impact. The passage resonates with William Morris's contentions in "The Beauty of Life" that "civilisation is threatened with a danger of her own breeding" as the unscrupulous seek self-gratification, with the result that they "deprive their whole race of all the beauty of life: a danger that the strongest and wisest of mankind, in striving to attain a complete mastery over nature, should destroy her simplest and widest-spread gifts." The ultimate effect, Morris warned, would be to bring forth a new "barbarism more ignoble, and a thousandfold more hopeless, than the first." Morris spoke further of the "possessions which should be common to all of us, of the green grass, and the leaves, and the waters, of the very light and air of heaven"; however, he added, "the Century of Commerce has been too busy to pay any heed to" these necessities of a rewarding life. Like Morris's admonition, "April" vociferously counters Emerson's implicit approbation of use value's justifying any environmental damage. Similarly, Patrick D. Murphy's essay on ecofeminism decries upholding "use value or exchange value as the criterion of worth" and instead expresses the "need to develop a criterion of ecological value, which emphasizes interrelationship, maintenance, and sustainment."[9]

Like the odd structure of "April," the rhyme scheme is irregular. Beginning with the expected *abb* of the Italian type, the rhyme falls into a disorderly sequence with odd pairings or no pattern at all. Thus, in the first dozen lines the rhymes jump from the *abb* of the first three to *cacddefef* and conclude thereafter with *gg*. Additionally, the final pair of lines forms a detached unit, as if tapping into a Shakespearean sonnet's paradigmatic conclusion in a couplet. The gap serves to punctuate the previous message about the damaging effect and high cost of human intervention in nature for selfish gains. Thus, the misshapen sonnet appearing at the beginning of the poem mimics formally the ruination of the natural world. This broken structure initiates a pattern of damaged sonnet forms that dissolve into chaos as the poem proceeds.

The next section of "April" consists of a quatrain, a "sestet," and a second quatrain, in another variation of a dismembered sonnet. In the first quatrain, only through the absence of individuals bent on control at any cost can the natural world thrive.

> Sweet April morning! by what wide mischance
> Is it that things more lovely are, in fact,
> Where men are few, or steeped in ignorance,
> Than where a crowd of thinkers plan and act?

In the "sestet" of this segment, the consequences of selfish intervention reach a horrific level, equated with tormenting and anguishing treatment, as if nature has been thrown on a metaphoric rack like a medieval prisoner refusing to accede willingly to a disastrous course of action.

> For such mischance is beauty's self a lie?
> Because she shrinks away and seems to die
> When rude man, in the hurry of his need,
> Tortures her into usefulness? when greed
> By twisting fair and good things into gold
> Makes "progress" one with wealth, and young men old?

The passage evokes Frankenstein's nightmarish experiments in the pursuit of self-aggrandizement. Moreover, the poem alludes to the false practice of alchemy and its mistaken assumptions in the hunt for riches by characterizing the transformation of nature as a process of contortion and distortion. As John Ruskin decries in speaking of unworthy human activity in *Sesame and Lilies*, "You have despised nature; that is to say, all the deep and sacred sensations of natural scenery."[10] The implicit reference in "April" to the Marxist idea of use value again appears in attacking the notion of "usefulness" so significant in Emerson's *Nature*.

The poem's reference to "progress," foregrounded and questioned through quotation marks, takes issue with the Victorian veneration of the forward movement that civilization supposedly was following. Indeed, progress took on the contours of an honored mission. To Thomas Babington Macaulay, writing of his influential midcentury assessments of the nation, "[t]he history of England" was synonymously and "emphatically the history of progress." He considered his countrymen "the greatest and most highly civilized people that ever the world saw" and claimed that "great progress [had gone] on" while humanity had "been almost constantly advancing in knowledge." Herbert Spencer asserted that progress is guided by a law promoting an evolution into greater complexity.[11] In "April," however, "progress" merely serves as a synonym for affluence, which not only derives from exploitation of nature but drains the lifeblood of individuals by turning "young men old."

The final quatrain of this sonnet fragment imparts relief that human powers are at least somewhat limited in the abuse of nature. "'Tis well there are some feats beyond our reach," the quatrain begins, and the next pair of lines confirms the point in asserting, "'Tis well we cannot climb the rainbow's arc / With earthly tread, to make its glory dark." The closing line of the quatrain disrupts the pattern of a sonnet conclusion in ending with enjambment rather than definitive resolution. By failing to resolve the thought in the line, the poem initiates an even more intense breakdown of the sonnet form, for the next segment of seven lines exists on its own, without an accompanying fragment to reach fourteen lines. Through this anomaly, the nonconforming stanza becomes foregrounded, and it takes on special urgency as the segment emphasizes the despoliation of nature that wrongful human activity has caused. The final line of the preceding quatrain leads into the irregular stanza that expresses relief; human misguidance cannot be taught to the natural world and thereby replicate the disastrous changes wrought by rampant industrialization, untrammeled growth, and ravaged landscape.

> 'Tis well no art of man can ever teach
>
> The wind and song-bird trammelled, thought-bound speech,
> Or build sick cities on the mighty sea,
> Or make one billow's curve less wildly free.
> And though on earth we crowd achievements so
> That little flowers have hardly room to grow,
> Price-labelled prose may reach not very high;
> We cannot "civilise" and spoil the sky.

The expressed sentiments resonate with Ruskin's admonition in *The Two Paths* about unrestrained exploitation. "[E]very day puts new machinery at your disposal," Ruskin points out, "and increases, with your capital, the vastness of your undertakings." He continues,

[H]ow much of it do you seriously intend within the next fifty years to
be coal-pit, brickfield, or quarry? For the sake of distinctness of conclusion,
I will suppose your success absolute: that from shore to shore the whole of
the island is to be set as thick with chimneys as the masts stand in the docks
of Liverpool: and there shall be no meadows in it; no trees; no gardens; only
a little corn grown upon the housetops, reaped and threshed by steam. . . .
[T]he smoke having rendered the light of the sun unserviceable, you work
always by the light of your own gas: that no acre of English ground shall be
without its shaft and its engine; and therefore, no spot of English ground
left, on which it shall be possible to stand, without a definite and calculable
chance of being blown off it, at any moment, into small pieces.[12]

The next sections of "April" return to the fragmented sonnet form as a glimmer
of hope issues forth that a realization of the harm caused will lead to positive
change. Although the "sonnet" is misshapen, as were the earlier ones, it seems to
augur a rebuilding process that could return a broken sonnet to its proper form.
The last fragment breaks the sonnet structure into a nine-line section followed
by a five-line closure. In this case, although the nine-line piece ends with enjambment and thus the attendant disarray that characterized the similar incom-
plete segment appearing earlier, the gap here suggests more of a gesture toward
mending the sonnet rather than undermining it; the gap seems to be announcing
an optimistic crescendo rather than a despairing descent. The opening phrase
proclaims the thematic alteration to prepare for the desired regret that will lead
humanity away from its detrimental path.

> Yet stay! we weep this beauty that we soil,
> And shrink from turning all our play to toil;
> But this fair thought may shine athwart our tears,
> And hope gleam April-wise on gloomy fears;
> The reign of fitness is not over yet,
> We never wholly lose what we regret.
> If he be man who blots the sunny sky
> With breath of avarice, and smoke of gain,
> Yet man he is who feels relenting pain
>
> For beauty's sickness; hates to see her die.
> The poet in the bosom of the best
> Shall never starve; because the law is just
> By which it lives, in which we put this trust
> That all fair things from final loss Love's Strength may wrest.

The imagery of incessant industrial destruction infuses the first eight lines, with besmirched beauty and a discolored sky, for instance. Greed is depicted as a kind of life force fueling industrial blight through the "breath of avarice," and the supposed "gain" achieved is revealed to be as insubstantial as "smoke." Yet the poetic fragment indicates a positive movement through a progression toward a cohesive sonnet. Following this quasi-octave that delineates environmental devastation comes a turn to the most optimistic part of "April"; thus, the prospective healing of the sonnet form mirrors the thematic optimism of the poem's conclusion.

Another Bevington poem moves from the macrocosmic plane of "April" to the microcosmic level of an individual flower to decry domination. Like "April," "The Story of a Scarlet Flower" denounces exploitation of nature but does so in veiled terms. The latter poem traces the plight of a white blossom from vibrancy to a likely death, as "[a] rude hand plucked it to cast away," the first stanza explains. Composed of tercets, the poem traces the flower's fate in straightforward fashion as the stanzas proceed. Although thrown to a roadside, the flower survives, "deeply wounded, and yet not slain," but reveals "a scarlet stain" from its mistreatment. As an emblem of nature despoiled by human interference, the flower suffers repeated abuse. "[T]he soul of the flower was perishing," the poem advises, for "[s]ome trampled it down in the race for wealth" and would "breathe the breath of its poisoned health." With the continued assault, "the flower-soul bled, and bled," as "[t]he white soul prisoned beneath the red" begged for help while it lingered on the edge of death. Ultimately, this representation of nature is recovered by a passer-by who recognizes its fate and vows to "give thee tenderest, sternest care" until "thy petals grow white and exceedingly fair." The nurturing succeeds, "[a]nd the scarlet cooled to a purer hue; / Till the white flower soul looked sweetly through." With this positive outcome, the poem offers the prospect that the natural world can be recuperated through an attitudinal change from domination to preservation.

One technique in *Key-Notes* that argues against unseemly domination of nature is that it frequently places humans in a peripheral position, whereas the natural realm occupies the foreground. Plumwood speaks of the prevalent practice of "backgrounding," which relates to the traditional feminizing of nature that places it, as well as women, in a subordinate role deemed inferior to the masculinized realm of culture. Nature, like women, serves as a background for male human endeavor in this process of "instrumentalisation," says Plumwood.[13] Such an approach works as a tactic of subjugation because nature becomes merely an insignificant setting against which human activity can be highlighted as the primary focus of interest. In Bevington's work, however, human presence is often minimized by being situated on the margins of a poem, whether in terms of stanzaic locale or degree of activity. "February," for example, relegates human entry into the poem almost entirely to the second of two stanzas. "March" calls attention to an individual merely in passing as a metaphor for a flower's delicacy; direct mention of humanity occurs only deep within the poem, while the emphasis even there remains on natural elements. Similarly, "July" situates nature as the opening and prevalent form of imagery, with the human questioning of "Purpose" emerging periodically but being overshadowed by natural sights and sounds. Exceptions to this marginalizing practice tend to appear when Bevington is stressing human inferiority in relationships with nature.

These poems additionally portray nature as highly active, as opposed to the passive depiction that generally signals inferiority in literary and other contexts, and activity is a vehicle for foregrounding nature. Bevington's verse not only configures nature as an agent but also reverses the scenario of a supposed human superiority by appropriating human traits and conferring them on nature. In effect, human manifestations lose power and instead nature becomes relatively more puissant. Predicates and other parts of speech depict nature's workings to suggest not a personification of nature that would place it in a submissive position as a means of harnessing it within language but a wresting away of the dominating verbiage. Rather than simply reversing the domination binary, the approach provides a way to reevaluate nature as an active presence. "January," for example, indicates that a nascent bud can "hide" hope, "caress" the flower's boundary, and "bless" the season's harsh qualities. "February" comments upon a "[s]pring-smile" and a "weeping" sunrise. "March" reveals that a frail flower, "[l]inked hand in hand" with the mighty wind, demonstrates "courage to be lovely in the cold" and "wakes into a smile." In "June," harebells are "nodding" and defiant, oaks are "dividing," and flowers "thank" and are "[s]o busy." The poem "October" witnesses the earth "lying patiently" while "summer holds / A failing hand," "meet[s]" winter, "smiles" as its life ebbs, and "bids" the autumn to "mourn." The speaker of "September" cedes virtually all agency to nature, asking that it take control, and the poem minimizes the human presence with diminutive descriptions. The second stanza says, for example, "Ah! mellow splendours of the autumn day, / Do with me all the life-ward things ye may; / Kindle me." The short third stanza and the beginning of the fourth beseech the evening,

> O star-specked purple of the autumn night!
> *Hint* all thou canst of purpose infinite,
> *Even in my small spirit's* human strife,
>
> Even in *my so ragged little life.*
> *Prop up* the habit of unseeing trust,

That hopes in goodness just because it must.
(emphasis added)

Language and Silence

The many examples illustrating nature's agency and lessons in Bevington's poems imply that the natural world communicates through a unique kind of language. In this third "front" of *Key-Notes*, the language is transmitted not only through a host of sounds but also through nonverbal cues. In "July," for example, the brief second stanza and opening lines of the third stanza make that point.

> A heaped-up blackness gathers in the west
> As the sun dips, and July's dewless night
> Grows thundrous as it ages. Hours for rest
>
> Are loud with clamour, lanced with lurid light,
> And fitful, frenzied gusts, all armed with hail,
> Deafen the darkness.

Nature's language, in whatever form, conveys meaning and holds value on its own terms, without assuming an intermediary role whereby it simply represents raw material to be manipulated into coherence as symbolic of larger human concerns. To Emerson, in contrast, nature's communications hold no value until filtered through human cognition into a viable source of meaning. Emerson begins his chapter "Language" in *Nature* by asserting that one "use which Nature subserves to man is that of Language," especially in a spiritual register. Thus, "[t]he use of the outer creation is to give us language for the beings and changes of the inward creation," which Emerson accentuates in asserting that "[e]very natural fact is a *symbol* of some spiritual fact" and "[e]very appearance in nature corresponds to *some state of the mind*" (emphasis added). Furthermore, Emerson claims, "All the facts in natural history taken by themselves, have no value, but are barren like a single sex"; however, "marry [natural history] to human history, and it is full of life." In effect, "the whole of nature is a metaphor of the human mind."[14]

In disavowing nature's utterances, Emerson's appraisal brings to mind the "Protagoras Myth." As David W. Gilcrest explains in a study of environmental poetics, the myth accords humans higher status than nature because of language skills. In one view cited by Gilcrest, the myth "serves to distinguish between 'dumb' creation and the linguistically cultured species" of humans. Christopher

Manes makes the related point in "Nature and Silence" that the cultural estima-
tion of humans as the sole speaking entities requires that nature itself be considered as silent. In the course of Western civilization, Manes maintains, nature has
been transformed from its animistic status as "a shifting, autonomous, articulate
identity that cuts across the human/nonhuman distinction," wherein human
speech is simply "a subset of the speaking of the world" rather than an exclu-
sive trait. He locates the perceptual change beginning in the medieval era with
the dissolution of the animistic viewpoint and the rise of humanism during the
Renaissance. "[N]ature has grown silent in our discourse," Manes remarks, and
humanism's reverence for rational thought and cognitive ability ultimately has
led to "an immense realm of silences, a world of 'not-saids' called nature." The
acceptance of the Great Chain of Being added to the belief in human superiority,
and with the Renaissance, Manes observes, humanity alone received credit for
speech. With that supposition came the perception that nature does not speak,
Manes explains. As Luce Irigaray says, speech has been privileged over silence,
with nature and women scornfully relegated to the latter category.[15]

Instead of Emerson's judgment that nature is wholly mediated and valuable
only in terms of its service to human cognition, Bevington's "July," as well as
other verses in *Key-Notes*, offers a far more productive assessment in considering
nature as a speaking subject. In that regard, Bevington's poetry resonates with
modern theorizations of nature's own forms of language, beginning with a premise that Patrick Murphy describes as the "need to recognize the existence of the
'other' as a self-existent entity, a thing-in-itself." If nature is considered a speaking
subject, however, the question arises as to the way that speech is conveyed, since
it will always be filtered through human language. To Murphy, "[t]he point is not
to speak for nature but to work to render the signification presented us by nature
into a verbal depiction by means of speaking subjects." As a result, he says, nature
can become a speaker rather than simply the linguistic object, which requires
humans to communicate nature's stories more effectively. Yet this objective is not
easily attained. As Catriona Sandilands inquires, "[W]hat is the authentic voice
of nature?" Any transmission of the voice means mediating it so that it becomes
understandable, Sandilands argues. Michael J. McDowell similarly acknowledges
in an ecological piece, "Every literary attempt to listen to voices in the landscape
or to 'read the book of nature' is necessarily anthropocentric" since "[i]t's our
language . . . and we inevitably put our values into the representation."[16]

Offering an approach for responding to the difficulty of transmitting nature's
voice is Gilcrest's assessment of a viable "spokesperson." Gilcrest rejects the notion
that a desirable "'spokesperson' for nature is one that *speaks as* the nonhuman"

in favor of "one [who] *speaks for* the nonhuman by *speaking on its behalf.*" Thus, the preferred position is championing nature's cause, Gilcrest says, not presuming a mimetic role. Like Murphy, Sandilands, and McDowell, Gilcrest cites the difficulties inherent in an attempt to present nature's voice since it is necessarily filtered and shaped by human language. Nevertheless, the effort can help humanity form a more mindful relationship with nature, he suggests.[17]

Bevington's "Summer Song" grapples with this vexing issue of communication by urging an individual to listen intently to nature's voice and seek to convey it as accurately as is feasible. Like Alice Meynell through her ecopoetics, Bevington validates an immersion in nature to understand its workings. Composed of four tercets, "Summer Song" mimics the structure of a song, with each stanza resembling a different group of notes. The poem's first two lines are characterized by sibilance that suggests the smooth lyrical quality of a pleasurable song: "Sing! Sing me a song that is fit for to-day, / Sing me a song of the sunshine, a warm sweet lay." The sense experiences of these lines—sound, vision, and a form of touch through warmth—are supplemented in the stanza's third line by the smell of hay, as well as additional sight imagery designating the hues of "[b]lue larkspur, and bold white daisies."

The middle stanzas proceed to set out the steps needed for creating the song, with sense experience again stressed. In the second stanza, the speaker counsels that nature must be absorbed as if providing the breath of life and that the lessons nature offers must be heeded. In the third stanza, the speaker's advice takes on greater urgency through a series of commands.

> Breathe: breathe into music a summer-day tune,
> Learnt of the bloom-heavy breezes and honey of noon,
> Full of the scent, and the glow, and the passion of June.
>
> You shall sit in the shadow to learn it, just under the trees;
> You shall let the wind fan you and kiss you, and hark to the bees;
> You shall live in the love-laden present, and dream at your ease.

As the poem moves into its final stanza, nature joins in the song as if signaling approval of its construction, and the final line reprises the sibilance of the poem's opening.

> And skylarks shall trill all in concert up, up in the blue,
> And the bee and the lazy-winged butterfly dance to it too,
> While you sing me a song of the summer that's ancient and new.

With the closing phrase, the poem indicates that while nature endures, it remains fresh through generations, and the song mimics the harmony that the individual lines have conveyed.

Another poem, "A Song of Silence," could serve as a response to Renaissance humanism and the centuries-long inheritance of its tenet that nature is mute and lacking any pretense to the linguistic ability that elevates humanity above the nonhuman world. Yet, as Irigaray contends, silence "is, or it creates, a place where we finally can listen to the other," where "I can listen to the music of the wind in the leaves, and also to the sound of the wood." These comments help to explain the seeming oxymoronic title of Bevington's poem, in that silence would seem incapable of presenting any form of song or other linguistic act. However, the poem repeatedly emphasizes the speaker's recognition of and attentiveness to nature's multifarious languages that belie the presumption of silence. With that rationale, the ballad form of the poem seems entirely consistent with its theme. Relevant here is Irigaray's revelation "I enjoy listening to the earth," for "[i]n listening I rediscover bliss, the wonder of attentive perception, the happiness of sonorous flesh." To Irigaray, nature's voice, "[n]either sound nor words, . . . is animated silence." Bound with nature's voice is the underlying agency that produces it. "Where it seems that nothing exists, there remains one presence, or a thousand," she says.[18]

In "A Song of Silence," noun and verb forms of hearing repeatedly promote mindful listening to natural surroundings. Surprisingly, though, the sources of sounds appear chimerical owing to their seeming impossibility. Through this fantastical impression, however, the poem defamiliarizes the natural world as a means of jarring humanity into reevaluating the misguided impression of a silent environment. Along with repetition of the reactions of hearing and listening that suffuse the poem comes a picture of a highly active nature. In contrast, the speaker occupies an ancillary position as one absorbing the ambient sounds. Despite multiple iterations of "I" and its accompanying placement as the subject of poetic sentences, the speaker is merely a receptor and exists on the periphery of nature's actions.

The change in perspective whereby an individual becomes aware of nature's form of language requires an entirely new way of assessing one's surroundings in "A Song of Silence," which the speaker signals in the poem's opening pair of lines. They present a kind of leap into and acceptance of an unrecognized linguistic capacity of nonhuman elements in announcing, "Over the edge of silence / My hearing went tripping one day." The lines usher forth a catalog of unexpected sounds, as the speaker comments, "And I heard all the tiny laughter / Of tiniest lives at play." In addition to the unexpected laughter comes the sound of growth in the second quatrain, characterizing various types of verbiage and the startling noise as a flower is born, amplified by persistent /b/ alliteration.

> I heard the rhythm of growing
> Wherever the herbage stood,
> Wherever the flowers blossomed
> The boom of the bursting bud.

The sheer breadth of the natural world is depicted through the poem's movement from this ground-level activity to considerably higher land in the third stanza, which is followed by a progression further upward to the stellar universe in the fourth quatrain. In so doing, the poem emphasizes its point that nature in its entirety carries a kind of linguistic capacity that an alert listener can learn to recognize and appreciate. The third quatrain locates its interest at an apex, "high on a cloud-capt upland." Synesthetic experience also emerges in the third quatrain, as the speaker contemplates the snowy ground where glittering snowflakes are not merely seen but heard: "I found the beauty of snow, / I heard how the crystal sparkles, / I heard how the crystals grow." As in the second quatrain, the stanza calls attention to nature's growth process, which seems an odd attribution for snow crystals. Yet the unexpected reference furthers the poem's defamiliarization, especially since the subsequent stanza indicates that the growth occurs at the unexpected time of night, when the sun's nurturing and reflecting rays have long disappeared.

In the fourth stanza, the range of nature's language is made infinite through its extension into the stellar realm of the universe.

> All night, while the far stars twinkle
> A crisp, clear tune of their own;
> Till clouds grow crimson at dawning
> To a major, mellower tone.

Again, synesthesia intertwines the sense experiences. The glimmering of the stars changes from a phenomenon registered through vision to one comprehended by sound. In similar fashion, the altered coloration of the clouds to a "major . . . tone" also transfers the sense response from sight to hearing. As in the two previous stanzas, the growth process is noted, in this case with the clouds' transformation in hue.

The final stanza equates the harmony of nature with music, as in "Summer Song," and each element of the nonhuman world contributes to the majesty of its supposed silence. The reader is again spurred to hear nature's voice and its fused components.

> The world is all set to music;
> O listen, listen with me!
> Each separate life is a thread of song,
> And the whole is a symphony.

Aside from the revelatory world that "silent" nature presents, the poem carries an implicit warning to attend to its voice. To an animist, nature is "a world of autonomous speakers whose intents . . . one ignores at one's peril," Manes notes. Moreover, listening to nature's voice engenders in humans the desire to protect the nonhuman environment. As Hans Peter Duerr asserts in a book on humanity and nature, "[P]eople do not exploit a nature that speaks to them."[19]

Repudiating Essentialism

As this study's introductory chapter imparted, the disparate approaches associated with ecofeminism have traditionally adhered to the belief that nature and women experience an oppression connecting the two entities in significant ways. *Key-Notes*, however, does not directly address this shared subjugation but instead concentrates on the cultural perspective regarding nature virtually alone. Nonetheless, the poetry undermines essentialist concepts holding that nature, like women, can be reduced to a homogenous, immutable, and inferior essence that sweepingly defines and constrains members of a group, thereby ignoring individual differences and departures from an ostensible norm. In effect, *Key-Notes* recuperates nature from the delimiting essentialist perceptions that have customarily marginalized it through supposed similarities to women experiencing their own devaluation.

Essentialism leads to the fourth "front," which undercuts cultural perceptions of a readily delineated essence of a feminized nature, attached to materiality and literality. Margaret Homans's distinctions between the literal and figurative conceptions of nature are instructive here, as illustrated in her *Women Writers and Poetic Identity* by her discussion of the work of Dorothy Wordsworth, in contrast to the verse penned by her brother William. In William Wordsworth's view, "an imbalance of power" invariably exists "between the mind and nature, in favor of the mind"; that is, as Homans puts it, "[n]ature teaches him to look beyond nature." Dorothy Wordsworth, however, valued "an absolute transparency of language," even "exclud[ing] from her vocabulary any language that would permit symbolic readings of nature." Homans succinctly characterizes the different outlooks in

this manner: "William looks at nature for the sake of the mind, whereas Dorothy
. . . looks at nature for its own sake." Rather than privilege the imagination in a
binary relationship, Dorothy "turns the possibility of a creating self back toward
nature." To William, nature attained value through the mechanism of the mind,
while for Dorothy, the significance rested in nature considered simply on its own
terms. Dorothy's writing evidences effort to present the natural world without an
overwhelming human presence, Homans observes. Dorothy's language aims to
project a reverence for nature rather than attempting to overwhelm it, Homans
relates.[20]

Such a perspective unsettles traditional gender-based comparisons deeming
the figurative as the superior component of the dichotomy formed with the literal. Another Homans text, *Bearing the Word*, asserts that women are conventionally linked to the literal realm, as they supposedly are bound to the natural
and material world, whereas men are connected with "the more highly valued
figurative" arena. In this scenario, the literal is associated with error and a failure
to understand properly and thus serves as a marker of inferiority. In a Lacanian
register, Homans points out that "[t]he symbolic order . . . depends on the identification of the woman with the literal" as well as "the denial that the literal has
any connection with masculine figurations." Literality, with its supposed correspondences to femininity, materiality, and nature, occupies "a position just outside language," functioning as "the object to which the figure refers but that the
figure sanitarily replaces."[21]

Bevington's poetry, however, reclaims the literal and accords it primary attention. Instead of seeing nature as merely serving as an emblem of meaning through
the workings of the mind, her poetry recognizes and values nature for its own
sake. *Key-Notes*'s "June," for example, observes "the most beautiful brightness of
dewdrop-filled daisies at dawn," the "fullness of life in the flowers," and the "joy
in the fledgling's new flight." "December" stresses the point in the penultimate
stanza:

> Meanings are made and fastened by our moods,
> Things only mean themselves; each fact proclaims
> By its existence, but that it exists:
> What is—not what it stands for—is the theme
> Of Nature's teaching.

Poem after poem depicts the particularities of natural elements in expressive detail that enables appreciation on this literal plane, without reducing nature to its
use value in the imaginative process.[22]

The implicit association of nature and women, seen with the literal/figurative dichotomy, carries profound implications for cultural perceptions of the environment. Emerson's text on occasion feminizes nature, referring to "her secret" and "her first works," for instance, additionally recognizing "my beautiful mother." Of course, Bevington's later contemporaries, literary and otherwise, followed the practice in also considering nature as female, and nineteenth-century writing is replete with references according feminine traits to nature. With few exceptions, however, Bevington avoided gendering nature as female, generally adopting the feminine pronoun only as a means of accentuating and protesting traditional devaluations of the natural world.[23] In breaking apart nature's customary connection with women and the delimiting gender affiliations involved, *Key-Notes* can position nature in a far more advantageous manner to transcend the presumed connection to inferiority and subjugation.

Bevington does feminize nature in a few instances in *Key-Notes*, however. In "April," nature receives the feminine pronoun on multiple occasions, which at first glance seems to contradict the notion that Bevington's poetry upsets the feminization of nature. Yet "April" juxtaposes feminized nature against masculinized culture to underscore and interrogate the adversarial relationship that has long existed. With the feminine pronoun, the poem foregrounds the harmful dichotomy that enables culture to dominate and damage nature. Although "June" also gives the earth a feminine pronoun, the effect is to call attention to its inappropriate invocation and a subsequent resolution. The opening stanza adopts the conventional gendering of nature, as the "earth shakes her short sleep away, / And turns her to meet the long future of one more intense summer day." As the poem lists natural elements in positive terms, no gendered pronouns appear. The next reference to "earth," coming as the poem moves toward its conclusion, establishes a contrast between the magnificence of nature detailed to this point and the conventional derision accorded it as a dangerous and ominous presence: "Things seem all youthful and faithful, and life all earnest and glad; / Who can believe 'tis the same old earth men say is so sinful and sad!" The poem's only other gendered reference comes in the penultimate stanza, which comments, "So certain the bee is of finding the sweetness her life has desired." The choice of the bee is an interesting one, for in reality it is the female that performs the labor, which breaks apart customary assumptions of male rather than female work when considered in the human realm. Also complicating gender affiliations is the fact that the worker bee usually does not reproduce because it is infertile. Another gendered pronoun appears in "March," but it is not a feminine pronoun and it is not to impose conventional terminology upon nature. The pronoun instead refers to divinity in nature, following the customary identification of God—specifically named in the poem—as male.

Bevington further suggests a new means of appraising nature without essentialist complications in utilizing ungendered speakers. Such poems provide no hints as to the speaker's biological sex, for the situations related apply to any individual. Although frequently the first-person singular pronoun appears, the poems give equivalent emphasis to the first-person plural pronoun, which suggests a strategic maneuver. With ample references to "I" and "me," the poetry situates the reader on a localized level, encouraging personal absorption and involvement in a verse's particular scenario. Meanwhile, the frequent usage of "we" and "our" helps to create the genderless shared ground, for the pronouns imply unfettered inclusiveness whereby every reader can experience a sense of common involvement in a poem's concern. Occasional addresses to natural elements with the second-person pronoun heighten the reader's feeling of participation in a poem's movement as well, while establishing communication with nature on a level plane where speaker and listener meet on the metaphoric shared ground. In some cases, the archaic form of "ye" or "thy" appears, suggesting respectfulness to the entity being cited. By generally refraining from third-person pronominal forms, the poetry avoids a sensation of separation that an omniscient voice imparts with its authoritative stance. Instead, Bevington's poetry continually strives to promote a feeling of desired community through its speakers' words.

Embodied Spirituality

The fifth "front" of Bevington's ecofeminism centers on embodied spirituality, as was presented in the discussion of Constance Naden's materialist work. Embodied spirituality comes from a substantively different perspective than traditional Christian thought. Although at first glance the two approaches may seem alike in that both adopt conventional religious terms in describing spiritual states, they are based on very different foundations. Proponents of embodied spirituality speak of the need to "reshape the concept of God," as theologian Rosemary Radford Ruether phrases the idea in referencing theologian McFague's view, to move from a male divinity separated from and dominating nature to a conception whereby God nourishes the earth in its entirety. This approach reassesses traditional understanding of spiritual being so that divinity and the earth are no longer divided, Ruether states. The world is reframed as a divine body requiring dutiful attention, asserts McFague, and through this reconfiguration, nature becomes a sacred site. The concept of embodied spirituality can illuminate Bevington's occasional adoption of religious verbiage, which otherwise seems odd coming from an individual who turned from Christianity; however, the spiritual language suggests that the natural world deserves an elevated status and a deep respect, which conventional Christian thought confers upon sacred entities.[24]

The ecofeminist emphasis on embodiment initiates as well a breakdown of the figurative/literal dichotomy seen earlier in regard to the role of nature either as a tool for imaginative development or as a material entity valuable in itself. A gender aspect pertains to spirituality also, in that the Christian divinity is male; with masculinity associated, in part, with abstract and higher-level thought in Western civilizational history, a sharp contrast exists in regard to the literal, material world. In Christianity resides a definitive antithetical relationship between idealized heaven—a disembodied realm populated by formless and pure souls—and the material world of earth, bound to negative associations of sinfulness, error, and physicality. With the traditional coupling of materiality and women in Western thought, this inferior realm of the physical world is consigned to the lesser sphere of the literal. With embodied spirituality, however, that division breaks apart, for this spirituality is inextricably allied with materiality. The gender binary cannot endure as the figurative slides into the literal.

The recognition of spiritual presence that appears in Emerson's *Nature* is related in much different terms than the embodiment approach yet at first glance may not seem particularly problematic. Emerson approvingly quotes, for example, the premise that "visible nature must have a spiritual and moral side," and he validates "[a] life in harmony with nature, the love of truth and of virtue." Additionally, Emerson avers that "nature [is] always the ally of Religion." "[M]oral law," he posits, "lies at the centre of nature and radiates to the circumference," constituting "the pith and marrow of every substance, every relation, and every process." However, various observations, which he presented in rather ambiguous language, seem to diminish nature by again considering it inferior to humanity. Emerson states that "[t]he world proceeds from the same spirit as the body of man," but the intimation of equivalent significance immediately dissolves with the apparent disclaimer that "[i]t is a remoter and inferior incarnation of God, a projection of God in the unconscious." Although appearing as "the present expositor of the divine mind," the world "is a fixed point whereby we may measure our departure," he says. Once again, nature seems to be relegated to the role of a mediator or a vehicle in service to human objectives, as the following passage suggests:

> We learn that . . . behind nature, throughout nature, spirit is present; that spirit is one and not compound; that spirit does not act upon us from without, that is, in space and time, but spiritually, or through ourselves. Therefore, that spirit, that is, the Supreme Being, does not build up nature

around us, but puts it forth through us, as the life of the tree puts forth new branches and leaves through the pores of the old. As a plant upon the earth, so a man rests upon the bosom of God; he is nourished by unfailing fountains, and draws, at his need, inexhaustible power. Who can set bounds to the possibilities of man?[25]

Bevington's "September," however, provides a decided contrast in appraising nature, in part by the poem's resemblance to a prayer, in multiple configurations: a beseeching tone, imparted in one instance through the reference to "thine"; the intimation of divine illumination conveyed through the introductory image of the sun's light; and the supplicatory predicates "show" and "teach" reinforcing the desire for guidance. The beginning of the second stanza reiterates this plea, with the speaker asking,

> O to be patient still, in gentle faith!
> To smile with no defiance in the heart,
> To deem that whole of which my life is part
> Worthy my life's expense.

The language of devotion appears, with the apostrophic opening and line-ending reference to belief, as well as the speaker's willingness to recognize the self as part of a larger "whole." The thematic elements wind throughout the poem, with religious vocabulary abundantly invoked in portraying nature's guiding effect on human endeavor and a desirable submersion of self to its workings.

"March" provides another trenchant lesson involving spiritual connection, revealing a special presence within nature through the conjunction of antithetical qualities designating power and fragility. The idea of unity emerges in the opening two lines' parallel format, their stated connection, and the equivalent attention from the divinity traced through the stanza: "Wild winds of March! ruthless and stern, and cold: / Wild flowers of March! that tenderly unfold." The poem begins by establishing a binary between strength and weakness, but the uneven conflict between these opposites gradually dissipates through a recognition that one spirit governs them both and enables them to coexist productively. In the first of two stanzas, the "blustering" March winds carry "a voice of sovereign fury" in their "rudest breath." In contrast, the flowers, which will "tenderly unfold," resemble "a peasant's child" in their vulnerability. Despite the obvious disparity in strength between the wind and the flower, the stanza moves quickly from this difference to stress that they "come ye thus together" because "[o]ne speaks in both"; this "god is everywhere" and governs "the strong and weak with equal care." This point resonates with the biblical reference to the wind as a representation of God:

"And suddenly there came a sound from heaven as of a rushing mighty wind" to the apostles, whereby "they were all filled with the Holy Ghost" (Acts 2:2, 2:4). "March" identifies the wind with a masculine pronoun, later capitalized to "God." The poem argues in the second stanza, "One law demands the twain," which enables the bud to survive the bitter wind and to flourish. In asserting that "God is in the wind, / As in the still small voice with which meanwhile / The meek, pale primrose wakes into a smile," the poem locates a spiritual element flowing through nature. Indeed, "a still small voice" is a biblical phrase (1 Kings 19:12). That presence affirms the ability of nature to serve as a model and guide to humanity, as the speaker apostrophizes, "O little flower! teach me to be bold, / And, like thyself, keep courage in life's bitter cold!"

In comparable fashion, "July" stresses the harsh aspects associated with nature in an unrelenting catalog. As in "March," the wind is a prime image, manifested in the opening stanza as "a savage, sudden gust," a force that "flings aloft a dust / Choking the thirsty leaves," and in the third stanza as "fitful, frenzied gusts, all armed with hail" so intense that they "[d]eafen the darkness." Such dismal sights and sounds bring to the speaker a sense of dismay that causes a questioning of a spiritual component, with the speaker wondering later in the third stanza, "Did we not sing of Purpose over-soon, / Judging too hopefully the light o'erhead?" in the far more harmonious spring. The speaker immediately chides, however, that such a response ignores the "equal truth in gloom" and asks in the final stanza, "O soul! that trembles lest it lose its trust / Must thou doubt Goodness if thou wouldst be just?" The "soul" is readily informed that "murk earth-clouds, muttering this sultry night" conceal a calm sky that will reappear, indicating thereby in the poem's closing lines that "the quiet smile / Of heaven was there, though hidden, all the while."

One could speculate on the different spiritual approaches adopted by Bevington and Emerson, attributing the diversity in part to the two writers' gender status, which could explain the former's ecofeminist embodied perspective and the latter's disembodied view. Another possible reason stems from the writers' nationalities and the assumption that worldviews could be molded to some extent by the divergent cultural discourses encompassing the two individuals and their dissimilar ways of processing the world around them. Bevington's ideas were primarily filtered through evolutionary thought, grounded in scientific objectivity; in contrast, Emerson's opinions were shaped by the tenets of transcendentalism, based on subjective judgments of one's placement in the universe. An evolutionary scenario is concerned with a particularized, close-up analysis of the elements of nature—in effect, an interest in embodiment—whereas a transcendental schematic is directed toward a more generalized, amorphous inquiry of human judgments about the world at large.[26]

Heeding Nature's Lessons

Critical to achieving a unity with nature, which Bevington's poetry so carefully endorses, is perceiving nature as a model for behavior and learning from the many lessons being relayed. Indeed, this final "front" involves another aspect of an ecofeminist respect for nature. Numerous *Key-Notes* poems underscore the significance of nature's teachings and the need for humans to perceive its realm as a potential source of wisdom. Nature becomes a wise text deserving attention, setting out through wide-ranging examples the desirable paths for an individual to follow.

For Emerson, however, the text of nature apparently served as a resource to be plundered. Although he asserts that "[a] life in harmony with nature, the love of truth and of virtue, will purge the eyes to understand her text," Emerson then imparts a sense of penetration. "By degrees we may come to know the primitive sense of the permanent objects of nature," he writes, "so that the world shall be to us an open book, and every form significant of its hidden life and final cause." The remark brings to mind Frankenstein's "fervent longing to penetrate the secrets of nature" as he "pursued nature to her hiding-places" in aggressive fashion. In decided contrast, Bevington's poems provide insights into nature's teachings, explicating the wealth of knowledge stored within diverse components that a respectful and educable student should value. As Donna Haraway observes, "The codes of the world are not still, waiting only to be read," for "[t]he world is not raw material for humanization."[27] In Bevington's "June," for example, the speaker announces, in the second stanza, not an invasive agenda but an attentiveness and willingness to absorb the teachings of nature's text.

> I will hark to the innocent secret in whisperings of tall, flowered grass,
> I will read the white lesson of daylight in breeze-wreathed clouds as they
>   pass,
> And, with fullest surrender of spirit to the free efflorescence of
>   things,
> I will think not a thought that is duller than glint of a dragon-fly's
>   wings;
> My heart shall be tender and trustful, and hold not a heavier care
> Than a butterfly, fluttering 'mong roses at noon, might carry, nor
>   know it was there.

Through an immersion in nature, then, humanity undergoes a transformative effect that dramatically enhances the quality of life.

A primary lesson of nature in *Key-Notes* addresses human despair, proceeding in part from an individual's limited vision and self-absorption. "February," for instance, opens with a bleak picture indicating "days of greyness and of gloom," with "the heavens expressionless and sad," and subsequently invokes funereal imagery in noting that a sign of spring "has not yet freshened from the tomb." The movement of the poem entails a descent paralleling the emotional fall that despair engenders. Other images reiterate the point, as when the "gleamy sunrise" deteriorates "mostly into weeping [and] melts away" onto "every dripping, leafless bough." However, the birds perched upon the branches continue their song with an instinctive realization "that yet again / Life shall grow lovely," which precludes the question a person would ask as to "how?" along with the query's accompanying sense of discomfort. The birds' acceptance of the patterns of life contrasts sharply with the human disinclination to do so, encumbered as humans are by an inability to see beyond personal difficulties and a narrow scope. Equally divided into a pair of twelve-line stanzas, the poem moves from the situation of the bird to that of the person in the final line of the first stanza by referencing "[w]e, self-bound, human weaklings!" The placement of the human at the end of the stanza otherwise devoted to the natural realm reflects the need for people to perceive themselves not as being separated from nature but as needing to heed its examples of profitable existence and

> Of hardly-garnered, inward hopefulness.
> So to translate a present dim distress
> To mean "the future shall but shine the more."
> 'Tis what we know, and what we partly know
> Hinders our sight, at times when, dim and grey,
> Soulless as death, shrivels the bloom away
> From lovely things; and if our hope would go
> Further than sight can lead us, 'tis with pain
> And strivings of the will that we attain
> Such trustfulness as makes the small bird sing
> Of sunshine, shaking sky-tears from its wing,
> Knowing the gloom must gladden into spring.

Such an undertaking, the stanza cautions, requires a determined reorientation of instinctive responses that necessitates both "pain / And strivings of the will." Expanding communion with nature, however, brings an emotional reward that disperses the speaker's despair.

The sonnet "May" offers another insight into the need to conquer despair, opening with the insistent command "Die not, my hope! It is the month of May" before proceeding to identify the signs of promise in the natural world. As the sonnet continues, it issues another command, again basing its rationale on nature's signs: "Fail not, my courage, while the world is gay / With wealth of sunlit green, and liquid song." The contrapuntal format followed in this example, comparing a human condition to natural elements that act as implicit disciplinary agents to regulate the speaker's behavior, appears again elsewhere in the poem. Thus, the speaker determines, "I will not own a frown upon the air / That all the sweet young flowers find so fair." With references to potential human failings—losing hope, lacking courage, and displaying surrender—contrasted to the speaker's surroundings, a didactic relationship obtains, with nature positioned as the sapient mentor figure. By the poem's conclusion, the speaker's emulation of nature has proven successful. The ambient "liquid song" or "tender air" becomes reflected in the speaker's own "song," and despair is deflected: "The gravest reading of my song shall be / A wistful gladness steadied by a cast-off care."

"My Flower" imparts a similar thought in its opening lines, describing the brief blossoming of the titular plant that had "waited all through the year to bloom, / Waited, and weathered the wind, the gloom, / Pent, and folded, and shaded." The flower blooms for a mere hour, the second stanza relates, "[a] gift withdrawn at the giving!" The speaker wonders in the next stanza whether instead of enduring "[t]he pain of waiting" it would be preferable to "nip the buds lest they shed their flowers / In the swift, sweet warmth of meridian hours?" In the final stanza, the speaker realizes that one must accept the reality of nature's sequence of birth, maturation, and death "[w]ith not too heavy a sorrow!" since the flower's "broken heart hath power / To yield new beauty to-morrow." The poem's advice is clear: one should learn from the workings of nature to guide one's own existence.

In addition to such instruction, nature offers a persistent lesson validating patience and acceptance of the unchangeable. In "September," the speaker implores nature for guidance as the poem opens:

> O sunshine in September! golden-green
> Through beechen woods, lap in thy mellow sheen
> The vista of my days; show hope afar,
> And teach me to accept the things that are
> With such a patient grace as is thine own,
> Though one more summer be for ever flown.

The speaker reveals despair over the progress of a life seen as a futile one but in the second stanza comes to recognize that "[l]oss is not death"; instead, perhaps it is "just the clipping of bold wings / Where flight were harmful." Moreover, in the poem's concluding sentiments, the speaker endeavors to appraise the process of aging in a metaphorical September not as a dismal descent but rather as a subsequent stage to "summer's passion" wherein one comprehends that "life be yet worth living." Instead of facing the future with despair, the speaker instead begs the "September sun" to hold out hope for a meaningful morrow. Even though "the flowers are daily fading so," the speaker asks the sun to "[h]int, if thou truly mayest, that autumn light / Is not all memory." Rather, the speaker wishes that the fading light will usher forth "long, long sight / That dares look on." The dim light will resist "the deadening grey / Of coming winter" to enable the speaker to recognize "a gladness on the way."

Although "September" occasionally raises the prospect of unavoidable death, its acceptance becomes the overriding lesson in "October." As the speaker observes the frost-laden morning signaling the approach of winter and nature's own form of death, the environment again provides a model of behavior, for the earth accepts the seasonal change as part of the cycle of life. Attempting to absorb nature's lesson, the speaker muses that the summer projects neither hope nor despair; mortality cannot be avoided, nature readily realizes, and accepts this fate. Religious verbiage laces the poem, as it did in "September," but in more explicit form, for "October" directly mentions God. In "October," nature's response to mortality reveals a positioning within a larger order. Acceptance of this overall pattern likewise enables an individual to recognize that the self will disappear but the effects of a life well led will continue beyond death. The poem brings the solace of hope, as the closing stanza indicates.

> Catch the vast measure of the march of man
> And read a cycle in an hour; for he,
> And only he, may live immortally
> Who lives, the while he lives, in tune with life
> That lives for ever. Prophet! having lived
> And quickened with thy word some further soul
> And sent a-ringing through eternity
> The chord thy hand was formed to strike, and leave,
> Thou shalt, October-wise, resign thy breath
> Glad with faint echoings from a future life
> Grown beautiful and great beyond thine hour of death.

Nature again provides the model for the speaker.

This final "front," like the others, provides striking connections to ecofeminist beliefs and identifies Bevington's poetic voice as indeed indicative of the philosophy to be unveiled generations later. This poet's departures from Emersonian thought offer important reminders that flawed attitudes toward nature based on misplaced perceptions about human superiority cause damage to all. Although arguing for individual rights in the 1882 poem "My Little Task," the question Bevington raises in the following lines from the poem seems equally relevant here: "What, with this fencèd human mind, / What can I do to help my kind?"[28] The answer, for readers willing to heed it, rests in the pages of *Key-Notes*.

NOTES

Introduction: Nascent Ecofeminism

1. M. A. Stodart, "Poetesses and Fleshly Poets," 135. It is certainly possible that scholars may identify other women poets whose work prominently addressed ecofeminist matters.

2. Ynestra King, "The Ecology of Feminism and the Feminism of Ecology," 409; Catriona Sandilands, "From Natural Identity to Radical Democracy," 84; Susan Griffin, "Ecofeminism and Meaning," 219–20.

3. Luce Irigaray, *Sexes and Genealogies*, 4.

4. Kate Rigby, "Ecocriticism," 125; Chris J. Cuomo, *Feminism and Ecological Communities: An Ethic of Flourishing*, 34; Karen J. Warren and Jim Cheney, "Ecological Feminism and Ecosystem Ecology," 186; Scott Hess, *William Wordsworth and the Ecology of Authorship: The Roots of Environmentalism in Nineteenth-Century Culture*, 5; Gretchen T. Legler, "Ecofeminist Literary Criticism," 227; Simon C. Estok, "Theorizing in a Space of Ambivalent Openness: Ecocriticism and Ecophobia," 208; Raymond Williams, *Keywords: A Vocabulary of Culture and Society*, 219.

5. Stacy Alaimo, "Material Engagements: Science Studies and the Environmental Humanities," 71; Erika Cudworth, *Developing Ecofeminist Theory: The Complexity of Difference*, 104; Legler, "Ecofeminist Literary Criticism," 229; Griffin, "Ecofeminism and Meaning," 217.

6. Luce Irigaray, *Key Writings*, 220; Carolyn Merchant, *The Death of Nature: Women, Ecology, and the Scientific Revolution*, xv; Griffin, "Ecofeminism and Meaning," 216; Rosemarie Tong, *Feminist Thought: A More Comprehensive Introduction*, 238; King, "Ecology of Feminism," 407; Val Plumwood, *Feminism and the Mastery of Nature*, 32.

7. Thomas Carlyle, *Past and Present*, 174.

8. Gretchen T. Legler, "Toward a Postmodern Pastoral: The Erotic Landscape in the Work of Gretel Ehrlich," 24; Donna Coffey, "Introduction: A Sense of Place," 132.

9. Stacy Alaimo, *Undomesticated Ground: Recasting Nature as Feminist Space*, 3; Penelope Brown and L. J. Jordanova, "Oppressive Dichotomies: The Nature/Culture Debate," 232; Havelock Ellis, *Man and Woman*, 395.

10. Carolyn Merchant, *Reinventing Eden: The Fate of Nature in Western Culture*, 22, 118. As Merchant observes, "Eve, rather than Adam, communicates with nature in the form of the serpent" and "is the first to ingest the fruit produced by nature on the tree of knowledge of good and evil" (117–18).

11. Tong, *Feminist Thought*, 240; Merchant, *Death of Nature*, 2, 6, 4, 7, 127.

12. Nicolaus Copernicus, *Copernicus: On the Revolutions of the Heavenly Spheres*, 50; Paracelsus, *Selected Writings*, 26 (second ellipsis appears in original); Friedrich Nietzsche,

Beyond Good and Evil, para. 239; Gerard Manley Hopkins, "That Nature Is a Heraclitean Fire," in Jerome Hamilton Buckley and George Benjamin Woods, eds., *Poetry of the Victorian Period*, 789; Carlyle, *Past and Present*, 7.

13. Gillian Beer, *Darwin's Plots: Evolutionary Narrative in Darwin, George Eliot and Nineteenth-Century Fiction*, 9, 69, 70, 70 (Darwin quote), 70–71 (Tyndall quote); Ellis, *Man and Woman*, 394–95.

14. Plumwood, *Feminism and the Mastery of Nature*, 36; Alaimo, *Undomesticated Ground*, 42.

15. Tong, *Feminist Thought*, 239; Lynn White Jr., "The Historical Roots of Our Ecologic Crisis," 1205.

16. Merchant, *Death of Nature*, 164, 165, 168, 169.

17. Francis Bacon, "The Great Instauration," 20; Francis Bacon, *De Sapientia Veterum*, 270; Francis Bacon, *Novum Organum*, 10, 72; Francis Bacon, *De Augmentis*, 343.

18. Martin Luther, quoted in Susan Griffin, *Woman and Nature: The Roaring inside Her*, 9; Merchant, *Death of Nature*, 16; René Descartes, *A Discourse on Method*, pt. 6; Griffin, *Woman and Nature*, 22; King, "Ecology of Feminism," 409; Luce Irigaray, *To Be Two*, 71.

19. Ynestra King, "Healing the Wounds: Feminism, Ecology, and the Nature/Culture Dualism," 117; Tong, *Feminist Thought*, 238; Patrick Curry, *Ecological Ethics: An Introduction*, 128, 127; Tong, *Feminist Thought*, 258; Lori Gruen, "On the Oppression of Women and Animals," 442; Cuomo, *Feminism and Ecological Communities*, 35–36, 136, 137.

20. Karen J. Warren, *Ecofeminist Philosophy: A Western Perspective on What It Is and Why It Matters*, 48–49; Karen J. Warren, "The Power and the Promise of Ecological Feminism," 21, 20–21; Cudworth, *Developing Ecofeminist Theory*, 2, 7, 8, 9.

21. Donna Haraway, "Situated Knowledges: The Science Question in Feminism and the Privilege of Partial Perspective," 592; Legler, "Ecofeminist Literary Criticism," 232; Luce Irigaray, in Luce Irigaray and Michael Marder, *Through Vegetal Being*, 37; Irigaray, *To Be Two*, 1; Murray Bookchin, *Remaking Society: Pathways to a Green Future*, 102.

22. Griffin, *Woman and Nature*, 5; Merchant, *Death of Nature*, 13 (Aristotle quote), 16.

23. Charles Darwin, *The Descent of Man, and Selection in Relation to Sex*, 580; Patrick Geddes and J. Arthur Thomson, *The Evolution of Sex*, 267, 271; W. K. Brooks, "The Condition of Women from a Zoological Point of View I," 154.

24. Legler, "Ecofeminist Literary Criticism," 233; Alaimo, *Undomesticated Ground*, 10; Stacy Alaimo and Susan Hekman, eds., *Material Feminisms*, 5; Noël Sturgeon, *Ecofeminist Natures: Race, Gender, Feminist Theory, and Political Action*, 28.

25. Haraway, "Situated Knowledges," 591, 592, 593, 594.

26. Alaimo, *Undomesticated Ground*, 12, 10, 4; Sherry B. Ortner, "Is Female to Male as Nature Is to Culture?," 47; Plumwood, *Feminism and the Mastery of Nature*, 37.

27. J. McGrigor Allan, "On the Real Differences in the Minds of Men and Women," ccx; Cesare Lombroso, *The Man of Genius*, 138; J. McGrigor Allan, "Influence of Sex on Mind III: Historical Evidence," 230; Allan, "On the Real Differences," ccvi; Brooks, "Condition of Women," 155; Grant Allen, "Woman's Place in Nature," 263; Frederic Harrison, "The Emancipation of Women," 446; Harry Campbell, *Differences in the Nervous Organisation of Man and Woman: Physiological and Pathological*, 173. The supposition

of female mental inferiority was eventually revised, however, though not in women's favor, when female students prospered in educational programs that were reluctantly opened to them. The argument then shifted to express concern that expanding intellectual pursuits would compromise vital reproductive energy.

28. Ortner, "Is Female to Male," 41, 40, 41. Unlike women's situation, "man's physiology" is viewed as "free[ing] him more completely to take up the projects of culture," says Ortner. Another perception is that "woman's *body and its functions* . . . place her in *social roles* that in turn are considered to be at a lower order of the cultural process than man's." A woman's body also "give[s] her a different *psychic structure* . . . seen as being closer to nature" (42).

29. Ortner, "Is Female to Male," 44, 41, 45; King, "Ecology of Feminism," 410.

30. Griffin, "Ecofeminism and Meaning," 217, 220, 221.

31. Karen J. Warren, "A Feminist Philosophical Perspective," 131, 119, 124.

32. Gillian McCulloch, *The Deconstruction of Dualism in Theology*, 72; Sallie McFague, "An Earthly Theological Agenda," 90; Tong, *Feminist Thought*, 252; Carol J. Adams, *Ecofeminism and the Sacred*, 2.

33. McCulloch, *Deconstruction of Dualism*, 65; Rosemary Radford Ruether, "Toward an Ecological-Feminist Theology of Nature," 145; Rosemary Radford Ruether, *Integrating Ecofeminism, Globalization, and World Religions*, 123.

34. Sallie McFague, *The Body of God: An Ecological Theology*, 20, 27; Sallie McFague, *Models of God: Theology for an Ecological, Nuclear Age*, 71; McFague, "Earthly Theological Agenda," 90, 94; McFague, *Models of God*, 74; Roger S. Gottlieb, ed., *This Sacred Earth: Religion, Nature, Environment*, 386.

35. Ariel Salleh, review of *Staying Alive: Women, Ecology, and Development*, 206; Greta Gaard, *Ecological Politics: Ecofeminists and the Greens*, 17, 14; Françoise d'Eaubonne, "The Time for Ecofeminism," 202; Carolyn Merchant, "Perspectives on Ecofeminism," 18; Greta Gaard, "New Directions for Ecofeminism: Toward a More Feminist Ecocriticism," 646; Coffey, "Introduction," 131; Andrea Campbell, ed., *New Directions in Ecofeminist Literary Criticism*, vii; Warren, *Ecofeminist Philosophy*, 21. Salleh adds that d'Eaubonne's text was not translated until about fifteen years after its original publication (review, 206). With a particular interest in bioregionalism, Coffey comments that the modern approach reminds of the "eighteenth- and nineteenth-century texts that celebrate the beauty and utility of particular places." Coffey adds that the texts call attention to the fact "that one's relationship to nature is always mediated, and to a certain extent limited and constrained by social factors, including class, gender, and race" ("Introduction," 131). In ecofeminism's formational years, gender issues represented the key concern, but the focus began to broaden and include questions of class, race, and other vital considerations. Cuomo comments of the early period, "The most developed positions . . . looked simply at gender, as though 'woman' could be sliced away from race, sexuality, and other identities and social locations" (*Feminism and Ecological Communities*, 26).

36. Warren, "The Power and the Promise," 23; Marti Kheel, *Nature Ethics: An Ecofeminist Perspective*, 209; Cudworth, *Developing Ecofeminist Theory*, 1; Curry, *Ecological Ethics*, 130; Timothy Clark, *The Cambridge Introduction to Literature and the Environment*, 111; Kate Sandilands, "Ecofeminism and Its Discontents: Notes toward a Politics of Diversity,"

90; Plumwood, *Feminism and the Mastery of Nature*, 1. Because ecofeminism began to make its mark in the late twentieth century, much of the theorization was published before or shortly after the turn of the century, which explains the plethora of early citations included in this study.

37. Plumwood, *Feminism and the Mastery of Nature*, 8–9; Sandilands, "Ecofeminism and Its Discontents," 90; Carol J. Adams and Lori Gruen, eds., *Ecofeminism: Feminist Intersections with Other Animals and the Earth*, 3; Cuomo, *Feminism and Ecological Communities*, 112; Sturgeon, *Ecofeminist Natures*, 28–29.

38. Cuomo, *Feminism and Ecological Communities*, 117; Catriona Mortimer-Sandilands, "Eco/Feminism on the Edge," 306–7; Cuomo, *Feminism and Ecological Communities*, 113; Alaimo, *Undomesticated Ground*, 8; Greta Gaard, "Ecofeminism Revisited: Rejecting Essentialism and Re-Placing Species in a Material Feminist Environmentalism," 26; Charis Thompson, "Back to Nature? Resurrecting Ecofeminism after Poststructuralist and Third-Wave Feminisms," 507; Gaard, "Ecofeminism Revisited," 41, 31; Mortimer-Sandilands, "Eco/Feminism on the Edge," 306; Gaard, "Ecofeminism Revisited," 27.

39. Simon C. Estok, "The Ecophobia Hypothesis: Re-membering the Feminist Body of Ecocriticism," 71; Clark, *Cambridge Introduction*, 4; Estok, "Ecophobia Hypothesis," 78; Clark, *Cambridge Introduction*, 111.

40. Gaard, "Ecofeminism Revisited," 27; Gaard, "New Directions for Ecofeminism," 660, 644. The term "ecofeminism" deserves recuperation owing to its emphasis on both ecology and feminism.

41. Tobias Menely and Jesse Oak Taylor, eds., *Anthropocene Reading: Literary History in Geologic Times*, 3; Jesse Oak Taylor, *The Sky of Our Manufacture: The London Fog in British Fiction from Dickens to Woolf*, 5.

42. Friedrich Engels, *The Condition of the Working Class in England*, 64, 109.

43. I. G. Simmons, *An Environmental History of Great Britain: From 10,000 Years Ago to the Present*, 150, 151.

44. Alice Meynell, "The Climate of Smoke," in *London Impressions: Etchings and Pictures in Photogravure*, n.p.; Mathilde Blind, *The Ascent of Man*, 63; Taylor, *Sky of Our Manufacture*, 1, 2, 1–2. Taylor discusses Meynell's views about the aesthetics of the London fog. Meynell "grant[s] aesthetic agency to the climate itself to produce effects, which are in turn mirrored in the work of impressionist painters," he says (167). Taylor also notes "[t]he ambivalence with which Meynell approaches the aestheticization of pollution" (168).

45. Engels, *Condition of the Working Class*, 110, 111.

46. Heidi C. M. Scott, *Chaos and Cosmos: Literary Roots of Modern Ecology in the British Nineteenth Century*, 49; Simmons, *Environmental History*, 166; James Winter, *Secure from Rash Assault: Sustaining the Victorian Environment*, 166; Simmons, *Environmental History*, 154.

47. Winter, *Secure from Rash Assault*, 83, 97; Karl Marx, quoted in Carolyn Merchant, *Ecology*, 57; Scott, *Chaos and Cosmos*, 47.

48. Simmons, *Environmental History*, 161, 174; "The Purification of the Thames," 71; Edmund Saul Dixon, "Dirty Cleanliness," 121; Engels, *Condition of the Working Class*, 60; Simmons, *Environmental History*, 161.

49. Friedrich Engels, quoted in Merchant, *Ecology*, 56.

50. John Ruskin, quoted in David Carroll, "Pollution, Defilement and the Art of Decomposition," 72; Mark Frost, "Reading Nature: John Ruskin, Environment, and the Ecological Impulse," 14; John Ruskin, *Fors Clavigera*, 86, 91, 92, 86; John Ruskin, "Fiction, Fair and Foul," 436; Ruskin, *Fors Clavigera*, 92–93; John Ruskin, *Modern Painters*, vol. 5, pt. 6, sec. 2; John Ruskin, quoted in Winter, *Secure from Rash Assault*, 184.

51. Thomas Carlyle, "Signs of the Times," 34, 43, 34, 43, 48; Thomas Carlyle, *Sartor Resartus*, 150, 205.

52. Gerard Manley Hopkins, "Binsey Poplars," n.p.; Gerard Manley Hopkins, "Inversnaid," in Buckley and Woods, *Poetry of the Victorian Period*, 786–87; Peter Coates, *Nature: Western Attitudes since Ancient Times*, 155; William Morris, *News from Nowhere*, 162, 112–13, 5–6, 141; Taylor, *Sky of Our Manufacture*, 203, 204.

53. Thomas H. Ford, "Punctuating History circa 1800: The Air of *Jane Eyre*," 78; Jonathan Bate, *Romantic Ecology: Wordsworth and the Environmental Tradition*, 40; David Pepper, *Modern Environmentalism: An Introduction*, 188, 189; Clark, *Cambridge Introduction*, 13; Bate, *Romantic Ecology*, 40; Clark, *Cambridge Introduction*, 16; Bate, *Romantic Ecology*, 9; Clark, *Cambridge Introduction*, 18.

54. Bate, *Romantic Ecology*, 9, 8, 39, 14 (Mill quote), 9; Hess, *William Wordsworth*, 12.

55. John Parham, "Was There a Victorian Ecology?," 163; Linda K. Hughes, *The Cambridge Introduction to Victorian Poetry*, 3, 4.

56. Frost, "Reading Nature," 13; Coates, *Nature*, 142. Haeckel defined "ecology" this way: "By ecology we mean the body of knowledge concerning the economy of nature—the investigation of the total relations of the animal both to its inorganic and to its organic environment." Haeckel "includ[ed] above all, its friendly and inimical relations with those animals and plants with which it comes directly or indirectly into contact." He added that "in a word, ecology is the study of all those complex interrelations referred to by Darwin as the conditions of the struggle for existence" (quoted in Robert P. McIntosh, *The Background of Ecology: Concept and Theory*, 7–8).

57. Barri J. Gold, "Energy, Ecology, and Victorian Fiction," 216, 215; Laurence W. Mazzeno and Ronald D. Morrison, *Victorian Writers and the Environment: Ecocritical Perspectives*, 1; Parham, "Was There a Victorian Ecology?," 156, 156–58; Nicholas Frankel, "The Ecology of Victorian Poetry," 631.

58. Parham, "Was There a Victorian Ecology?," 169; Frankel, "Ecology of Victorian Poetry," 630; Jesse Oak Taylor, "Where Is Victorian Ecocriticism?," 879; Gold, "Energy, Ecology, and Victorian Fiction," 214.

59. James Diedrick, *Mathilde Blind: Late-Victorian Culture and the Woman of Letters*, 228, 211, 224, 226; Angela Leighton, *Victorian Women Poets: Writing against the Heart*, 223; Emma Donoghue, *We Are Michael Field*, 27; Angela Leighton, in Angela Leighton and Margaret Reynolds, eds., *Victorian Women Poets: An Anthology*, 558.

60. Linda K. Hughes, "A Club of Their Own," 238; Patricia Rigg, *Julia Augusta Webster: Victorian Aestheticism and the Woman Writer*, 26; Marysa Demoor, *Their Fair Share: Women, Power and Criticism in the* Athenaeum, *from Millicent Garrett Fawcett to Katherine Mansfield, 1870–1920*, 109–20 (on Webster as reviewer), 104–9 (on Blind as reviewer); Blind, quoted in Diedrick, *Mathilde Blind*, 129; Ana I. Parejo Vadillo, "New Woman Poets and the Culture of the *Salon* at the *Fin de Siècle*," 28.

61. Leighton, in Leighton and Reynolds, *Victorian Women Poets: An Anthology*, 477; Philip E. Smith II, "Robert Lewins, Constance Naden, and Hylo-Idealism," 305; Charles LaPorte, "Atheist Prophecy: Mathilde Blind, Constance Naden, and the Victorian Poetess," 428.

62. Linda K. Hughes, "Daughters of Danaus and Daphne: Women Poets and the Marriage Question," 486. Hughes indicates that this perception "was all the more important because poetry sold less widely than novels" so that "*succès d'estime* was all the more important" (486).

Perhaps the New Woman connections suggest that ecofeminist ideas offer another aspect to be considered in theorizing the controversial figure's interests, specifically in poetry. Further study about such possible linkages would be an interesting addition to criticism on Victorian poetry.

63. Leighton, *Victorian Women Poets: Writing against the Heart*, 164.

64. Diedrick, *Mathilde Blind*, 204, 205, 217.

65. Sally Mitchell, "New Women, Old and New," 582; Marion Thain, *"Michael Field": Poetry, Aestheticism and the* Fin de Siècle, 13; Mary Sturgeon, *Michael Field*, 20; Thain, *"Michael Field,"* 13.

66. Talia Schaffer, *The Forgotten Female Aesthetes: Literary Culture in Late-Victorian England*, 164, 159, 160; Vadillo, "New Woman Poets," 22; Schaffer, *Forgotten Female Aesthetes*, 164.

67. Emily R. Anderson, "Constance Naden (1858–1889)," 284; Marion Thain, "Birmingham's Women Poets: Aestheticism and the Daughters of Industry," 49; Linda K. Hughes, ed., *New Woman Poets: An Anthology*, 2.

68. Jackie Dees Domingue, ed., *Collected Essays of Louisa Sarah Bevington*, viii; Hughes, *New Woman Poets*, 7; Vadillo, "New Woman Poets," 28.

69. Christine Sutphin, *Augusta Webster: Portraits and Other Poems*, 34, 36.

70. Menely and Taylor, *Anthropocene Reading*, 12, 13; Benjamin Morgan, "Scale as Form: Thomas Hardy's Rocks and Stars," 140.

71. Peter C. Gould, *Early Green Politics: Back to Nature, Back to the Land, and Socialism in Britain 1880–1900*, viii, 4.

72. Irigaray, *Key Writings*, 67–68, 67.

73. Karen I. Burke, "Masculine and Feminine Approaches to Nature," 189, 190 (on the 1986 speech by Irigaray, titled "A Chance to Live"); Christopher Cohoon, "The Ecological Irigaray?," 206, 207; Margaret Whitford, *Luce Irigaray: Philosophy in the Feminine*, 95.

74. Coral Lansbury, *The Old Brown Dog: Women, Workers, and Vivisection in Edwardian England*, 84.

Chapter 1: Augusta Webster

1. Luce Irigaray, *Speculum of the Other Woman*, 163.

2. Vita Sackville-West, "The Women Poets of the 'Seventies," 125; Leighton, *Victorian Women Poets: Writing against the Heart*, 173; Theodore Watts, "Mrs. Augusta Webster," 355; Leighton, *Victorian Women Poets: Writing against the Heart*, 172. Leighton characterizes Webster's views on feminism this way: "Not an out-and-out radical, Webster's opinions grow out of a middle current of liberal thinking in the nineteenth century" (173).

3. Augusta Webster, *A Housewife's Opinions*, 98, 99, 101, 91, 41.

4. Webster, *A Housewife's Opinions*, 242.

5. Mackenzie Bell, "Augusta Webster," 105; Rigg, *Julia Augusta Webster*, 192, 193, 240, 189, 239. Dorothy Mermin comments that Webster was "[t]he first woman writer of note to hold elective office" (*Godiva's Ride: Women of Letters in England, 1830–1880*, 56).

6. Rigg, *Julia Augusta Webster*, 18; Christina Rossetti, *The Family Letters of Christina Georgina Rossetti*, 96; Webster, *A Housewife's Opinions*, 275, 277, 271, 273.

7. Webster, *A Housewife's Opinions*, 173, 175, 173, 243, 231.

8. Bell, "Augusta Webster," 107; Isobel Armstrong, *Victorian Poetry: Poetry, Poetics, and Politics*, 324; Marysa Demoor, "A Mode(rni)st Beginning?: The Women of the 'Athenaeum' 1890–1910," 274. Rigg maintains that "Webster's 'arrival' as a lyric poet" came with the publication of *A Book of Rhyme* (*Julia Augusta Webster*, 217). Mermin comments that Webster "began publishing with ballads and romances in apparent imitation of Barrett Browning's early works, and also with explorations of women's traditional location within nature, identifying with a dandelion, a flock of birds, and a serpent imprisoned in a chest at the bottom of a lake" (*Godiva's Ride*, 79). Sutphin observes, "Reviewers of Webster's poetry noted the influence of Tennyson and Elizabeth Barrett Browning and typically invoked Robert Browning in discussing her monologues" (*Augusta Webster*, 16).

As Sutphin notes, "Of course, during Webster's time controversy raged concerning fit subjects and appropriate forms for poetry" (*Augusta Webster*, 35). Sutphin also comments that "Webster succeeded with critics in spite of the fact that her subjects and techniques often defied gender stereotypes, or perhaps she succeeded because of such defiance" (31). As Sutphin surmises of reviewer reactions, "Webster's work managed to negotiate successfully between her culture's constructions of femininity and masculinity" in her efforts aimed at "expanding middle-class women's sphere" (33). Not all critics expressed admiration, however. In the 1903 *Victorian Poets*, for instance, Edmund Clarence Stedman sniffed that "*A Book of Rhyme* adds to the impression that, with all her uncommon gifts, she is too versatile and facile: most of her poetry is good, but she has yet to write a poem or drama of the highest class" (443–44).

9. All quotes from poems in this chapter come from *A Book of Rhyme*. Although other poems may mention flowers in passing, those flowers, unlike the rose, are generally unspecified by name and are fleeting rather than prominent images.

10. Thomas Bewick, *A History of British Birds*, xxvi; Haraway, "Situated Knowledges," 593.

11. Julia Kristeva, "Women's Time," 18, 16.

12. Alfred Tennyson, *Tennyson's "The Princess,"* lines 172–75. H. Buxton Forman stated in *Our Living Poets* that some of Webster's poems "derive from Tennyson and Mrs. Browning, and in a lesser degree from Browning and Miss Rossetti" (173).

13. Warren, "The Power and the Promise," 20, 22.

14. Legler, "Ecofeminist Literary Criticism," 228.

15. Thomas Gray, "Elegy Written in a Country Churchyard," in James Noggle and Lawrence Lipking, eds., *The Norton Anthology of English Literature*, vol. C, *The Restoration and the Eighteenth Century*, 3051; Ortner, "Is Female to Male," 42, 43.

16. Isobel Armstrong, *Language as Living Form in Nineteenth-Century Poetry*, 35.

17. Charlotte Smith, "To Night," in Deidre Shauna Lynch and Jack Stillinger, eds., *The Norton Anthology of English Literature*, vol. D, *The Romantic Period*, 55.

18. Robert Browning, "Andrea del Sarto," in Buckley and Woods, *Poetry of the Victorian Period*, 289, lines 97–98.

19. Plumwood, *Feminism and the Mastery of Nature*, 4.

20. Luce Irigaray, "There Can Be No Democracy without a Culture of Difference," 201.

21. Irigaray has commented on the "one 'path,' the one historically assigned to the feminine: that of *mimicry*" (*The Irigaray Reader*, 124).

22. Webster, *A Housewife's Opinions*, 231.

23. In a sense, Webster anticipates later-century women's poetry wherein "mothers and lovers are ambiguously confused," as Leighton observes of the confused pairings (Leighton and Reynolds, *Victorian Women Poets: An Anthology*, xxviii).

24. Emily Harrington, "'Appraise Love and Divide': Measuring Love in Augusta Webster's *Mother and Daughter*," 268; Melissa Valiska Gregory, "Augusta Webster Writing Motherhood in the Dramatic Monologue and Sonnet Sequence," 41–42.

25. Margaret Homans, *Women Writers and Poetic Identity: Dorothy Wordsworth, Emily Brontë, and Emily Dickinson*, 16; Leighton, in Leighton and Reynolds, *Victorian Women Poets: An Anthology*, xxxviii.

Chapter 2: Mathilde Blind

1. Richard Garnett, *Memoir*, 38; Mathilde Blind, "Shelley's View of Nature as Contrasted with Darwin's," 9; Mathilde Blind, introduction to *The Journal of Marie Bashkirtseff*, by Marie Bashkirtseff, trans. Mathilde Blind, 695. As Paula Alexandra Guimarães comments, Blind sought to "capture the resonances between human individuals and the natural world" ("'Over My Boundless Waste of Soul': Echoes of the Natural World, or a Feminine *Naturphilosophie*, in the Poetry of Emily Brontë and Mathilde Blind," para. 30).

2. George Perkins Marsh, *Man and Nature: George Perkins Marsh*, 36; William Cronon, foreword to *Man and Nature: George Perkins Marsh*, x; Marsh, *Man and Nature*, 36–37, 40–41, 42. Marsh condemned "man" for "his reckless destruction of the natural protection of the soil" and lamented that "[h]e has broken up the mountain reservoirs" that nourished livestock and watered crops; "he has destroyed the fringe of semi-aquatic plants which skirted the coast and checked the drifting of the sea sand"; and "[h]e has ruthlessly warred on all the tribes of animated nature whose spoil he could convert to his own uses" (38, 39).

3. Irigaray, in Irigaray and Marder, *Through Vegetal Being*, 38; Irigaray, *Thinking the Difference*, 5; Irigaray, *To Be Two*, 73; Irigaray, "There Can Be No Democracy," 198. Irigaray precedes the comment about going further by stating that "[m]ankind is traditionally carnivorous, sometimes cannibalistic. So men must kill to eat, must increase their domination of nature in order to live or to survive, . . . must defend by any means the small patch of land they are exploiting here or over there" (*Thinking the Difference*, 5).

4. Diedrick, *Mathilde Blind*, 25 (friend quote); Blind, quoted in Garnett, *Memoir*, 9–10; Diedrick, "Mathilde Blind"; Blind, quoted in Diedrick, "Mathilde Blind," 30.

5. Theodore Watts-Dunton, "Miss Blind," 796; Garnett, *Memoir*, 18; "Women Who Write," n.p.

6. "The Ascent of Man," 87; Blind, *Ascent of Man*, 97. The anonymous *Athenaeum* reviewer added, "We have known her book to be read in the Underground Railway, and the

reader to be so absorbed in its contents as to be carried unawares several stations past his destination" (87). "The poem achieved a degree of popularity, if not notoriety," says Jason R. Rudy, "through its use of varied metrical structures, driving rhythmic impulses and vivid imagery" ("Rapturous Forms: Mathilde Blind's Darwinian Poetics," 444). Moreover, as James Diedrick remarks, the poem "anticipates the intense preoccupation with gender that characterizes Blind's subsequent writing" ("'The Hectic Beauty of Decay': Positivist Decadence in Mathilde Blind's Late Poetry," 634).

7. Blind, *Ascent of Man*, 98, 100, 101, 50. Critics have discussed the maternal images in *Ascent*. Diedrick, for instance, speaks of "the centrality of female creative power—both biological and poetic—to Blind's attempt to weave a new, humanist mythology from the resistant threads of Darwinian theory" (*Mathilde Blind*, 214). Helen Groth speaks of "Blind's portrayal of earth and sea as a heaving maternal body" ("Victorian Women Poets and Scientific Narratives," 338).

8. Blind, "Nûît," in *The Poetical Works of Mathilde Blind*, 385; Bonnie J. Robinson, "'Individual Incorporate': Poetic Trends in Women Writers, 1890–1918," 4. With the exception of *The Ascent of Man* and "Entangled," all quotations of Blind poems in this study are from *The Poetical Works of Mathilde Blind*.

9. Mathilde Blind, "Mary Wollstonecraft," 390; Blind, introduction to *Journal of Marie Bashkirtseff*, 696; Mathilde Blind, *Madame Roland* (London: Allen, 1886); Blind, "Shelley," 88–89, 89. For details on such writings, see James Diedrick's essay "Mathilde Blind's (Proto-) New Women."

10. Diedrick, *Mathilde Blind*, 129; Garnett, *Memoir*, 18–19; Blind, quoted in Diedrick, *Mathilde Blind*, 224; Garnett, *Memoir*, 41.

11. Garnett, *Memoir*, 18; "Women's Suffrage: A Reply," 50.

12. Garnett, *Memoir*, 18; Blind, quoted in Diedrick, *Mathilde Blind*, 188; Diedrick, *Mathilde Blind*, 198.

13. Mathilde Blind [Claude Lake, pseud.], "Entangled," in *Poems*, 62.

14. John Keats, "La Belle Dame sans Merci," in Lynch and Stillinger, *Norton Anthology of English Literature*, vol. D, *The Romantic Period*, 924.

15. Irigaray, "There Can Be No Democracy," 198. As Irigaray remarks, "Man cultivates nature and manages its conservation, but often at the price of birth and growth." As a result, "[t]he cultivation of nature becomes exploitation" (*An Ethics of Sexual Difference*, 100).

16. Thomas Hardy, *Tess of the d'Urbervilles*, 404, 406, 404, 405.

17. Richard Jefferies, *The Hills and the Vale*, 134, 134–35, 135, 136; Irigaray, *To Be Two*, 69. Jefferies's description includes other haunting details about "the savage force": a wire on the machine "stretches and strains as if it would snap and curl up like a tortured snake; the engine pants loudly and quick; the plough . . . eats its way through a tougher place." Another machine resembles a "monster [that] puffs and pants and belches smoke, while the one that has done its work uncoils its metal sinews" (135).

18. Michael Field, "Wheat-Miners," in *The Wattlefold*, 13.

19. William Wordsworth, "Lines Composed a Few Miles above Tintern Abbey," in Lynch and Stillinger, *Norton Anthology of English Literature*, vol. D, *The Romantic Period*, 289.

Chapter 3: Michael Field

1. Legler, "Ecofeminist Literary Criticism," 232; Catrin Gersdorf, "Ecocritical Uses of the Erotic," 178, 180, 182.

2. Greta Gaard, "Toward a Queer Ecofeminism," 133; Audre Lorde, *Sister Outsider: Essays and Speeches*, 53; Catriona Sandilands, "Desiring Nature, Queering Ethics: Adventures in Erotogenic Environments," 177, 180; Gaard, "Toward a Queer Ecofeminism," 118.

3. Homer, *The Odyssey*, bk. 5, lines 226–27, 63–74; bk. 9, lines 30–32; Virgil, *The Aeneid of Virgil*, bk. 6, lines 47–56.

4. Charles Paul Segal, *Landscape in Ovid's "Metamorphoses,"* 8, 9.

5. Ovid, *Metamorphoses*, bk. 1, lines 549–50, 553–56; bk. 5, lines 388, 391, 394–96, 399–401; bk. 9, lines 347–48; bk. 4, lines 312–313, 314–315, 317, 319–20, 371–73.

6. Michael Field, *Works and Days*, 48. The relationship between the land and the goddess in "The Sleeping Venus" has drawn other critical notice as well. Jill R. Ehnenn, for instance, cites the similarity between the description of the curvature of the terrain and that of Venus herself, additionally observing that the poem "clearly depicts her free from shame" ("Looking Strategically: Feminist and Queer Aesthetics in Michael Field's *Sight and Song*," 228). Erik Gray notes that "Field insists that Venus is deeply interfused with her background, with the landscape in which she reclines and from which she is inseparable" ("A Bounded Field: Situating Victorian Poetry in the Literary Landscape," 467). Identifying "two overlapping fields of vision" in the poem that include the body and the land, Gray remarks that "they are depicted as perfectly continuous" (468). Krysta Lysack observes that in its description of Venus, the poem "lauds the fidelity between her 'curves' (line 15) and those of the surrounding pastures and sky and praises the erotic landscape of her body" ("Aesthetic Consumption and the Cultural Production of Michael Field's *Sight and Song*," 952). Julia F. Saville remarks that "[t]he poem repeatedly dwells on the correlations between the undulations of Venus's body and those of the landscape, insisting on both as feminine and shameless" ("The Poetic Imaging of Michael Field," 196–97). Saville maintains that Venus "lies absorbed in the pleasure of her own sexualized womanhood for the observation and admiration of other women as much as men" (198). These critics, however, do not address the eroticization of nature as an ecofeminist device.

7. Michael Field, "The Sleeping Venus," in *Sight and Song (1892) with Underneath the Bough (1893)*, 98–105.

8. Legler, "Toward a Postmodern Pastoral," 23, 22, 23, 24. Legler's essay is referring to American nature writing and describes the work of Wyoming poet Gretel Ehrlich, but the approach applies as well to Michael Field's verse.

9. Several critics have also discussed the autoerotic aspect of these lines. For example, Leighton makes note of the "self-delighting physical literalness which marks an extraordinary freeing of the female imagination"; moreover, "'delicious womanhood' is a welcome, sexualised description of an ideal too long associated with hearths and angels" (*Victorian Women Poets: Writing against the Heart*, 215). Ana I. Parejo Vadillo states that the poem "describes Venus in her full 'womanhood,'" and the poem describes Venus in an act of masturbation" ("*Sight and Song*: Transparent Translations and a Manifesto for the Observer," 30). Lysack asserts that "the sloping margins of the poem—as they curve inward following line 62—suggestively reproduce the curves of Venus's own body" ("Aesthetic Consumption," 952). Gray also comments on the formal aspect of the stanza: "Field

presents Giorgione's Venus as a figure of autoeroticism, an implication that is reinforced by the stanza-form: an inverted and attenuated sonnet, sestet followed by octave, with a quite literal 'enjambement' between the two—hand and thigh crossing from one half of the stanza to the other" ("Bounded Field," 467). To S. Brooke Cameron, the poem "is extraordinary precisely for its sexually charged description of feminine autoeroticism" ("The Pleasures of Looking and the Feminine Gaze in Michael Field's *Sight and Song*," 165). Ehnenn indicates that "'Sleeping Venus' represents autoerotic and homoerotic possibility for all women" ("Looking Strategically," 227).

10. Michael Field, "Venus and Mars," in *Sight and Song (1892) with Underneath the Bough (1893)*, 442–46.

11. Ann B. Shteir, *Cultivating Women, Cultivating Science*, 16; Harriet Ritvo, "Zoological Nomenclature and the Empire of Victorian Science," 336; René-Louis Desfontaines, quoted in François Delaporte, *Nature's Second Kingdom: Explorations of Vegetality in the Eighteenth Century*, 129; Londa Schiebinger, *Nature's Body: Gender in the Making of Modern Science*, 19, 21; Linnaeus, quoted in Thomas Laqueur, *Making Sex: Body and Gender from the Greeks to Freud*, 172; Schiebinger, *Nature's Body*, 13, 17; Alan Bewell, "'Jacobin Plants': Botany as Social Theory in the 1790s," 132, 134.

12. Erasmus Darwin, *The Loves of the Plants*, preface (on designations of plant types); Schiebinger, *Nature's Body*, 23. Darwin lays out Linnaeus's system of nomenclature in his poem's preface.

13. Laqueur, *Making Sex*, 172, 173; dismayed individual, quoted in James L. Larson, "Linnaeus and the Natural Method," 310; Johann Georg Siegesbeck, quoted in Delaporte, *Nature's Second Kingdom*, 145; Janet Browne, "Botany for Gentlemen: Erasmus Darwin and *The Loves of the Plants*," 599; Caroline Jackson-Houlston, "'Queen Lilies'?: The Interpenetration of Scientific, Religious and Gender Discourses in Victorian Representations of Plants," 86; William Smellie, quoted in Martin Priestman, *The Poetry of Erasmus Darwin: Enlightened Spaces, Romantic Times*, 72; Laqueur, *Making Sex*, 172–73; Charles Alston, quoted in Bewell, "'Jacobin Plants,'" 133; Goethe, quoted in Bewell, "'Jacobin Plants,'" 134.

14. Hugh Rose, quoted in Browne, "Botany for Gentlemen," 600; Linnaeus, quoted in James L. Larson, "The Species Concept of Linnaeus," 297; Linnaeus, quoted in Larson, "Linnaeus and the Natural Method," 306, 317; Linnaeus, quoted in Laqueur, *Making Sex*, 172.

15. Linnaeus, quoted in Laqueur, *Making Sex*, 172.

16. Schiebinger, *Nature's Body*, 28, 29; Desmond King-Hele, *Erasmus Darwin and the Romantic Poets*, 36, 68, 1, 100, 230.

17. Amy M. King, *Bloom: The Botanical Vernacular in the English Novel*, 72; Lisa L. Moore, "Queer Gardens: Mary Delaney's Flowers and Friendships," 65, 65–66; Richard Polwhele, quoted in Shteir, *Cultivating Women, Cultivating Science*, 28; Thomas Mathias, quoted in Tristanne Connolly, "Flowery Porn: Form and Desire in Erasmus Darwin's *The Loves of the Plants*," 606.

18. Anna Seward, quoted in Priestman, *Poetry of Erasmus Darwin*, 70; Darwin, *The Loves of the Plants*, canto 1, lines 62, 234, 301, 395, 307, 317, 319, 9–20.

19. Darwin, *The Loves of the Plants*, canto 1, lines 109–16, 119, 121–24, 141, 139–40, 97, 98; canto 4, lines 136, 135, 301–2, 203; canto 1, lines 281, 282; Shteir, *Cultivating Women, Cultivating Science*, 27.

20. Shteir, *Cultivating Women, Cultivating Science*, 157.

21. Nicolette Scourse, *The Victorians and Their Flowers*, 63 (Moriarty quote), 5 (Smith quote); Jackson-Houlston, "'Queen Lilies'?," 87; Fabienne Moine, *Women Poets in the Victorian Era: Cultural Practices and Nature Poetry*, 53, 93.

22. Webster, review of *Underneath the Bough*, 345. Webster is identified as the author of this review in Rigg's *Julia Augusta Webster*, 285n86.

23. Sexuality is an important aspect of all three paths. See Chris White's "Flesh and Roses: Michael Field's Metaphors of Pleasure and Desire" for a discussion of various poems not considered here. White indicates about the volume that it reveals "complex, implicitly sexual overtones" (55). Robert P. Fletcher calls the verses in *Underneath the Bough* "narratives of sexuality" and argues that "'Michael Field' both appropriates and subverts cultural narratives of desire that serve as frames for *Underneath the Bough*'s lyrics" ("'I Leave a Page Half-Writ': Narrative Discoherence in Michael Field's *Underneath the Bough*," 164, 165).

24. Michael Field, "Tiger-lilies," in *Underneath the Bough: A Book of Verse*, 90.

25. Quotations from "Great violets in the weedy tangle" and the rest of the poems in this chapter, except where stated otherwise, come from *Sight and Song (1892) with Underneath the Bough (1893)*.

26. Lisa L. Moore, *Sister Arts: The Erotics of Lesbian Landscapes*, 2; Elizabeth Bernath, "'Seeking Flowers to Comfort Her': Queer Botany in Blake's *Visions*, Darwin's *Loves* and Wollstonecraft's *Rights of Woman*," 115. For critical commentary on the significance of bees in Field poems, see White, "Flesh and Roses," 59–60, and especially the lengthy discussion in Thain's *"Michael Field,"* chap. 5. Thain says of Field's verse that "the bee is undoubtedly a useful conveyor of sexual significance" and that the insects' sexuality "is homoerotic just as much as it is heteroerotic" (142).

27. Michael Field, "LII," in Marion Thain and Ana Parejo Vadillo, eds., *Michael Field, the Poet: Published and Manuscript Materials*, 72–74.

28. Alison Syme, *A Touch of Blossom: John Singer Sargent and the Queer Flora of Fin-de-Siècle Art*, 69, 29–30; Annette Stott, "Floral Femininity: A Pictorial Definition," 66.

29. Paula Bennett, "Critical Clitoridectomy: Female Sexual Imagery and Feminist Psychoanalytic Theory," 242, 241, 244, 242, 243.

30. Martha Vicinus, "The Adolescent Boy: Fin-de-Siècle Femme Fatale?," 91; Moore, *Sister Arts*, 2; Syme, *A Touch of Blossom*, 12. Moore clarifies that "'lesbian' is not understood here as a kind of person but as an art-making practice, a form of relationship or community, and sometimes as a kind of art object" (2–3).

31. Ehnenn, "Looking Strategically," 223; Moine, *Women Poets*, 92, 93, 96, 97.

32. Jean Marsh, *The Illuminated Language of Flowers*, 15; Beverly Seaton, *The Language of Flowers: A History*, 170–71, 182; Molly Engelhardt, "The Language of Flowers in the Victorian Knowledge Age," 144 (disclaimer quote), 143–44.

33. Shteir, *Cultivating Women, Cultivating Science*, 158; Engelhardt, "Language of Flowers," 136; Marsh, *Illuminated Language of Flowers*, 12, 14, 14 (contemporary book quote), 17.

34. Engelhardt, "Language of Flowers," 148, 146, 136; Webster, review of *Underneath the Bough*, 345.

35. As recorded in the two poets' journal published in part as *Works and Days*, Michael Field attended a Pater lecture, attempted to visit him at his home, and demonstrated a familiarity with his aesthetic philosophy. Field wrote a sonnet in Pater's honor after his

death in which "Field faithfully presents the 'imaginary portrait' of a lover of beauty for whom the aesthetic experience resides in the body," Vadillo notes ("*Sight and Song*," 15). Saville comments that Field engaged in "simultaneous study of the aesthetic theories of Pater" ("Poetic Imaging," 180), while Thain says that Pater was "an aesthetic idol" of Michael Field's and "had a huge influence on their work" (*"Michael Field,"* 16). Wilde was an acquaintance who wrote to the Field poets in praise of a play they had written, and he received considerable coverage in *Works and Days*. Ehnenn indicates that Katharine Bradley had been part of "Ruskinian circles in the mid 1870s" but "[b]y 1880 the friendship had completely faded" ("Looking Strategically," 215).

36. Walter Pater, "Wordsworth," 419, 420, 424.

37. Walter Pater, *The Renaissance: Studies in Art and Poetry*, xx, xix, 190, 189; Field, *Works and Days*, 136.

38. Oscar Wilde, *The Decay of Lying*, 3, 5, 30–31, 31, 54, 31, 41, 54; Oscar Wilde, *The Picture of Dorian Gray*, 21.

39. Michael Field, preface to *Sight and Song*, in *Sight and Song (1892) with Underneath the Bough (1893)*, v; Vadillo, "*Sight and Song*," 32.

40. Ruskin, *Modern Painters*, vol. 1, pt. 1, sec. 1, chap. 6, secs. 1, 6, 5. Ruskin also demonstrates his interest in nature in *Proserpina* with numerous chapters on plant life. In a chapter on flowers Ruskin echoes Erasmus Darwin in saying that "the life and death of the blossom *itself* is always an eventful romance" (69).

41. Ruskin, *Modern Painters*, vol. 2, pt. 3, sec. 1, chap. 12, sec. 4; vol. 2, pt. 3, sec. 1, chap. 15, sec. 4.

42. Immanuel Kant, *The Critique of Judgement*, 160, 162, 167.

43. Allen Carlson, *Nature and Landscape: An Introduction to Environmental Aesthetics*, 2, 3; Allen Carlson, "Aesthetics of the Environment," 134.

44. Carlson, "Aesthetics of the Environment," 135, 136.

45. Angela Leighton, "Women Poets and the Fin-De-Siècle: Towards a New Aestheticism," 3; Kathy Alexis Psomiades, *Beauty's Body: Femininity and Representation in British Aestheticism*, 2; Mary Devereaux, "Feminist Aesthetics," 657; Devereaux, "Feminist Aesthetics," 659. Interestingly, one target of feminist aesthetics is Kantian theory, which Field's poetry conversely seems to embrace. Feminist aesthetics also challenges "neo-Kantian formalism" and "the trajectory of aesthetic thought associated with Oscar Wilde" and others in subsequent decades, Devereaux says. As she also explains, "[I]t would be no great exaggeration to say that critiques of 'Kant and formalism' have largely come to define what is meant by 'feminist critiques of aesthetics'" (657). For details of the feminist appraisal, see Devereaux, "Feminist Aesthetics," 657–60.

46. Talia Schaffer and Kathy Alexis Psomiades, *Women and British Aestheticism*, 11, 12, 18; Kathy Alexis Psomiades, "'Still Burning from This Strangling Embrace': Vernon Lee on Desire and Aesthetics," 29; Vadillo, "*Sight and Song*," 24.

Chapter 4: Alice Meynell

1. Irigaray, *Key Writings*, 220.

2. Lynn Keller, "Twenty-First Century Ecopoetry and the Scalar Challenges of the Anthropocene," 62; Ann Fisher-Wirth and Laura-Gray Street, *The Ecopoetry Anthology*, xxviii, xxix, xxx.

3. Forrest Gander, in Forrest Gander and John Kinsella, *Redstart: An Ecological Poetics*, 11, 15; Jed Purdy, "Losing Nature: Living in the Anthropocene," n.p.

4. J. Scott Bryson, *Ecopoetry: A Critical Introduction*, 3, 5, 5–6.

5. Leonard M. Scigaj, *Sustainable Poetry: Four American Ecopoets*, 11; Lawrence Buell, *The Environmental Imagination: Thoreau, Nature Writing, and the Formation of American Culture*, 7–8; Scott Knickerbocker, *Ecopoetics: The Language of Nature, the Nature of Language*, 7–8; Irigaray, *To Be Two*, 71.

6. Stacy Alaimo, "Trans-Corporeal Feminisms and the Ethical Space of Nature," 238, 249; Karen Barad, "Posthumanist Performativity: Toward an Understanding of How Matter Comes to Matter," 146; Stacy Alaimo, *Bodily Natures: Science, Environment, and the Material Self*, 2; Laird Christensen, "The Pragmatic Mysticism of Mary Oliver," 140. Although Christensen is speaking here of a particular poet's view, the comment would apply as well to Meynell's ecopoetics.

7. Alice Meynell, quoted in June Badeni, *The Slender Tree: A Life of Alice Meynell*, 52; Alice Meynell, *The Selected Letters of Alice Meynell: Poet and Essayist*, 23; Viola Meynell, quoted in Badeni, *Slender Tree*, 52; Badeni, *Slender Tree*, 52; Meynell, *Selected Letters*, 69. Unless otherwise indicated by a date later than 1875, the poems discussed in this chapter appeared in *Preludes*; quotations of the *Preludes* poems, as well as of the later poems, all come from *The Poems of Alice Meynell: Complete Edition*.

8. Linda Peterson, for example, observes that the 1875 collection "suggests an ambivalence about the direction her poetry would take, about its relation to a nineteenth-century women's lyric tradition, as well as to the poetry of male predecessors" ("Alice Meynell's *Preludes*, or Preludes to What Future Poetry?," 406). Peterson also comments, "A significant number of poems in *Preludes* seem appreciative of, or merely expansive on, the work of male poets, without suggesting a new direction for her own poetry" (418–19). Of one poem, "In Early Spring," Peterson contends that it "suggests that the young woman writing cannot imagine *herself* as a poet in the Wordsworthian tradition, that there is a secret in the nature poet that she cannot fathom and that she can represent this sort of poet only with the pronoun 'he'" (406). In contrast, Kathleen Anderson states that "Meynell succeeded in constructing a female poetic voice that generates and affirms itself, rather than being defined by the Not-Male" ("'I Make the Whole World Answer to My Art': Alice Meynell's Poetic Identity," 259). Sharon Smulders indicates that Meynell "tries to resolve the conflict between inherited structures—both formal and conceptual—and the woman poet" ("Looking 'Past Wordsworth and the Rest': Pretexts for Revision in Alice Meynell's 'The Shepherdess,'" 35). Beverly Ann Schlack says of *Preludes* that "Meynell insists upon her conjunction of woman, nature, and poetry" and points to gender elements in various verses ("The 'Poetess of Poets': Alice Meynell Rediscovered," 116). To some critics, Meynell is the speaker in various poems and is attempting to establish her own poetic voice in response to tradition and gender challenges. See the cited critics for divergent readings of several of the poems addressed in this chapter.

In one pair of poems, gender designations offset each other in subheads, for one identifies a female poet speaking ("The Moon to the Sun") whereas the other refers to a male poet addressing another writer ("The Day to the Night"). Another poem includes the feminine pronoun to designate nature ("To Any Poet"), whereby Meynell is conforming to common practice. In a different poem ("West Wind in Winter"), the wind is identified as masculine, and in "Love of Narcissus," the featured poet is male, likely in reference to male Romantic poets such as Wordsworth.

9. Michael Field, "Poets," in *The Wattlefold*, 70; Irigaray, *To Be Two*, 5.

10. Jonathan Culler, *The Pursuit of Signs: Semiotics, Literature, Deconstruction*, 138, 139, 143.

11. Alice Meynell, "The Foot," 43, 44.

12. Alice Meynell, "Grass," 60, 63–64, 61–62. Meynell gained greater fame "in her day" for her essays than for her poetry, Leighton notes (*Victorian Women Poets: Writing against the Heart*, 256).

13. Alice Meynell, "In July," 181, 182, 181, 183.

14. Meynell, "In July," 182, 182–83.

15. Alice Meynell, "Rushes and Reeds," 41, 41–42; Alice Meynell, "Rain," 12, 13.

16. Linda H. Peterson, "Writing Nature at the *Fin de Siècle*: Grant Allen, Alice Meynell, and the Split Legacy of Gilbert White," 85, 82; Jefferies, *The Hills and the Vale*, 273–74, 275; Peterson, "Writing Nature," 85.

17. Jefferies, quoted in Peterson, "Writing Nature," 85; Gilbert White, *The Natural History of Selborne*, 41, 45, 52, 61. Peterson observes that "Meynell's essays . . . follow White's lead but develop their own mode of 'looking closely'" (*Becoming a Woman of Letters: Myths of Authorship and Facts of the Victorian Market*, 190). Peterson also comments, "In writing these innovative nature essays, Meynell speaks to an uneasiness she had registered in *Preludes*: the assumption that Nature yields up a higher meaning, a nature philosophy, to the Romantic poet" (191). Subsequent discussion in this chapter also comes to such a conclusion on the flawed poet.

18. Alice Meynell, "Tennyson," 81, 83, 87, 88, 89.

19. Schlack offers a gendered reading of the poem, with "the woman-moon-poet singing to her man-sun-poet" ("'Poetess of Poets,'" 117). Emily Harrington, in contrast, relates the moon to future generations of poets. She also sees the moon "changing its quality" through its reflection of sunlight "so that the light it gives belongs to" predecessor and descendant poets (*Second Person Singular: Late Victorian Women Poets and the Bonds of Verse*, 134).

20. To Harrington, "[e]ach poet renews the other" (*Second Person Singular*, 135).

21. Yopie Prins, "Patmore's Law, Meynell's Rhythm," 279; Percy Bysshe Shelley, "Ode to the West Wind," in Lynch and Stillinger, *Norton Anthology of English Literature*, vol. D, *The Romantic Period*, 793; Alice Meynell, "Winds of the World," 23. Meynell's familiarity with Shelley is indisputable, as is his effect upon her. She remarked that she "discovered" Shelley in adolescence and credited him for altering her perspective on spirituality, indicating, "I thought the whole world was changed for me thenceforth" (quoted in Viola Meynell, *Alice Meynell: A Memoir*, 41). Moreover, one of Meynell's introductions to various books of collected poems by others included one of poems by Shelley.

22. The masculine pronoun is fitting here in making a poet a Narcissus since the mythological figure is male.

23. Luce Irigaray, *This Sex Which Is Not One*, 187.

24. Hess, *William Wordsworth*, 29; Wordsworth, "Lines Composed a Few Miles above Tintern Abbey," in Lynch and Stillinger, *Norton Anthology of English Literature*, vol. D, *The Romantic Period*, 290; William Wordsworth, *The Fourteen-Book "Prelude,"* bk. 14,

lines 450–53; Hess, *William Wordsworth*, 40. In the 1805 *Prelude*, the quoted lines appear at the end of bk. 13. In W. J. B. Owen's edited version of the poem, *The Fourteen-Book "Prelude,"* the lines appear at the end of bk. 14. The sole difference between the two versions is the capitalization of "Man" in Owen's volume. Hess points to a "process of capturing, carrying away, and then returning to the image in a more private setting" (29).

25. Homans, *Women Writers*, 38.

26. Meynell's familiarity with Wordsworth is apparent not only through the daisy poems but also because she wrote an introduction to a collection of his poems. Further, Meynell was a frequent reader of Wordsworth in her youth. As she described it, "In quite early childhood I lived upon Wordsworth. I don't know that I particularly enjoyed him, but he was put into my hands, and to me, Wordsworth's poetry was the normal poetry *par excellence*" (quoted in Viola Meynell, *Alice Meynell*, 41). Also see Peterson for a reading of the daisy poems (*Becoming a Woman of Letters*, 191).

27. William Wordsworth, "To the Daisy," in Nicholas Halmi, ed., *Wordsworth's Poetry and Prose: Authoritative Texts*.

28. William Wordsworth, "Preface to *Poems*," 140, 141, 145, 146, 152, 153.

Chapter 5: Constance Naden

1. [Constance Naden], "Hylozoic Materialism," 313; Constance Naden [C.A., pseud.], "Correspondence: Hylo-Idealism," 242; Irigaray, *Key Writings*, 220. Naden used the initials "C.A." and "C.N." for some of her writings, as well as the pseudonym "Constance Arden," and she published some of her works anonymously. In her childhood, the baptized Naden attended church services when living with her grandparents and later attended a school operated by "two Unitarian ladies," William R. Hughes notes (*Constance Naden: A Memoir*, 7, 9). James R. Moore describes Naden's grandparents as "old-fashioned churchgoers of the Calvinist persuasion. In their 'Puritan house' no lively entertainments took place and 'worldly' amusements were banned" ("The Erotics of Evolution: Constance Naden and Hylo-Idealism," 227). In an 1891 essay, R. W. Dale indicates that some of the poems in her 1881 *Songs and Sonnets of Springtime* evidence "the falling away of early religious faith" ("Constance Naden," 514).

2. *Encyclopaedia Britannica*, 11th ed. (1911), s.v. "hylozoism," https://en.wikisource.org/wiki/1911_Encyclop%C3%A6dia Britannica/Hylozoism; Nour Alarabi, "Constance Naden's Philosophical Poetry," 849; Smith, "Robert Lewins, Constance Naden, and Hylo-Idealism," 305.

3. Constance Naden [Constance Arden, pseud.], "The Philosophy of Thomas Carlyle," 319; Constance Naden, "On Mental Physiology and Its Place in Philosophy," 81, 81–82; Constance Naden [Constance Arden, pseud.], "The Brain Theory of Mind and Matter," 124; Constance Naden, *What Is Religion?*, 20–21.

4. Naden, *What Is Religion?*, 22, 27–28, 22, 23.

5. Naden, *What Is Religion?*, 24; [Constance Naden], "Hylo-Idealism: The Creed of the Coming Day," 170, 171; Constance Naden [Constance Arden, pseud.], "The Identity of Vital and Cosmical Energy," 253; Naden, "Hylo-Idealism: The Creed," 173.

6. Robert Lewins, *Humanism versus Theism*, 12; Naden, "Philosophy of Thomas Carlyle," 315; Naden, "Brain Theory," 125, 128; Naden, "Correspondence," 242; Constance Naden [Constance Arden, pseud.], "Hylo-Idealism: A Defence," 704.

7. Naden, "The Identity," 255, 254; Naden, "Brain Theory," 126.

8. Naden, "Brain Theory," 124, 129; Naden, *What Is Religion?*, 18.

9. Moore, "Erotics of Evolution," 248; Constance Naden, "The Nebular Theory." Quotations of "The Nebular Theory" and all other Naden poems in this chapter are from *The Complete Poetical Works of Constance Naden.*

10. Marilyn Bailey Ogilvie, "Robert Chambers and the Nebular Hypothesis," 229; Herbert Spencer, "Recent Astronomy and the Nebular Hypothesis"; Robert Chambers, quoted in Ogilvie, "Robert Chambers," 226; Rush Emery, "The Nebular Theory," 461. Chambers's book, Ogilvie explained, "populariz[ed] evolutionary ideas," which "establish[ed] it as a significant work in the history of science even though its intrinsic scientific value is not great"; she added, "The clientele to whom the book especially appealed was not too concerned with errors in fact and unsupported generalizations" ("Robert Chambers," 214). Such failings, however, "caused it to be an anathema to both scientists and clergymen, who . . . agreed that the ideas in [the book] were potentially harmful to those untrained in scientific procedures and unaware of the book's inherent religious heresies" (214). See Ogilvie's essay for an explanation of the nebular theory.

11. Alarabi comments that Naden's poem "is referring . . . to the idea of Monism: matter is the source of life; it unites the body with the sun and the stars" ("Constance Naden's Philosophical Poetry," 855). Rather than "look for answers in religion and mythologies," the poem indicates that "science can offer more reliable explanations" (855). Monism "is the prominent concept" in the poem, Alarabi notes (855).

12. George Landow, "Atheism," n.p.; Percy Bysshe Shelley, "The Necessity of Atheism," n.p.

13. Charles Bradlaugh, "Humanity's Gain from Unbelief," n.p.; George Eliot, quoted in James A. Haught, *2000 Years of Disbelief: Famous People with the Courage to Doubt*, 142, 143; Annie Besant, *My Path to Atheism*, n.p.

14. Marion Thain asserts that Naden "use[s] religious language to describe the material world" and adds that "Lewins and Naden really did make a religion out of their science-based materialism" ("'Scientific Wooing': Constance Naden's Marriage of Science and Poetry," 160).

Naden does adopt a somewhat varied position in arguing that God is simply a product of human thought, a point not addressed in the ecofeminist references presented here.

15. Rosemary Radford Ruether, "Ecofeminism: Symbolic and Social Connections of the Oppression of Women and the Domination of Nature," 396; Ursula King, *The Search for Spirituality: Our Global Quest for a Spiritual Life*, 136; Ruether, *Integrating Ecofeminism*, 124–25.

16. McFague, "Earthly Theological Agenda," 97; Ruether, *Integrating Ecofeminism*, 124.

17. Sallie McFague, "The Scope of the Body: The Cosmic Christ," 267; McFague, *Body of God*, 48, 17; McFague, "Earthly Theological Agenda," 95; Irigaray, *Sexes and Genealogies*, 77; Ruether, "Ecofeminism," 396. Perhaps one thread of Naden's rejection of Christianity derives from the religion's definitive rejection of the body. The position is a paradoxical one in that, as McFague identifies it, "Christianity is the religion of the incarnation *par excellence*" (*Body of God*, 16). McFague cites several Christian tenets that focus on embodiment, including the incarnation, Christ's adoption of human form, the

resurrection, and the equation of the Eucharist with Christ's body. The distaste for the body is a relatively recent position, in that in its early years respect rather than dismissal was the dominant reaction. Over the centuries, however, Christianity as "a religion of the body" has "germinated into full-blown distrust of the body" and an attendant marginalization of nature as well as the female form (14). Abhorrence of the human body has translated into a distaste for the earth's body that prevails today (16).

18. Naden, "The Identity," 254; McCulloch, *Deconstruction of Dualism*, 73, 102; McFague, *Models of God*, 74; McFague, *Body of God*, 16; Ruether, "Toward an Ecological-Feminist Theology," 145, 146.

19. Sallie McFague, *Super, Natural Christians: How We Should Love Nature*, 19, 17, 19, 18 (Garb quote); Adams, *Ecofeminism and the Sacred*, 1; Ruether, "Ecofeminism," 396.

20. Irigaray, *Key Writings*, 155; Riane Eisler, "The Gaia Tradition and the Partnership Future: An Ecofeminist Manifesto," 23, 23–24, 30.

21. The song, also known as "The Battle Hymn of the Republic," was written by Julia Ward Howe during the US Civil War.

22. The oak tree has traditionally been linked with strength because of its long life. Shakespeare associates the willow with death in *Hamlet*, in which Ophelia falls from a willow tree to die by drowning, and in *Othello*, in which Desdemona sings the "Willow Song" shortly before she is murdered.

23. Irigaray, *To Be Two*, 2.

24. Irigaray, *This Sex Which Is Not One*, 116, 112.

25. Irigaray, *To Be Two*, 2.

26. As Alarabi points out, "[W]hite light consists of all the colours of the spectrum" ("Constance Naden's Philosophical Poetry," 855).

Chapter 6: L. S. Bevington

1. A prolific author, Louisa Sarah Bevington is perhaps best recognized for a determined commitment to evolutionary ideas within her noncanonical oeuvre of verse as well as prose, gaining thereby the admiration of Charles Darwin and the support of Herbert Spencer. In an 1891 introduction to Bevington's verse in a collection of poets' works, contemporary Alfred H. Miles comments that *Key-Notes* "found fame chiefly in scientific circles" and that biologist Roy Lankester had "brought it under the notice of Darwin, who read it after not having opened a volume of verse for fifteen years" (*The Poets and the Poetry of the Nineteenth Century*, 228). Miles goes on, "It is not surprising that [Bevington] should have broken the spell which for fifteen years had confined Darwin to the world of prose, for her part is emphatically that of the poetess of evolutionary science" (229). Spencer, Miles reports, was instrumental in the reprinting of four Bevington poems in *Popular Science Monthly*, and Bevington penned an essay in defense of evolution through Spencer's influence (228). Bevington's work brought recognition in the literary world as well, of course, with Robert Browning commenting to her, "I venture to recognize in your verses much power and beauty of various kinds" (quoted in Domingue, "An Unpublished Browning Letter to Louisa Sarah Bevington," 38).

2. The quotation used as the epigraph appears in Emerson's 1850 *Representative Man* essay "Swedenborg; or, the Mystic." Bevington's knowledge of Emerson's work is evident,

not only through the epigraph in *Key-Notes* but also through an epigraph in a subsequent volume of her poetry and a quotation in one of her essays as well: Bevington's 1882 *Poems, Lyrics and Sonnets* includes an epigraph from Emerson's essay "Poetry and Imagination" from his *Letters and Social Aims*, and her essay "The Moral Colour of Rationalism" includes a quotation of Emerson (181). The extent of Bevington's familiarity with Emerson's oeuvre is unclear, however; no biography or personal journal has appeared, and few letters still exist. See Domingue, *Collected Essays*, vi, for details of Bevington's remaining letters.

3. See Domingue's introduction to *Collected Essays* for further information on the two versions of *Key-Notes* (ii).

Miles notes Bevington's longtime interest in the natural world, for "[h]er father encouraged her in the observation and love of nature, and at a very early age she wrote childish verses about natural objects" (*The Poets and the Poetry*, 227).

In various essays supportive of atheistic notions, Bevington attributes moral growth to evolution rather than to religious influence. In "The Moral Colour of Rationalism," an 1881 *Fortnightly Review* piece, for example, Bevington rejects the idea that the "duty of mutual helpfulness" stems from Christ's teachings, believing instead that it occurs "because of the simple, natural fact that [people] are knit by their common needs, and mutual powers of helpfulness" (185). Another essay, published in two parts with the identical title "Modern Atheism and Mr. Mallock" in October and December 1879 issues of *The Nineteenth Century* and garnering a wide audience, attributes morality to secular influences while responding vigorously to attacks on atheism. In the October essay, Bevington "den[ies], emphatically and utterly," that the ability to respond productively to a "difficult and stormy crisis" affecting "human virtue" will be derived from "the failing vitality of religious creeds" (603). In the December conclusion, Bevington asserts that "in the evolutional view of man's social condition we seem to have a firm basis for a clear theory of morals, quite independent of the comings and goings of religious creeds" (1000). With such arguments, Bevington established herself as an insistent defender of evolution and a determined opponent of religion.

Regarding feminism, Domingue remarks, "Bevington rarely referred to women's issues in her political essays because as an anarchist she advanced everyone's entitlement to self-autonomy," striving to aid "the oppressed of both sexes without emphasis on feminist issues" (*Collected Essays*, viii). Domingue mentions that in this era of feminist interest, "for some the anarchist movement was a way to transcend an entanglement of gender in order to create meaning for themselves within society as a whole" (viii–ix).

4. Mary Mellor, *Feminism & Ecology*, 1; Plumwood, *Feminism and the Mastery of Nature*, 4; McFague, "Earthly Theological Agenda," 91.

5. King, "Ecology of Feminism," 408; Legler, "Ecofeminist Literary Criticism," 230; Ralph Waldo Emerson, *Nature*, 11, 11–12, 13.

6. Emerson, *Nature*, 7, 10, 36, 37.

7. Except when otherwise noted, all quotations of Bevington poems in this chapter are from *Key-Notes*.

8. Emerson, *Nature*, 16, 25, 50–51, 95.

9. William Morris, "The Beauty of Life," n.p.; Patrick D. Murphy, "Prolegomenon for an Ecofeminist Dialogics," 42.

10. John Ruskin, *Sesame and Lilies*, 64.

11. Thomas Babington Macaulay, "Sir James Mackintosh," 102, 103, 97; Herbert Spencer, "Progress: Its Law and Cause," 10.

12. John Ruskin, *The Two Paths*, n.p.

13. Plumwood, *Feminism and the Mastery of Nature*, 21.

14. Emerson, *Nature*, 32, 33, 35, 41.

15. David W. Gilcrest, *Greening the Lyre: Environmental Poetics and Ethics*, 38, 39; Christopher Manes, "Nature and Silence," 15, 18, 18–20, 17, 21, 25; Irigaray, in Irigaray and Marder, *Through Vegetal Being*, 49.

16. Patrick D. Murphy, "Ground, Pivot, Motion: Ecofeminist Theory, Dialogics, and Literary Practice," 148, 152, 153; Sandilands, "Natural Identity," 77; Michael J. McDowell, "The Bakhtinian Road to Ecological Insight," 372. Murphy posits that viewing the other as an entity capable of speech involves addressing "pivotal questions" as to "the degree to which language is recognized as one type of sign system, the degree to which volition is assumed as a prerequisite for becoming a speaking subject, and the degree to which the other speaking subjects who do not use the *parole* of human beings can 'speak' in a sign system that can be understood by humans" ("Prolegomenon," 45). To Murphy, the nonhuman speaks "by means of various 'dialects'" without the need for "volition to do so" (47).

17. Gilcrest, *Greening the Lyre*, 62, 63, 43–44.

18. Irigaray, in Irigaray and Marder, *Through Vegetal Being*, 50; Irigaray, *To Be Two*, 4, 1.

19. Manes, "Nature and Silence," 15, 16 (Duerr quote).

20. Homans, *Women Writers*, 54, 56, 74, 75, 86.

21. Margaret Homans, *Bearing the Word: Language and Female Experience in Nineteenth-Century Women's Writing*, 4, 10. In an essay on Mary Oliver's poetry, Diane S. Bonds also turns to Homans's work in assessing the poet's response to Emerson's *Nature* ("The Language of Nature in the Poetry of Mary Oliver," *Women's Studies* 21 [1992]: 1–15).

22. Although Bevington accords nature spiritual importance, which may seem a contradictory coupling in one regard, the connection is made on a literal level, as will become evident later in this chapter.

23. Emerson, *Nature*, 10, 30, 73. The feminine pronoun is usually associated with the passage of time (month, year, season) in Bevington's poetry. These designations of linear time, which carry a strong association to masculinity, complicate and undermine the feminization of nature's time, with its cyclical movements. See Julia Kristeva's essay "Women's Time" for the delineation.

24. Ruether, "Ecofeminism," 396; Ruether, *Integrating Ecofeminism*, 125; McFague, *Models of God*, 77; McFague, "Earthly Theological Agenda," 95. "Despite her claims to leave religion behind, its symbols were nevertheless ingrained in her work," Domingue observes of Bevington (*Collected Essays*, ii).

25. Emerson, *Nature*, 44, 52, 53, 80–81, 79–80.

26. No evidence has been found that Bevington embraced transcendentalism.

27. Emerson, *Nature*, 44, 44–45; Mary Shelley, *Frankenstein*, 41, 55; Haraway, "Situated Knowledges," 593.

28. L. S. Bevington, "My Little Task," in *Poems, Lyrics, and Sonnets*, n.p.

WORKS CITED

Adams, Carol J., ed. *Ecofeminism and the Sacred*. New York: Continuum, 1993.

Adams, Carol J., and Lori Gruen, eds. *Ecofeminism: Feminist Intersections with Other Animals and the Earth*. New York: Bloomsbury, 2014.

Alaimo, Stacy. *Bodily Natures: Science, Environment, and the Material Self*. Bloomington: Indiana University Press, 2010.

———. "Material Engagements: Science Studies and the Environmental Humanities." *Ecozon* (2010): 69–74.

———. "Trans-Corporeal Feminisms and the Ethical Space of Nature." In *Material Feminisms*, ed. Stacy Alaimo and Susan Hekman, 237–64. Bloomington: Indiana University Press, 2008.

———. *Undomesticated Ground: Recasting Nature as Feminist Space*. Ithaca, NY: Cornell University Press, 2000.

Alaimo, Stacy, and Susan Hekman, eds. *Material Feminisms*. Bloomington: Indiana University Press, 2008.

Alarabi, Nour. "Constance Naden's Philosophical Poetry." *Literature Compass* 9, no. 11 (2012): 848–60.

Allan, J. McGrigor. "Influence of Sex on Mind III: Historical Evidence." *Knowledge* 1 (Jan. 13, 1882): 230–31.

———. "On the Real Differences in the Minds of Men and Women." *Journal of the Anthropological Society of London* 7 (1869): cxcv–ccxix.

Allen, Grant. "Woman's Place in Nature." *Forum* 7 (1889): 258–63.

Anderson, Emily R. "Constance Naden (1858–1889)." In *Nineteenth-Century British Women Writers: A Bio-Bibliographical Critical Sourcebook*, ed. Abigail Burnham Bloom, 283–86. Westport, CT: Greenwood, 2000.

Anderson, Kathleen. "'I Make the Whole World Answer to My Art': Alice Meynell's Poetic Identity." *Victorian Poetry* 41, no. 2 (2003): 259–76.

Arden, Constance. *See* Naden, Constance.

Armstrong, Isobel. *Language as Living Form in Nineteenth-Century Poetry*. Sussex, UK: Harvester, 1982.

———. *Victorian Poetry: Poetry, Poetics, and Politics*. London: Routledge, 1993.

"The Ascent of Man." Anonymous review of *The Ascent of Man*, by Mathilde Blind. *Athenaeum* (July 20, 1889): 87–88.

Bacon, Francis. *De Augmentis*. In *The Works of Francis Bacon*, vol. 4, ed. James Spedding, Robert Leslie Ellis, and Douglas Denon Heath. Cambridge: Cambridge University Press, 2011.

————. *De Sapientia Veterum*. In *Francis Bacon: The Essays*, ed. John Pitcher. Harmondsworth, UK: Penguin, 1985.

————. "The Great Instauration." In *The Works of Francis Bacon*, vol. 4, ed. James Spedding, Robert Leslie Ellis, and Douglas Denon Heath. Cambridge: Cambridge University Press, 2011.

————. "The Masculine Birth of Time." In *The Philosophy of Francis Bacon*, ed. Benjamin Farrington. Chicago: Phoenix, 1964.

————. *Novum Organum*. Ed. Joseph Devey. New York: P. F. Collier & Son, 1902. https://www.gutenberg.org/files/45988/45988-h/45988-h.htm.

Badeni, June. *The Slender Tree: A Life of Alice Meynell*. Padstow: Tabb House, 1981.

Barad, Karen. "Posthumanist Performativity: Toward an Understanding of How Matter Comes to Matter." In *Material Feminisms*, ed. Stacy Alaimo and Susan Hekman, 120–54. Bloomington: Indiana University Press, 2008.

Bate, Jonathan. *Romantic Ecology: Wordsworth and the Environmental Tradition*. London: Routledge, 1991.

Beer, Gillian. *Darwin's Plots: Evolutionary Narrative in Darwin, George Eliot and Nineteenth-Century Fiction*. London: Routledge & Kegan Paul, 1983.

Bell, Mackenzie. "Augusta Webster." In *The Victorian Poets*, ed. William E. Fredeman. New York: Garland, 1986.

"Belles Lettres." *Westminster Review* 116 (1881): 563–64.

Bennett, Paula. "Critical Clitoridectomy: Female Sexual Imagery and Feminist Psychoanalytic Theory." *Signs* 18, no. 2 (1993): 235–59.

Bernath, Elizabeth. "'Seeking Flowers to Comfort Her': Queer Botany in Blake's *Visions*, Darwin's *Loves* and Wollstonecraft's *Rights of Woman*." In *Blake, Gender and Culture*, ed. Helen P. Bruder and Tristanne J. Connolly, 111–22. London: Pickering & Chatto, 2012.

Besant, Annie. *My Path to Atheism*. 3rd ed. London: Freethought, 1885. http://www.gutenberg.org/files/37234/37234-h/37234-h.htm.

Bevington, L. S. *Key-Notes*. 1879. N.p.: Dodo, n.d.

————. "Modern Atheism and Mr. Mallock." *Nineteenth Century* 32 (October 1879): 585–603.

————. "Modern Atheism and Mr. Mallock." *Nineteenth Century* 34 (December 1879): 999–1020.

————. "The Moral Colour of Rationalism." *Fortnightly Review* 36 (1881): 179–94.

————. *Poems, Lyrics, and Sonnets*. London: Elliot Stock, 1882. Available at the Victorian Women Writers Project, Indiana University, https://webapp1.dlib.indiana.edu/vwwp/welcome.do.

Bewell, Alan. "'Jacobin Plants': Botany as Social Theory in the 1790s." *Wordsworth Circle* 20, no. 3 (1989): 132–39.

Bewick, Thomas. *A History of British Birds*. Vol. 1. Newcastle, UK: Longman, 1826.

Blind, Mathilde. *The Ascent of Man*. London: T. Fisher Unwin, 1899.

————. Introduction to *The Journal of Marie Bashkirtseff*. Trans. Mathilde Blind. 1891. London: Virago, 1985.

————. "Mary Wollstonecraft." *New Quarterly Magazine* (July 1878): 390–412.

———— [Claude Lake, pseud.]. *Poems*. London: Alfred W. Bennett, 1867. Available at the Victorian Women Writers Project, Indiana University, https://webapp1.dlib. indiana.edu/vwwp/welcome.do.

————. *The Poetical Works of Mathilde Blind*. Ed. Arthur Symons. London: T. Fisher Unwin, 1900.

————. "Shelley." *Westminster Review* 38 (July 1870): 75–97.

————. "Shelley's View of Nature as Contrasted with Darwin's." London, 1886. Available at the Victorian Women Writers Project, Indiana University, https:// webapp1.dlib.indiana.edu/vwwp/welcome.do.

Bookchin, Murray. *Remaking Society: Pathways to a Green Future*. Boston: South End, 1990.

Bradlaugh, Charles. "Humanity's Gain from Unbelief." London: Freethought, 1889. http://www.victorianweb.org/religion/bradlaugh2.html.

Bradley, Katharine, and Edith Cooper. *See* Field, Michael.

Brooks, W. K. "The Condition of Women from a Zoological Point of View I." *Popular Science Monthly* 15 (1879): 145–55.

Brown, Penelope, and L. J. Jordanova. "Oppressive Dichotomies: The Nature/Culture Debate." In *Women in Society*, 224–41. London: Virago, 1981.

Browne, Janet. "Botany for Gentlemen: Erasmus Darwin and *The Loves of the Plants*." *Isis* 80, no. 4 (1989): 592–621.

Bryson, J. Scott. *Ecopoetry: A Critical Introduction*. Salt Lake City: University of Utah Press, 2002.

Buckley, Jerome Hamilton, and George Benjamin Woods, eds. *Poetry of the Victorian Period*. 3rd ed. New York: HarperCollins, 1965.

Buell, Lawrence. *The Environmental Imagination: Thoreau, Nature Writing, and the Formation of American Culture*. Cambridge: Harvard University Press, 1995.

Burke, Karen I. "Masculine and Feminine Approaches to Nature." In *Luce Irigaray Teaching*, 189–200. New York: Continuum, 2008.

Cameron, S. Brooke. "The Pleasures of Looking and the Feminine Gaze in Michael Field's *Sight and Song*." *Victorian Poetry* 51, no. 2 (2013): 147–75.

Campbell, Andrea, ed. *New Directions in Ecofeminist Literary Criticism*. Newcastle upon Tyne, UK: Cambridge Scholars Publishing, 2008.

Campbell, Harry. *Differences in the Nervous Organisation of Man and Woman: Physiological and Pathological*. London: H. K. Lewis, 1891.

Carlson, Allen. "Aesthetics of the Environment." In *A Companion to Aesthetics*, 2nd ed., ed. Stephen Davies, et al., 134–36. Malden: Wiley-Blackwell, 2009.

————. *Nature and Landscape: An Introduction to Environmental Aesthetics*. New York: Columbia University Press, 2009.

Carlyle, Thomas. *Past and Present*. New York: AMS, 1974.

————. *Sartor Resartus*. London: Chapman and Hall, 1896.

————. "Signs of the Times." In *The Spirit of the Age: Victorian Essays*, ed. Gertrude Himmelfarb. New Haven, CT: Yale University Press, 2007.

Carroll, David. "Pollution, Defilement and the Art of Decomposition." In *Ruskin and the Environment: The Storm-Cloud of the Nineteenth Century*, ed. Michael Wheeler, 58–75. Manchester, UK: Manchester University Press, 1995.

Christensen, Laird. "The Pragmatic Mysticism of Mary Oliver." In *Ecopoetry: A Critical Introduction*, ed. J. Scott Bryson, 135–52. Salt Lake City: University of Utah Press, 2002.

Clark, Timothy. *The Cambridge Introduction to Literature and the Environment*. Cambridge: Cambridge University Press, 2011.

Coates, Peter. *Nature: Western Attitudes since Ancient Times*. Berkeley: University of California Press, 2005.

Coffey, Donna. "Introduction: A Sense of Place." *Women's Studies* 31, no. 2 (2002): 131–40.

Cohoon, Christopher. "The Ecological Irigaray?" In *Ecocritical Theory: New European Approaches*, ed. Axel Goodbody and Kate Rigby, 206–14. Charlottesville: University of Virginia Press, 2011.

Connolly, Tristanne. "Flowery Porn: Form and Desire in Erasmus Darwin's *The Loves of the Plants*." *Literature Compass* 13, no. 10 (2016): 604–16.

"Contemporary Poets and Versifiers." *Edinburgh Review* (October 1893): 470–99.

Copernicus, Nicolaus. *Copernicus: On the Revolutions of the Heavenly Spheres*. Trans. A. M. Duncan. New York: Barnes & Noble, 1976.

Cronon, William. Foreword to *Man and Nature: George Perkins Marsh*, by George Perkins Marsh, ed. David Lowenthal. Seattle: University of Washington Press, 2003.

Cudworth, Erika. *Developing Ecofeminist Theory: The Complexity of Difference*. London: Palgrave Macmillan, 2005.

Culler, Jonathan. *The Pursuit of Signs: Semiotics, Literature, Deconstruction*. Ithaca, NY: Cornell University Press, 1981.

Cuomo, Chris J. *Feminism and Ecological Communities: An Ethic of Flourishing*. London: Routledge, 1998.

Curry, Patrick. *Ecological Ethics: An Introduction*. Cambridge, UK: Polity, 2011.

Dale, R. W. "Constance Naden." *Contemporary Review* 59 (1891): 508–22.

Darwin, Charles. *The Descent of Man, and Selection in Relation to Sex*. New York: Hurst, n.d.

Darwin, Erasmus. *The Loves of the Plants*, pt. 2 of *The Botanic Garden; A Poem, in Two Parts*. 2nd ed. London, 1790. https://www.gutenberg.org/files/10671/10671-8.txt.

D'Eaubonne, Françoise. "The Time for Ecofeminism." Trans. Ruth Hottell. 1974. In *Ecology*, 2nd ed., ed. Carolyn Merchant, 201–14. Amherst, NY: Humanity, 2008.

Delaporte, François. *Nature's Second Kingdom: Explorations of Vegetality in the Eighteenth Century*. Trans. Arthur Goldhammer. Cambridge, MA: MIT, 1982.

Demoor, Marysa. "A Mode(rni)st Beginning? The Women of the 'Athenaeum' 1890–1910." In *The Turn of the Century: Modernism and Modernity in Literature and the Arts*, ed. Christian Berg, Frank Durieux, and Geert Lernout, 270–81. Berlin: Walter de Gruyter, 1995.

———. *Their Fair Share: Women, Power and Criticism in the* Athenaeum, *from Millicent Garrett Fawcett to Katherine Mansfield, 1870–1920*. Aldershot, UK: Ashgate, 2000.

Descartes, René. *A Discourse on Method*. https://www.gutenberg.org/files/59/59-h/59-h.htm#part4.

Devereaux, Mary. "Feminist Aesthetics." In *The Oxford Handbook of Aesthetics*, ed.
Jerrold Levinson, 647–66. Oxford: Oxford University Press, 2005.

Diedrick, James. "'The Hectic Beauty of Decay': Positivist Decadence in Mathilde
Blind's Late Poetry." *Victorian Literature and Culture* 34, no. 2 (2006): 631–48.

———. "Mathilde Blind." *Dictionary of Literary Biography*, vol. 199, 28–39. Detroit:
Gale, 1999.

———. *Mathilde Blind: Late-Victorian Culture and the Woman of Letters*.
Charlottesville: University of Virginia Press, 2016.

———. "Mathilde Blind's (Proto-) New Women." *The Latchkey: Journal of New Woman
Studies*. http://www.thelatchkey.org/Latchkey9/essay/Diedrick.htm.

Dixon, Edmund Saul. "Dirty Cleanliness." *Household Words* 18, no. 435 (July 24,
1858): 121–23. Available at Dickens Journals Online, University of Buckingham,
www.djo.org.uk.

Domingue, Jackie Dees, ed. *Collected Essays of Louisa Sarah Bevington*. Ann Arbor, MI:
Scholars, 2010.

———. "An Unpublished Browning Letter to Louisa Sarah Bevington." *ANQ* 13, no. 3
(2000): 37–41.

Donoghue, Emma. *We Are Michael Field*. Bath, UK: Absolute, 1998.

Ehnenn, Jill R. "Looking Strategically: Feminist and Queer Aesthetics in Michael Field's
Sight and Song." *Victorian Poetry* 42, no. 3 (2004): 213–60.

———. "'Our Brains Struck Fire Each from Each': Disidentification, Difference, and
Desire in the Collaborative Aesthetics of Michael Field." In *Economies of Desire at
the Victorian Fin de Siècle: Libidinal Lives*, ed. Jane Ford, Kim Edwards Keates, and
Patricia Pulham, 180–204. New York: Routledge, 2016.

Eisler, Riane. "The Gaia Tradition and the Partnership Future: An Ecofeminist
Manifesto." In *Reweaving the World: The Emergence of Ecofeminism*, ed. Irene
Diamond and Gloria Feman Orenstein, 23–34. San Francisco: Sierra Club, 1990.

Ellis, Havelock. *Man and Woman: A Study of Human Secondary Sexual Characters*. New
York: Arno, 1974.

Emerson, Ralph Waldo. *Nature*. Boston: Beacon, 1985.

Emery, Rush. "The Nebular Theory." *Appleton's Journal* 8, no. 187 (Oct. 26, 1872):
461–63.

Engelhardt, Molly. "The Language of Flowers in the Victorian Knowledge Age."
Victoriographies 3, no. 2 (2013): 136–60.

Engels, Friedrich. *The Condition of the Working Class in England*. Trans. and ed. W. O.
Henderson and W. H. Chaloner. Stanford, CA: Stanford University Press, 1958.

Estok, Simon C. "The Ecophobia Hypothesis: Re-membering the Feminist Body of
Ecocriticism." In *International Perspectives in Feminist Criticism*, ed. Greta Gaard,
Simon C. Estok, and Serpil Oppermann, 70–83. New York: Routledge, 2013.

———. "Theorizing in a Space of Ambivalent Openness: Ecocriticism and Ecophobia."
Interdisciplinary Studies in Literature and Environment 16, no. 2 (2009): 203–25.

Field, Michael [Katharine Bradley and Edith Cooper]. *Sight and Song (1892) with
Underneath the Bough (1893)*. Oxford: Woodstock, 1993.

———. *Underneath the Bough: A Book of Verses*. Portland, ME: Thomas B. Mosher, 1898.

————. *The Wattlefold: Unpublished Poems by Michael Field*. Ed. Emily C. Fortey. Oxford: Basil Blackwell, 1930.

————. *Works and Days*. Ed. T. Moore and D. C. Moore. London: John Murray, 1933.

Fisher-Wirth, Ann, and Laura-Gray Street. *The Ecopoetry Anthology*. San Antonio, TX: Trinity University Press, 2013.

Fletcher, Robert P. "'I Leave a Page Half-Writ': Narrative Discoherence in Michael Field's *Underneath the Bough*." In *Women's Poetry, Late Romantic to Late Victorian: Gender and Genre, 1830–1900*, ed. Isobel Armstrong and Virginia Blain, 164–82. London: St. Martin's, 1999.

Ford, Thomas H. "Punctuating History circa 1800: The Air of *Jane Eyre*." In *Anthropocene Reading: Literary History in Geologic Times*, ed. Tobias Menely and Jesse Oak Taylor, 78–95. University Park: Pennsylvania State University Press, 2017.

Forman, H. Buxton. *Our Living Poets*. 1871. New York: Garland, 1986.

Frankel, Nicholas. "The Ecology of Victorian Poetry." *Victorian Poetry* 41, no. 4 (2003): 629–35.

Frost, Mark. "Reading Nature: John Ruskin, Environment, and the Ecological Impulse." In *Victorian Writers and the Environment: Ecocritical Perspectives*, ed. Laurence W. Mazzeno and Ronald D. Morrison, 13–28. London: Routledge, 2017.

Gaard, Greta. "Ecofeminism Revisited: Rejecting Essentialism and Re-Placing Species in a Material Feminist Environmentalism." *Feminist Formations* 23, no. 2 (2011): 26–53.

————. *Ecological Politics: Ecofeminists and the Greens*. Philadelphia: Temple University Press, 1998.

————. "New Directions for Ecofeminism: Toward a More Feminist Ecocriticism." *Interdisciplinary Studies in Literature and Environment* 17, no. 4 (2010): 643–65.

————. "Toward a Queer Ecofeminism." *Hypatia* 12, no. 1 (1997): 114–37.

Gander, Forrest, and John Kinsella. *Redstart: An Ecological Poetics*. Iowa City: University of Iowa Press, 2012.

Garnett, Richard. *Memoir*. In *The Poetical Works of Mathilde Blind*, ed. Arthur Symons. London: T. Fisher Unwin, 1900.

Geddes, Patrick, and J. Arthur Thomson. *The Evolution of Sex*. New York: Charles Scribner's Sons, 1889.

Gersdorf, Catrin. "Ecocritical Uses of the Erotic." *Bucknell Review* 44, no. 1 (2000): 175–91.

Gilcrest, David W. *Greening the Lyre: Environmental Poetics and Ethics*. Reno: University of Nevada Press, 2002.

Gold, Barri J. "Energy, Ecology, and Victorian Fiction." *Literature Compass* 9, no. 2 (2012): 213–24.

Gottlieb, Roger S., ed. *This Sacred Earth: Religion, Nature, Environment*. 2nd ed. New York: Routledge, 2004.

Gould, Peter C. *Early Green Politics: Back to Nature, Back to the Land, and Socialism in Britain 1880–1900*. Sussex, UK: Harvester, 1988.

Gray, Erik. "A Bounded Field: Situating Victorian Poetry in the Literary Landscape." *Victorian Poetry* 41, no. 4 (2003): 465–72.

Gregory, Melissa Valiska. "Augusta Webster Writing Motherhood in the Dramatic Monologue and Sonnet Sequence." *Victorian Poetry* 49, no. 1 (2011): 27–51.

Griffin, Susan. "Ecofeminism and Meaning." In *Ecofeminism: Women, Culture, Nature*, ed. Karen J. Warren, 213–26. Bloomington: Indiana University Press, 1997.

———. *Woman and Nature: The Roaring inside Her*. New York: Harper & Row, 1978.

Groth, Helen. "Victorian Women Poets and Scientific Narratives." In *Women's Poetry, Late Romantic to Late Victorian: Gender and Genre, 1830–1900*, ed. Isobel Armstrong and Virginia Blain, 325–51. London: Centre for English Studies, 1999.

Gruen, Lori. "On the Oppression of Women and Animals." *Environmental Ethics* 18, no. 4 (1996): 441–44.

Guimaräes, Paula Alexandra. "'Over My Boundless Waste of Soul': Echoes of the Natural World, or a Feminine *Naturphilosophie*, in the Poetry of Emily Brontë and Mathilde Blind." *Nineteenth-Century Gender Studies* 7, no. 2 (2011). www.ncgsjournal.com.

Halmi, Nicholas, ed. *Wordsworth's Poetry and Prose: Authoritative Texts, Criticism*. New York: Norton, 2014.

Haraway, Donna. "Situated Knowledges: The Science Question in Feminism and the Privilege of Partial Perspective." *Feminist Studies* 14, no. 3 (1988): 575–99.

Hardy, Thomas. *Tess of the d'Urbervilles*. New York: Penguin, 1978.

Harrington, Emily. "'Appraise Love and Divide': Measuring Love in Augusta Webster's *Mother and Daughter*." *Victorian Poetry* 50, no. 3 (2012): 259–77.

———. *Second Person Singular: Late Victorian Women Poets and the Bonds of Verse*. Charlottesville: University of Virginia Press, 2014.

Harrison, Frederic. "The Emancipation of Women." *Fortnightly Review* 56 (1891): 437–52.

Haught, James A. *2000 Years of Disbelief: Famous People with the Courage to Doubt*. Amherst, NY: Prometheus, 1996.

Hess, Scott. *William Wordsworth and the Ecology of Authorship: The Roots of Environmentalism in Nineteenth-Century Culture*. Charlottesville: University of Virginia Press, 2012.

Homans, Margaret. *Bearing the Word: Language and Female Experience in Nineteenth-Century Women's Writing*. Chicago: University of Chicago Press, 1986.

———. *Women Writers and Poetic Identity: Dorothy Wordsworth, Emily Brontë, and Emily Dickinson*. Princeton, NJ: Princeton University Press, 1980.

Homer. *The Odyssey*. Trans. Robert Fitzgerald. Garden City, NY: Anchor, 1963.

Hopkins, Gerard Manley. "Binsey Poplars." https://www.poetryfoundation.org/poems/44390/binsey-poplars.

Hughes, Linda K. *The Cambridge Introduction to Victorian Poetry*. Cambridge: Cambridge University Press, 2010.

———. "A Club of Their Own." *Victorian Literature and Culture* 35, no. 1 (2006): 233–60.

———. "Daughters of Danaus and Daphne: Women Poets and the Marriage Question." *Victorian Literature and Culture* 34, no. 2 (2006): 481–93.

———, ed. *New Woman Poets: An Anthology*. London: The Eighteen Nineties Society, 2001.

Hughes, William R. *Constance Naden: A Memoir*. London: Bickers & Son, 1890.

Irigaray, Luce. *An Ethics of Sexual Difference*. Trans. Carolyn Burke and Gillian C. Gill. Ithaca, NY: Cornell University Press, 1993.

———. *The Irigaray Reader*. Ed. Margaret Whitford. Cambridge, UK: Blackwell, 1991.

———. *Key Writings*. London: Continuum, 2004.

———. *Sexes and Genealogies*. Trans. Gillian C. Gill. New York: Columbia University Press, 1993.

———. *Speculum of the Other Woman*. Trans. Gillian C. Gill. Ithaca, NY: Cornell University Press, 1985.

———. "There Can Be No Democracy without a Culture of Difference." In *Ecocritical Theory: New European Approaches*, ed. Axel Goodbody and Kate Rigby, 194–205. Charlottesville: University of Virginia Press, 2011.

———. *Thinking the Difference: For a Peaceful Revolution*. Trans. Karin Montin. London: Athlone, 1994.

———. *This Sex Which Is Not One*. Trans. Catherine Porter and Carolyn Burke. Ithaca, NY: Cornell University Press, 1985.

———. *To Be Two*. Trans. Monique M. Rhodes and Marco F. Cocito-Monoc. New York: Routledge, 2001.

Irigaray, Luce, and Michael Marder. *Through Vegetal Being*. New York: Columbia University Press, 2016.

Jackson-Houlston, Caroline. "'Queen Lilies'?: The Interpenetration of Scientific, Religious and Gender Discourses in Victorian Representations of Plants." *Journal of Victorian Culture* 11, no. 1 (2006): 84–110.

Jefferies, Richard. *The Hills and the Vale*. Oxford: Oxford University Press, 1980.

Kant, Immanuel. *The Critique of Judgement*. Trans. James Creed Meredith. Oxford: Clarendon, 1952.

Keller, Lynn. "Twenty-First Century Ecopoetry and the Scalar Challenges of the Anthropocene." In *The News from Poems: Essays on the 21st-Century American Poetry of Engagement*, ed. Jeffrey Gray and Ann Keniston, 47–63. Ann Arbor, MI: University of Michigan Press, 2016.

Kheel, Marti. *Nature Ethics: An Ecofeminist Perspective*. Lanham, MD: Rowman & Littlefield, 2008.

King, Amy M. *Bloom: The Botanical Vernacular in the English Novel*. Oxford: Oxford University Press, 2003.

King, Ursula. *The Search for Spirituality: Our Global Quest for a Spiritual Life*. N.p.: BlueBridge, 2008.

King, Ynestra. "The Ecology of Feminism and the Feminism of Ecology." In *Feminist Theory: A Reader*, 3rd ed., ed. Wendy K. Kolmar and Frances Bartkowski, 407–12. Boston: McGraw Hill, 2008.

———. "Healing the Wounds: Feminism, Ecology, and the Nature/Culture Dualism." In *Reweaving the World: The Emergence of Ecofeminism*, ed. Irene Diamond and Gloria Feman Orenstein, 106–21. San Francisco: Sierra Club, 1990.

King-Hele, Desmond. *Erasmus Darwin and the Romantic Poets*. New York: St. Martin's, 1986.

Knickerbocker, Scott. *Ecopoetics: The Language of Nature, the Nature of Language*. Amherst: University of Massachusetts Press, 2012.

Kristeva, Julia. "Women's Time." Trans. Alice Jardine and Harry Blake. *Signs* 7 (1981): 13–35.

Landow, George. "Atheism." Victorian Web. http://www.victorianweb.org/religion /atheism.html.

Lansbury, Coral. *The Old Brown Dog: Women, Workers, and Vivisection in Edwardian England.* Madison: University of Wisconsin Press, 1985.

LaPorte, Charles. "Atheist Prophecy: Mathilde Blind, Constance Naden, and the Victorian Poetess." *Victorian Literature and Culture* 34, no. 2 (2006): 427–41.

Laqueur, Thomas. *Making Sex: Body and Gender from the Greeks to Freud.* Cambridge: Harvard University Press, 1990.

Larson, James L. "Linnaeus and the Natural Method." *Isis* 58, no. 3 (1967): 304–20.

———. "The Species Concept of Linnaeus." *Isis* 59, no. 3 (1968): 291–99.

Legler, Gretchen T. "Ecofeminist Literary Criticism." In *Ecofeminism: Women, Culture, Nature*, ed. Karen J. Warren, 227–38. Bloomington: Indiana University Press, 1997.

———. "Toward a Postmodern Pastoral: The Erotic Landscape in the Work of Gretel Ehrlich." In *The ISLE Reader: Ecocriticism, 1993–2003*, ed. Michael P. Branch and Scott Slovic, 22–32. Athens: University of Georgia Press, 2003.

Leighton, Angela. *Victorian Women Poets: Writing against the Heart.* Charlottesville: University Press of Virginia, 1992.

———. "Women Poets and the Fin-de-Siècle: Towards a New Aestheticism." *Victorian Review* 23, no. 1 (1997): 1–14.

Leighton, Angela, and Margaret Reynolds, eds. *Victorian Women Poets: An Anthology.* Oxford: Blackwell, 1995.

Lewins, Robert. *Humanism versus Theism.* London: Freethought, 1887.

Lombroso, Cesare. *The Man of Genius.* London: Walter Scott, 1891.

Lorde, Audre. *Sister Outsider: Essays and Speeches.* Berkeley, CA: Crossing, 1984.

Lynch, Deidre Shauna, and Jack Stillinger, eds. *The Norton Anthology of English Literature.* 9th ed. Vol. D, *The Romantic Period.* New York: Norton, 2012.

Lysack, Krista. "Aesthetic Consumption and the Cultural Production of Michael Field's *Sight and Song*." *Studies in English Literature, 1500–1900* 45, no. 4 (2005): 936–60.

Macaulay, Thomas Babington. "Sir James Mackintosh." In *Critical, Historical, and Miscellaneous Essays and Poems*, vol. 2. New York: American, 1880.

Manes, Christopher. "Nature and Silence." In *The Ecocriticism Reader: Landmarks in Literary Ecology*, ed. Cheryll Glotfelty and Harold Fromm, 15–29. Athens: University of Georgia Press, 1996.

Marsh, George Perkins. *Man and Nature: George Perkins Marsh.* Ed. David Lowenthal. Seattle: University of Washington Press, 2003.

Marsh, Jean. *The Illuminated Language of Flowers.* Austin, TX: Holt, Rinehart, and Winston, 1978.

Marx, Karl. "Marx and Engels on Ecology." Ed. Howard L. Parsons. In *Ecology*, 2nd ed., ed. Carolyn Merchant. Amherst, NY: Humanity, 2008.

Mazzeno, Laurence W., and Ronald D. Morrison. *Victorian Writers and the Environment: Ecocritical Perspectives.* London: Routledge, 2017.

McCulloch, Gillian. *The Deconstruction of Dualism in Theology*. Carlisle, UK: Paternoster, 2002.

McDowell, Michael J. "The Bakhtinian Road to Ecological Insight." In *The Ecocriticism Reader: Landmarks in Literary Ecology*, ed. Cheryll Glotfelty and Harold Fromm, 371–91. Athens: University of Georgia Press, 1996.

McFague, Sallie. *The Body of God: An Ecological Theology*. Minneapolis: Fortress, 1993.

———. "An Earthly Theological Agenda." In *Ecofeminism and the Sacred*, ed. Carol J. Adams, 84–98. New York: Continuum, 1993.

———. *Models of God: Theology for an Ecological, Nuclear Age*. Philadelphia: Fortress, 1987.

———. "The Scope of the Body: The Cosmic Christ." In *This Sacred Earth: Religion, Nature, Environment*, 2nd ed., ed. Roger S. Gottlieb, 262–72. New York: Routledge, 2004.

———. *Super, Natural Christians: How We Should Love Nature*. Minneapolis: Fortress, 1997.

McIntosh, Robert P. *The Background of Ecology: Concept and Theory*. Cambridge: Cambridge University Press, 1985.

Mellor, Mary. *Feminism & Ecology*. New York: New York University Press, 1997.

Menely, Tobias, and Jesse Oak Taylor, eds. *Anthropocene Reading: Literary History in Geologic Times*. University Park: Pennsylvania State University Press, 2017.

Merchant, Carolyn. *The Death of Nature: Women, Ecology and the Scientific Revolution*. New York: Harper & Row, 1980.

———, ed. *Ecology*. 2nd ed. Amherst, NY: Humanity, 2008.

———. "Perspectives on Ecofeminism." *Environmental Action* 24, no. 2 (1992): 18–19.

———. *Reinventing Eden: The Fate of Nature in Western Culture*. New York: Routledge, 2003.

Mermin, Dorothy. *Godiva's Ride: Women of Letters in England, 1830–1880*. Bloomington: Indiana University Press, 1993.

Meynell, Alice. "The Foot." In *The Spirit of Place and Other Essays*. London: John Lane, 1899.

———. "Grass." In *The Colour of Life and Other Essays on Things Seen and Heard*. London: John Lane, 1896.

———. "In July." In *Essays*. Westport, CT: Greenwood, 1947.

———. *Later Poems*. London: John Lane, 1902.

———. *London Impressions: Etchings and Pictures in Photogravure*. Westminster, UK: Constable, 1898. www.gutenberg.org/ebooks/32842.

———. *The Poems of Alice Meynell: Complete Edition*. London: Oxford University Press, 1941.

———. "Rain." In *Essays*. Westport, CT: Greenwood, 1947.

———. "Rushes and Reeds." In *The Colour of Life and Other Essays on Things Seen and Heard*. London: John Lane, 1896.

———. *The Selected Letters of Alice Meynell: Poet and Essayist*. Ed. Damian Atkinson. Newcastle upon Tyne, UK: Cambridge Scholars, 2013.

———. "Tennyson." In *Prose and Poetry*. London: Jonathan Cape, 1947.

———. "Winds of the World." In *The Colour of Life and Other Essays on Things Seen and Heard*. London: John Lane, 1896.

Meynell, Viola. *Alice Meynell: A Memoir*. New York: Charles Scribner's Sons, 1929.

Miles, Alfred H., ed. *The Poets and the Poetry of the Nineteenth Century*. 1907. Vol. 9. New York: AMS, 1967.

Mitchell, Sally. "New Women, Old and New." *Victorian Literature and Culture* 27, no. 2 (1999): 579–88.

Moine, Fabienne. *Women Poets in the Victorian Era: Cultural Practices and Nature Poetry*. Farnham, UK: Ashgate, 2015.

Moore, James R. "The Erotics of Evolution: Constance Naden and Hylo-Idealism." In *One Culture: Essays in Science and Literature*, ed. George Levine, 225–57. Madison: University of Wisconsin Press, 1987.

Moore, Lisa L. "Queer Gardens: Mary Delaney's Flowers and Friendships." *Eighteenth-Century Studies* 39, no. 1 (2005): 49–70.

———. *Sister Arts: The Erotics of Lesbian Landscapes*. Minneapolis: University of Minnesota Press, 2011.

Morgan, Benjamin. "Scale as Form: Thomas Hardy's Rocks and Stars." In *Anthropocene Reading: Literary History in Geologic Times*, 132–49. University Park: Pennsylvania State University Press, 2017.

Morris, William. "The Beauty of Life." In *Hopes and Fears for Art*. London: Longmans, Green, 1919. http://www.gutenberg.org/files/3773/3773-h/3773-h.htm.

———. *News from Nowhere*. London: Routledge & Kegan Paul, 1970.

Mortimer-Sandilands, Catriona. "Eco/Feminism on the Edge." *International Feminist Journal of Politics* 10, no. 3 (2008): 305–13.

Murphy, Patrick D. "Ground, Pivot, Motion: Ecofeminist Theory, Dialogics, and Literary Practice." *Hypatia* 6, no. 1 (1991): 146–61.

———. "Prolegomenon for an Ecofeminist Dialogics." In *Feminism, Bakhtin, and the Dialogic*, ed. Dale M. Bauer and Susan Jaret McKinstry, 39–56. Albany: State University of New York Press, 1991.

Naden, Constance [Constance Arden, pseud.]. "The Brain Theory of Mind and Matter." *Journal of Science* (March 1883): 121–29.

———. *The Complete Poetical Works of Constance Naden*. London: Bickers & Son, 1894.

——— [C.A., pseud.]. "Correspondence: Hylo-Idealism." *Journal of Science* (April 1884): 242.

[———]. "Hylo-Idealism: The Creed of the Coming Day." In *Induction and Deduction*. London: Bickers & Son, 1890.

——— [Constance Arden, pseud.]. "Hylo-Idealism: A Defence." *Journal of Science* (December 1884): 697–705.

[———]. "Hylozoic Materialism." *Journal of Science* (June 1881): 313–18.

——— [Constance Arden, pseud.]. "The Identity of Vital and Cosmical Energy." *Journal of Science* (May 1882): 249–58.

———. "On Mental Physiology and Its Place in Philosophy." *Proceedings of the Aristotelian Society* 1, no. 3 (1890): 81–82.

——— [Constance Arden, pseud.]. "The Philosophy of Thomas Carlyle." *Journal of Science* (June 1882): 313–22.

———. *What Is Religion?* 1883. N.p.: Kessinger, n.d.

Nietzsche, Friedrich. *Beyond Good and Evil*. Trans. Helen Zimmern. https://www.gutenberg.org/files/4363/4363-h/4363-h.htm.

Noggle, James, and Lawrence Lipking, eds. *The Norton Anthology of English Literature*. 9th ed. Vol. C, *The Restoration and the Eighteenth Century*. New York: Norton, 2012.

Ogilvie, Marilyn Bailey. "Robert Chambers and the Nebular Hypothesis." *British Journal for the History of Science* 8, no. 3 (1975): 214–32.

Ortner, Sherry B. "Is Female to Male as Nature Is to Culture?" In *Readings in Ecology and Feminist Theology*, ed. Mary Heather MacKinnon and Moni McIntyre, 36–55. Kansas City, MO: Sheed & Ward, 1995.

Ovid. *Metamorphoses*. Trans. Rolfe Humphries. Bloomington: Indiana University Press, 1958.

Paracelsus. *Selected Writings*. Ed. Jolande Jacobi. Trans. Norbert Guterman. Princeton, NJ: Princeton University Press, 1988.

Parham, John. "Was There a Victorian Ecology?" In *The Environmental Tradition in English Literature*, ed. John Parham, 156–71. Aldershot, UK: Ashgate, 2002.

Pater, Walter. *The Renaissance: Studies in Art and Poetry*. Berkeley: University of California Press, 1980.

———. "Wordsworth." In *Walter Pater: Three Major Texts*, ed. William E. Buckler. New York: New York University Press, 1986.

Pepper, David. *Modern Environmentalism: An Introduction*. London: Routledge, 1996.

Peterson, Linda H. "Alice Meynell's *Preludes*, or Preludes to What Future Poetry?" *Victorian Literature and Culture* 34, no. 2 (2006): 405–26.

———. *Becoming a Woman of Letters: Myths of Authorship and Facts of the Victorian Market*. Princeton, NJ: Princeton University Press, 2009.

———. "Writing Nature at the *Fin de Siècle*: Grant Allen, Alice Meynell, and the Split Legacy of Gilbert White." *Victorian Review* 36, no. 2 (2010): 80–91.

Plumwood, Val. *Feminism and the Mastery of Nature*. Routledge: London, 1993.

Priestman, Martin. *The Poetry of Erasmus Darwin: Enlightened Spaces, Romantic Times*. Farnham, UK: Ashgate, 2013.

Prins, Yopie. "Patmore's Law, Meynell's Rhythm." In *The Fin-de-Siècle Poem: English Literary Culture and the 1890s*, ed. Joseph Bristow, 261–310. Athens: Ohio University Press, 2005.

Psomiades, Kathy Alexis. *Beauty's Body: Femininity and Representation in British Aestheticism*. Stanford, CA: Stanford University Press, 1997.

———. "'Still Burning from This Strangling Embrace': Vernon Lee on Desire and Aesthetics." In *Victorian Sexual Dissidence*, ed. Richard Dellamora, 21–41. Chicago: University of Chicago Press, 1999.

Purdy, Jed. "Losing Nature: Living in the Anthropocene." *Fieldwork* (blog), April 3, 2013. https://jedfieldwork.blogspot.com/search?q=Losing+Nature%3A+Living+in+the+Anthropocene.

"The Purification of the Thames." *Illustrated London News* 33, no. 928 (July 24, 1858): 71–72. http://www.victorianweb.org/periodicals/iln/thames.html.

Rigby, Kate. "Ecocriticism." In *Introducing Criticism in the 21st Century*, 2nd ed., ed. Julian Wolfreys, 122–54. Edinburgh, Scotland: Edinburgh University Press, 2015.

Rigg, Patricia. *Julia Augusta Webster: Victorian Aestheticism and the Woman Writer*. Madison, NJ: Fairleigh Dickinson University Press, 2009.

Ritvo, Harriet. "Zoological Nomenclature and the Empire of Victorian Science." In *Victorian Science in Context*, ed. Bernard Lightman, 334–53. Chicago: University of Chicago Press, 1997.

Robinson, Bonnie J. "'Individual Incorporate': Poetic Trends in Women Writers, 1890–1918." *Victorian Poetry* 38, no. 1 (2000): 1–14.

Rossetti, Christina. *The Family Letters of Christina Georgina Rossetti*. Ed. William Michael Rossetti. New York: Haskell House, 1968.

Rossetti, William. Introduction to *Mother and Daughter: An Uncompleted Sonnet Sequence*, by Augusta Webster. London: Macmillan, 1895.

Rudy, Jason R. "Rapturous Forms: Mathilde Blind's Darwinian Poetics." *Victorian Literature and Culture* 34, no. 2 (2006): 443–59.

Ruether, Rosemary Radford. "Ecofeminism: Symbolic and Social Connections of the Oppression of Women and the Domination of Nature." In *This Sacred Earth: Religion, Nature, Environment*, 2nd ed., ed. Roger S. Gottlieb, 388–99. New York: Routledge, 2004.

———. *Integrating Ecofeminism, Globalization, and World Religions*. Lanham, MD: Rowman & Littlefield, 2005.

———. "Toward an Ecological-Feminist Theology of Nature." In *Healing the Wounds: The Promise of Ecofeminism*, ed. Judith Plant, 145–50. Philadelphia: New Society, 1989.

Ruskin, John. "Fiction, Fair and Foul." In *The Genius of John Ruskin: Selections from His Writings*, ed. John D. Rosenberg. Boston: Routledge & Kegan Paul, 1979.

———. "Fors Clavigera." In *The Works of John Ruskin*, ed. E. T. Cook and Alexander Wedderburn, vol. 1. London: George Allen, 1907.

———. *Modern Painters*. Available at Project Gutenberg, www.gutenberg.org.

———. *Proserpina*. Vol. 1. New York: John Wiley & Sons, 1888. https://www.gutenberg.org/files/20421/20421-h/20421-h.htm.

———. *Sesame and Lilies*. New York: American, 1916.

———. *The Two Paths*. http://www.gutenberg.org/cache/epub/7291/pg7291-images.html.

Sackville-West, Vita. "The Women Poets of the 'Seventies." In *The Eighteen-Seventies*, ed. Harley Granville-Barker. New York: Macmillan, 1929.

Salleh, Ariel. Review of *Staying Alive: Women, Ecology and Development*, by Vandana Shiva. *Hypatia* 6, no. 1 (1991): 206–14.

Sandilands, Catriona. "Desiring Nature, Queering Ethics: Adventures in Erotogenic Environments." *Environmental Ethics* 23, no. 2 (2001): 169–88.

———. "From Natural Identity to Radical Democracy." *Environmental Ethics* 17 (Spring 1995): 75–91.

———. *The Good-Natured Feminist: Ecofeminism and the Quest for Democracy*. Minneapolis: University of Minnesota Press, 1999.

Sandilands, Kate. "Ecofeminism and Its Discontents: Notes toward a Politics of Diversity." *Trumpeter* 8, no. 2 (1991): 90–96.

Saville, Julia F. "The Poetic Imaging of Michael Field." In *The Fin-de-Siècle Poem: English Literary Culture and the 1890s*, ed. Joseph Bristow, 178–206. Athens: Ohio University Press, 2005.

Schaffer, Talia. *The Forgotten Female Aesthetes: Literary Culture in Late-Victorian England.* Charlottesville: University Press of Virginia, 2000.

Schaffer, Talia, and Kathy Alexis Psomiades. *Women and British Aestheticism.* Charlottesville: University Press of Virginia, 1999.

Schiebinger, Londa. *Nature's Body: Gender in the Making of Modern Science.* New Brunswick, NJ: Rutgers University Press, 2004.

Schlack, Beverly Ann. "The 'Poetess of Poets': Alice Meynell Rediscovered." *Women's Studies* 7, nos. 1–2 (1980): 111–26.

Scigaj, Leonard M. *Sustainable Poetry: Four American Ecopoets.* Lexington: University Press of Kentucky, 1999.

Scott, Heidi C. M. *Chaos and Cosmos: Literary Roots of Modern Ecology in the British Nineteenth Century.* University Park: Pennsylvania State University Press, 2014.

Scourse, Nicolette. *The Victorians and Their Flowers.* London: Croom Helm, 1983.

Seaton, Beverly. *The Language of Flowers: A History.* Charlottesville: University Press of Virginia, 1995.

Segal, Charles Paul. *Landscape in Ovid's "Metamorphoses."* Wiesbaden, Germany: Franz Steiner Verlag, 1969.

Shelley, Mary. *Frankenstein.* London: Penguin, 1992.

Shelley, Percy Bysshe. "The Necessity of Atheism." The Secular Web. https://infidels.org/library/historical/percy_shelley/necessity_of_atheism.html.

Shteir, Ann B. *Cultivating Women, Cultivating Science.* Baltimore: Johns Hopkins University Press, 1996.

Simmons, I. G. *An Environmental History of Great Britain: From 10,000 Years Ago to the Present.* Edinburgh, Scotland: Edinburgh University Press, 2001.

Smith, Philip E., II. "Robert Lewins, Constance Naden, and Hylo-Idealism." *Notes and Queries* 25, no. 4 (1978): 303–9.

Smulders, Sharon. "Looking 'Past Wordsworth and the Rest': Pretexts for Revision in Alice Meynell's 'The Shepherdess.'" *Victorian Poetry* 38, no. 1 (2000): 35–48.

Spencer, Herbert. "Progress: Its Law and Cause." In *Essays: Scientific, Political, and Speculative,* vol. 1. New York: D. Appleton, 1896.

———. "Recent Astronomy and the Nebular Hypothesis." *Westminster Review* 70 (July 1858): 104–27.

Stedman, Edmund Clarence. *Victorian Poets.* Boston: Houghton, Mifflin, 1903.

Stodart, M. A. "Poetesses and Fleshly Poets." In *The Victorian Poet: Poetics and Persona,* ed. Joseph Bristow, 134–39. London: Croom Helm, 1987.

Stott, Annette. "Floral Femininity: A Pictorial Definition." *American Art* 6, no. 2 (1992): 60–77.

Sturgeon, Mary. *Michael Field.* New York: Arno, 1975.

Sturgeon, Noël. *Ecofeminist Natures: Race, Gender, Feminist Theory, and Political Action.* New York: Routledge, 1997.

Sutphin, Christine. "Augusta Webster (1837–1894)." In *Nineteenth-Century British Women Writers: A Bio-Bibliographical Critical Sourcebook,* ed. Abigail Burnham Bloom, 405–7. Westport, CT: Greenwood, 2000.

———. *Augusta Webster: Portraits and Other Poems.* Peterborough, Canada: Broadview, 2000.

Syme, Alison. *A Touch of Blossom: John Singer Sargent and the Queer Flora of Fin-de-Siècle Art*. University Park: Pennsylvania State University Press, 2010.

Taylor, Jesse Oak. *The Sky of Our Manufacture: The London Fog in British Fiction from Dickens to Woolf*. Charlottesville: University of Virginia Press, 2016.

———. "Where Is Victorian Ecocriticism?" *Victorian Literature and Culture* 43, no. 4 (2015): 877–94.

Tennyson, Alfred. *Tennyson's "The Princess."* Ed. Katharine Lee Bates. New York: American, 1904.

Thain, Marion. "Birmingham's Women Poets: Aestheticism and the Daughters of Industry." *Cahiers Victoriens & Édouardiens* 74 (2011): 37–57, 275, 12.

———. *"Michael Field": Poetry, Aestheticism and the* Fin de Siècle. Cambridge: Cambridge University Press, 2007.

———. "'Scientific Wooing': Constance Naden's Marriage of Science and Poetry." *Victorian Poetry* 41, no. 1 (2003): 151–69.

Thain, Marion, and Ana Parejo Vadillo, eds. *Michael Field, the Poet: Published and Manuscript Materials*. Peterborough, Canada: Broadview, 2009.

Thompson, Charis. "Back to Nature? Resurrecting Ecofeminism after Poststructuralist and Third-Wave Feminisms." *Isis* 97, no. 3 (2006): 505–12.

Tong, Rosemarie. *Feminist Thought: A More Comprehensive Introduction*. 3rd ed. Charlotte: University of North Carolina Press, 2009.

Vadillo, Ana I. Parejo. "New Woman Poets and the Culture of the *Salon* at the *Fin de Siècle*." *Women: A Cultural Review* 10, no. 1 (1999): 22–34.

———. "*Sight and Song*: Transparent Translations and a Manifesto for the Observer." *Victorian Poetry* 38, no. 1 (2000): 15–34.

Vicinus, Martha. "The Adolescent Boy: Fin-de-Siècle Femme Fatale?" In *Victorian Sexual Dissidence*, ed. Richard Dellamora, 83–106. Chicago: University of Chicago Press, 1999.

Virgil. *The Aeneid of Virgil*. Trans. Rolfe Humphries. New York: Charles Scribner's Sons, 1951.

Warren, Karen J. *Ecofeminist Philosophy: A Western Perspective on What It Is and Why It Matters*. Lanham, MD: Rowman & Littlefield, 2000.

———. "A Feminist Philosophical Perspective." In *Ecofeminism and the Sacred*, ed. Carol J. Adams, 119–32. New York: Continuum, 1993.

———. "The Power and the Promise of Ecological Feminism." In *Ecological Feminist Philosophies*, ed. Karen J. Warren, 19–41. Bloomington: Indiana University Press, 1996.

Warren, Karen J., and Jim Cheney. "Ecological Feminism and Ecosystem Ecology." *Hypatia* 6, no. 1 (1991): 179–97.

Watts, Theodore. "Mrs. Augusta Webster." *Athenaeum* (Sept. 15, 1894): 355.

Watts-Dunton, Theodore. "Miss Blind." *Athenaeum* (Dec. 5, 1896): 796–97.

Webster, Augusta. *A Book of Rhyme*. N.p.: Dodo, n.d.

———. *A Housewife's Opinions*. London: Macmillan, 1879.

[———]. Review of *Underneath the Bough*. *Athenaeum* (Sept. 9, 1893): 345–46.

White, Chris. "Flesh and Roses: Michael Field's Metaphors of Pleasure and Desire." *Women's Writing* 3, no. 1 (1996): 47–62.

White, Gilbert. *The Natural History of Selborne*. Ware, UK: Wordsworth Editions, 1996.

White, Lynn, Jr. "The Historical Roots of Our Ecologic Crisis." *Science* 155.3767 (1967): 1203–7.

Whitford, Margaret. *Luce Irigaray: Philosophy in the Feminine*. London: Routledge, 1991.

Wilde, Oscar. *The Decay of Lying*. In *Oscar Wilde: Intentions*. Amherst, NY: Prometheus, 2004.

———. *The Picture of Dorian Gray*. London: Penguin, 1985.

Williams, Raymond. *Keywords: A Vocabulary of Culture and Society*. New York: Oxford University Press, 1985.

Winter, James. *Secure from Rash Assault: Sustaining the Victorian Environment*. Berkeley: University of California Press, 1999.

"Women's Suffrage: A Reply." *Fortnightly Review* 52 (July 1, 1889): 125–31. In *Literature of the Women's Suffrage Campaign in England*, ed. Carolyn Christensen Nelson. Peterborough, Canada: Broadview, 2004.

"Women Who Write." *Pall Mall Gazette* (June 1, 1889): n.p.

Wordsworth, William. *The Fourteen-Book "Prelude."* Ed. W. J. B. Owen. Ithaca, NY: Cornell University Press, 1985.

———. "Preface to *Poems*." In *Literary Criticism of William Wordsworth*, ed. Paul M. Zall. Lincoln: University of Nebraska Press, 1966.

INDEX

employment, 28, 37–38; Michael Field review, 111, 123; on marriage, 37, 38, 56; and suffrage, 36, 37; and women's rights, 27, 28, 35, 69
————works: "Belated," 58–59; *A Book of Rhyme*, 32, 35, 38, 51, 56, 60–61; "The First Spring Day," 38, 44–49; *A Housewife's Opinions*, 35–38, 56; *Mother and Daughter*, 59–60; "My Loss," 54–56; "Not to Be," 56–58; "The Old Dream," 38, 59–63; "Once," 51–54; "A Song of a Spring–Time," 38, 49–51; "The Swallows," 38, 39–44, 45, 46

White, Chris, 228nn23, 26
White, Gilbert, 142
White, Jr., Lynn, 9
Whitford, Margaret, 32
Wilde, Oscar, 124, 125, 126, 229n35
Williams, Raymond, 4
Winter, James, 21
Withering, William, 106–7
Wollstonecraft, Mary, 68–69
Wordsworth, Dorothy, 205–6
Wordsworth, William, 25, 89, 108, 124, 131, 154–55, 156–57, 205–6, 230n8, 231n8, 232n26